"A fascinating and detailed account of the work of ARCIC and the response of the two Communions in search of an answer to the question of whether Anglicans and Roman Catholics agree on the Eucharist. Even if some may not entirely agree with all of the use of the evidence, Bishop Colin's reflections will help us reconsider and perhaps refine the processes of response to, and reception of, the results of ecumenical dialogue."

—Dame Mary Tanner, European President of the WCC from 2006 to 2013

"Bishop Colin Buchanan's historical and theological study concentrates on one of the themes that was dealt with by the Anglican Roman-Catholic International Commission (ARCIC): the Eucharist . . . His careful analysis of all relevant documents leads to the conclusion that there is no substantial agreement on the eucharist between the two Communions . . . His arguments will certainly challenge ecumenists and theologians because they put the common opinion into question that ARCIC has reached a substantial agreement on the Eucharist."

—Adelbert Denaux, member of ARCIC II 1993–2004 and of ARCIC III 2011–17, and joint-author of the Final Report of ARCIC II

"Colin Buchanan gives a timely review of the ARCIC agreed statements on the Eucharist, and reveals the many disagreements that have been missed or ignored. Both Roman Catholic and Anglican theologians will need to ponder his arguments and conclusions."

—Bryan D. Spinks, Yale Institute of Sacred Music and Yale Divinity School

"In 1997 I enjoyed a coffee with Cardinal Ratzinger, later to become Pope Benedict XVI. I asked him point-blank: 'Why was the Congregation for the Doctrine of the Faith so negative towards The Final Report?' In strong Germanic English he replied: 'Because it did not comply with Catholic doctrine'. In this splendid book Colin Buchanan traces the hopes of successive Catholic and Anglican theologians as they sought to unite our two Communions. Perhaps this dream will be realized one day but Dr. Buchanan shows why this way of proceeding was doomed to fail."

—George Carey, Archbishop of Canterbury 1991–:

GW00578251

"This fascinating book by Colin Buchanan is both important and disturbing. In the end, it is a critical case study of one example of the reception of an agreed statement from a significant bilateral dialogue, ARCIC. *Did the Anglicans and Roman Catholics agree on the Eucharist?* is a challenge to the nature and purpose of all ecumenical dialogues, and to consensus ecumenism. From the perspective of the Anglican Communion and its theological ecumenical engagements, this book demands a careful reform and renewal of our processes of reception."

—**John Gibaut**, Director for Unity Faith and Order of the Anglican
        Consultative Council

Did the Anglicans and Roman Catholics Agree on the Eucharist?

Did the **Anglicans** and **Roman Catholics Agree** on the **Eucharist?**

A Revisit of the Anglican–Roman Catholic International Commission's Agreed Statements of 1971 and Related Documents

Colin Buchanan

Retired Bishop of the Church of England

PICKWICK *Publications* · Eugene, Oregon

DID THE ANGLICANS AND ROMAN CATHOLICS AGREE ON
THE EUCHARIST?
A Revisit of the Anglican–Roman Catholic International Commission's Agreed
Statements of 1971 and Related Documents

Pickwick Publications
An Imprint of Wipf and Stock Publishers
199 W. 8th Ave., Suite 3
Eugene, OR 97401

www.wipfandstock.com

PAPERBACK ISBN: 978-1-5326-3383-6
HARDCOVER ISBN: 978-1-5326-3385-0
EBOOK ISBN: 978-1-5326-3384-3

Cataloguing-in-Publication data:

Names: Buchanan, Colin.

Title: Did the Anglicans and Roman Catholics agree on the Eucharist? : a revisit
of the Anglican-Roman Catholic International Commission's agreed statements
of 1971 and related documents / by Colin Buchanan.

Description: Eugene, OR: Pickwick Publications, 2018 | Includes bibliographical
references and index.

Identifiers: ISBN 978-1-5326-3383-6 (paperback) | ISBN 978-1-5326-3385-0 (hard-
cover) | ISBN 978-1-5326-3384-3 (ebook)

Subjects: LCSH: Catholic Church—Relations—Anglican Communion. | Agreed
Statement on Eucharistic Doctrine. | Lord's Supper. | Anglican Communion—Re-
lations—Catholic Church.

Classification: LCC E185.9.M6 C58 2018 (print) | LCC E185.9.M6 (ebook)

I am grateful for permission to publish texts in this volume granted by the following
copyright-holders:

The Society for the Promotion of Christian Knowledge and the Catholic Truth Society in respect of documents contained in Anglican-Roman Catholic International
Commission I, *The Final Report*: London, SCPK and CTS, 1982.

The Secretary-General of the Anglican Consultative Council in respect of Anglican-
Roman Catholic International Commission II, *Clarifications On Eucharist and
Ministry*, CHP: ACC and PCPCU, 1994; and in respect of Anglican-Roman Catholic
International Commission III's Statement, *Walking Together on the Way*, 2018.

Manufactured in the U.S.A.   10/15/18

In grateful tribute to the memory of

Julian Charley
(1930–2017)

"I rarely write an article or deliver a paper on ecumenism without asking to myself: 'Would Julian agree with such an affirmation; would he confirm such a proposal?' And when the answer is 'no,' I feel obliged to look again at my text."

—Jean-Marie Tillard, Roman Catholic theologian, member of the Anglican–Roman Catholic International Commission, in a written tribute to Julian Charley on his retirement in 1997

Contents

Acknowledgments

I ACKNOWLEDGE WITH THANKS THE great help I have received from correspondence and conversation with the following:

The late Henry Chadwick, Julian Charley, Cormac Murphy-O'Connor, and Jean-Marie Tillard.

Solomon Amusan, Donald Anderson, Ross Bay, John Baycroft, Stephanie Bennett, Roger Bowen, Tim Bradshaw, Timothy Calligan, George Carey, Peter Carrell, Claire Charley, George Connor, Brian Douglas, Peter Foskett, John Gibaut, David Hamid, Christopher Hill, Bruce Kaye, Michael Kennedy, Kurt Koch, Peter Lee, Harold Miller, David Moxon, Andrew Norman, Elizabeth Paterson, Stephen Platten, Nicholas Sagovsky, Mark Santer, Charles Sherlock, William Steele, Amelia Sutcliffe, Stephanie Taylor, Mary Tanner, Sam Van Culin, and Jeremy Worthen.

Abbreviations

ACC	Anglican Consultative Council
ACO	Anglican Communion Office
APCK	Association for Promoting Christian Knowledge
ARCCNZ	Anglican–Roman Catholic Conversations in New Zealand
ARCIC	Anglican–Roman Catholic International Commission
ARCUSA	Anglican–Roman Catholic USA dialogue
BCP	Book of Common Prayer
CCU	Council for Christian Unity (of the Church of England General Synod)
CDF	Congregation for Defence of the Faith
CEEC	Church of England Evangelical Council
CHP	Church House Publishing
CIO	Church Information Office
CTS	Catholic Truth Society
DLT	Darton, Longman, and Todd
ET	English Translation
FOAG	Faith and Order Advisory Group (of General Synod)
GTUM	*Growing Together in Unity and Mission*
IARCCUM	International Anglican–Roman Catholic Council for Mission and Unity

JPC	Joint Preparatory Commission
NOL	*News of Liturgy*
OUP	Oxford University Press
PCPCU	Pontifical Council for Promoting Christian Unity
SPCK	Society for the Promotion of Christian Knowledge
SPCU	Secretariat for Promoting Christian Unity
WCC	World Council of Churches

Introduction

T HERE EXISTS NOW A continuous story of dialogue between Anglicans
and Roman Catholics covering more than fifty years since, in the
post-Vatican II days, Michael Ramsey's visit to Pope Paul VI in April 1966
kicked off the process. By steps set out below the visit led to the formation
in 1969 of the first Anglican–Roman Catholic International Commission
(ARCIC I), and then in 1983 to ARCIC II, and in 2011 to ARCIC III which
is still hard at work today.[1] The story is well told in literature to which this
book regular refers. It is regularly told as broadly a success story. However,
I judge that the particular title under which I now write, and the particular
method I follow, vary sufficiently from the existing telling of the story to
justify this separate study. There are here three major points of distancing
from the existing works.

A Thematic Treatment

First of all, this examines a single theme. It is solely concerned with
eucharistic doctrine. That means that its concerns include some background scene-setting in *Apostolicae curae* and *Saepius officio* (1896–97)
and in the Malines Conversations (1921–27); its concerns then cover the
Preparatory Commission (1967–68) and the actual ARCIC documents,
namely the initial Agreement of 1971 (*Eucharistic Doctrine*: the Windsor
Statement), the *Elucidation* in 1979, and *Clarifications* in 1994. The first

---

1. In July 2018, while this book was at the press, ARCIC III produced their first
statement, *Walking Together on the Way: Learning to Be the Church—Local, Regional,
Universal*. This is a massive statement, and, although its theme is ecclesiology, it includes
a kind of resumé of the eucharistic statements addressed in this present book, and thus
the three relevant paragraphs are reproduced in chapter 13 below and are the subject of
the new addendum that chapter forms.

two of these are bound up together in *The Final Report* of ARCIC I in 1982, whereas the third exists on its own as a product of ARCIC II. The official reports—whether *The Final Report* of ARCIC I or Adelbert Denaux, Nicholas Sagovsky and Charles Sherlock (eds.), *Looking Towards a Church Fully United* (London: SPCK, 2017), the officially commissioned report of ARCIC II—provide synchronous collections of documents across a range of themes; but they do not relate the texts on the eucharist of ARCIC I to the eucharistic part of *Clarifications* of ARCIC II—indeed, for indeterminate reasons which will be explored in the pages below, the ARCIC II collection does not include the text of *Clarifications* at all. The only publication that does include all these three Statements on the eucharist is Christopher Hill and Edward Yarnold (eds.), *Anglicans and Roman Catholics: The Search for Unity* (London: SPCK, 1994).[2] This volume does indeed bring together ARCIC I and ARCIC II material, but it does so at a date that does not well serve the purpose of this present study; for, although it contains the text of *Clarifications* (and of the Letter of Cardinal Cassidy responding to it but not the co-chairmen's Introduction), these were clearly incorporated at a late stage in a volume already in other respects prepared for publication. Thus the book as published contains weighty comments by members of both ARCICs on the previous ARCIC Statements and on the *Response* of the Pontifical Council for Promoting Christian Unity (PCPCU), but they all refer solely to those previous documents and were written before the writers could have any knowledge of *Clarifications*. As *Clarifications* necessarily gives rise to some intense enquiry, there remains in the Hill/Yarnold volume a considerable lacuna which this present volume addresses. The diachronic treatment here of the single theme, the eucharist, enables that particular enquiry to be pursued in a sustained and concentrated way. The comprehensive diachronic provision is brought up to date through the unforeseen timing that has enabled the relevant paragraphs of ARCIC III's major new document, *Walking Together on the Way* (2018), to be added also.

The limiting of the study to the single theme does, however, provide problems of context and of demarcation. Thus, in 1971 *Eucharistic Doctrine* fell on Anglicans out of a blue sky and was without competitors for ecumenical attention. But the coming of the further Statements meant that by 1979 the issues of papal authority were seizing headline attention; and there

2. The grouping of these three documents as "Statements" is for convenience, and is without prejudice to a question arising later as to whether *Clarifications* ought officially to be classified as a "Statement."

was also a rising Anglican murmur about an item missing from the agenda, one which ought to precede the other topics and underlie them, namely justification and salvation. Thus, the *Elucidation* on the eucharist gained much less publicity and interrogation than *Eucharistic Doctrine* had done. Background issues throughout have been the validity of Anglican orders, and the question of intercommunion; and by the 1990s the ordination of women and issues of same-sex relationships were similarly impacting the agenda; and when *Clarifications*, published in 1994, failed to arouse the interest and concern which it certainly merited, the years ran out, and it was the third Statement on Authority, *The Gift of Authority* (1999) which stirred the Anglican sensitivities. There is also no lack of keen participants and perceptive observers who reckon that ecumenism itself had in that decade become boring to church leaders and synods, so that, although lip-service was still paid, critical energies flagged.

The issue of demarcation particularly touches the Statements on Ministry and Ordination. From *Apostolicae curae* in 1896 onwards, the ordination questions have been closely bound up with eucharistic ones. Nevertheless ARCIC I drew this distinction between the two subjects from the start, and so I have limited the present enquiry by omitting all the Ministry texts, and by correspondingly not discussing the presidency of the eucharist. I apologize for the sharp exclusions this has entailed, but some boundary had to be established, and ARCIC itself had set the precedent.

Doctrine and Liturgy

A second feature of this study is that it attempts to keep liturgical texts in view while considering dogmatic theological propositions. I write as a liturgist, and am conscious that sacramental theology is regularly treated as a distinct (and even superior) category of theology which does not overlap with liturgical studies. The Anglican–Roman Catholic documents considered here have a strong tendency towards that separation: Roman Catholic liturgical texts never come into the official picture at all, and Anglican ones were equally out of sight originally. This did not go unnoticed by Joseph Ratzinger, then prefect of the Congregation for Defence of the Faith (CDF), later Pope Benedict XVI, in his own reflections on the ARCIC I *Final Report*:

> If the basic form of the liturgy of the early Church were accepted as a lasting heritage, ranking with conciliar creeds, this would

provide unifying hermeneutics which would render many points of contention superfluous. The Church's liturgy being the original interpretation of the biblical heritage has no need to justify itself before historical reconstructions: it is rather itself the standard, sprung from what is living, which directs research back to the initial stages. . . . The two levels we are referring to [historic and "living"] can be well illustrated by a formula in the ARCIC documents. As the authors unfold their theological vision, they repeatedly use the phrase "we believe." If I understand them aright, what it actually means is "it is our opinion": it is expressing the opinion of theologians. But it is only when "we believe" is transformed from "this is our opinion" to "this is our faith" by what has been thought out theologically that it is caught up into the full life stream of the Church; only in this way can unity be achieved.[3]

While Ratzinger may be over-sweeping, and perhaps also be somewhat hostile to his own (distinguished) Roman Catholic team on ARCIC I, he raises a serious question, for the liturgy unites the historic with the "living." But liturgical texts only enter the ARCIC story slowly; Anglican ones are summoned to provide secondary supportive documents; and even then the Roman texts remain almost entirely out of sight, and it is the Church of England 1662 Book of Common Prayer (hereafter simply "1662") which is laid under contribution. It is, however, mostly quoted to carry meanings beyond its capacity to bear. It should, of course, be noted that, whereas Roman Catholic texts are imposed throughout the worldwide Communion, and must be expounded in line with the Church's historic doctrinal position, in Anglicanism 1662 holds a much less precise position, though it does lie somewhere in every province's liturgical ancestry.[4] In many provinces 1662 has in time been superseded, and worldwide its use and standing has certainly declined. Nevertheless, when the successive Commissions, perhaps finding the XXXIX Articles unhelpful, have wished to cite Anglican liturgy, it is to 1662 they have turned, and it is then the task of Anglican liturgical scholarship to test the use they have made of it. I have included here three appendices to explore the ARCIC use of the Anglican liturgical heritage. But, that said, the principle of

3. Ratzinger, *Church, Ecumenism* (ET of chapter 4 on "Anglican–Catholic Dialogue: Its Problems and Hopes" by Dame Frideswide Sandeman) 85–86.

4. The Scottish Episcopal Church alone could be cited as an exception, though even it has given some currency to the 1662 eucharistic rite within the last two centuries.

including the liturgy as evidence of the stance of a Communion, although ARCIC came to it late, has to be applauded.

Roman Catholic and Reformed Positions

It is a given feature of Anglicanism that its sixteenth-century formularies stood close to reformed models, not least those of Calvin, and that those formularies have been the charter for evangelicalism within the Communion. There has, of course, been a great broadening of *de facto* Anglicanism, and in the first half of the twentieth century evangelicalism was largely eclipsed in the Church of England. Yet evangelicals, holding to the historic formularies, in principle have stood further from Rome than the "central" or anglo-catholic strands have done. So a third feature of this study has been that it focusses the need to unite the positions which within the two Communions stand furthest from each other. In simple terms, it is fairly useless to seek agreement on behalf of whole denominations, if it is simply those who already stood nearest to each other before the dialogue started who then happily reach an agreement. A classic instance of how thus to come to easy agreement is provided by the Malines Conversations in the 1920s—early assurances from the small band of anglo-catholics who were purporting to speak for the Church of England assured the Roman Catholics that they and the Anglicans were agreed on the doctrines of the supposedly seven sacraments; and that purported agreement was then taken as read, and the Conversationalists turned to other matters.[5] Quite apart from Halifax's preferences, the 1920s were not good times for the Church of England to provide learned evangelical representatives, so the question of across-the-board representation may not have been fully faced. But in the post-War years evangelicals in England were emerging from any ghetto in which they had been confined, and were getting above ground academically, and starting to raise a profile. This rising profile was also reflected in various other parts of the Anglican Communion. It was also visible to Roman Catholic observers. Thus it is interesting to read, in William Purdy's account of a seminal series of Anglican–Roman Catholic conferences in the 1950s and 1960s, this report about the Worth Conference addressing the theme of "The Eucharist"; namely, that Maurice Bévenot reported to

---

5. See the report of this on pp. 11–12 below.

Cardinal Heenan: "The Worth dialogue was good but was only with the 'Catholics' in the Church of England."[6]

While Roman Catholics were aware that they had little contact with evangelicals (and until the 1960s there was always a chance that unsophisticated live contact might simply lead to denunciation or confrontational attempts at conversion), the coming of this post-War resurgence of evangelicals was slowly being noticed within the Church of England itself. In the early 1960s they were still hardly represented on the Convocations, or among the University teachers of theology, or on official commissions of the Church of England, or on the bench of Bishops. I was myself appointed in 1964 to the Liturgical Commission overtly as a pioneer representative of a school of thought previously treated as irrelevant—and I not only discovered the pressures upon a "token" representative of a newly noticed school of thought, but also had to learn my role fast, as I immediately found myself addressing the creation of a new eucharistic liturgical text.

This recognition of a growing constituency in the Church of England was hastened by the open and accepting stance towards the rest of the Church of England taken by the 1,000 evangelicals at the first National Evangelical Anglican Congress at Keele in 1967. Archbishop Michael Ramsey, who himself attended the Congress as a guest, was particularly aware of Michael Green, the registrar of the London College of Divinity at that time; and he both appointed him to the Doctrine Commission and made him the youngest theological consultant at the 1968 Lambeth Conference. He went on in early 1969 to invite him to join the Anglican–Roman Catholic Commission which was in process of formation.[7] Michael Green, however, was just becoming principal of his College and was in charge of moving it to Nottingham as well as his other commitments, and he replied urging the appointment in his place of his colleague, Julian Charley. William Purdy, who mistakenly stated that Julian Charley was a "younger man" and charmingly added that he "had the recommendation of being a bachelor," records his appointment as follows:

> Julian Charley, interviewed at Lambeth, was told that "his Grace
> is eager to have someone who would be able to *represent in a very*

---

6. Purdy, *Search for Unity*, 47.

7. Michael Green had published scholarly papers on the doctrine of the eucharist, notably "Eucharistic Sacrifice in the New Testament" and "Christ's Sacrifice and Ours." He also went on to contribute with Eric Mascall "Eucharistic Sacrifice: Some Interim Agreement" as an appendix to Buchanan et al., *Growing into Union* in 1970.

definite way the conservative evangelical wing of the Church of England" (italics mine). He never failed this charge.[8]

As this rising evangelical movement in the Church of England was matched by similar movements elsewhere in the Anglican Communion, the arch-bishop's concern that it should be represented on ARCIC was timely and wise. Nevertheless, the Anglican team which Julian Charley joined on the Commission was well weighted in both churchmanship and scholarship towards the anglo-catholicism which in 1970 still held its fading hegemony within the Anglican Communion.

The Sundered Positions

Irrespective of the distribution of Anglican beliefs on the Commission, the principle should have been established that any agreements between Ro-man Catholics and Anglicans had to include on the Anglican side those who stood farthest from Rome. In simple terms that meant that the children of the Reformation, adhering to the doctrine of the Articles and the Book of Common Prayer and recovering their confidence and their apologetic vigor, had to recognize, in any verbal agreements which might be reached, the eucharistic faith which they themselves held. So, as a background to the history which follows, we examine in brief the points of the widest in-hderited gulf between the Roman Catholic and Protestant or evangelical positions. Admittedly there might be some Anglicans to agree with George Tavard's reading of the Reformation:

> It is generally admitted that the Church of England and the Catho-lic Church of the continent did not separate in the sixteenth cen-tury over fundamental points of faith.[9]

But this may be easier for a Roman Catholic to conclude than for an An-glican, and even so "generally admitted" overstates the somewhat slender

---

8. Purdy, *Search for Unity*, 125. The stated "recommendation" is probably the verdict of hindsight—Julian Charley "clicked" from the start with Jean-Marie Tillard, a promi-nent Roman Catholic theologian on the Commission, and their mutual understanding and cooperation became a key factor in the responsibilities that were entrusted to the two of them to do much of the most sensitive drafting together. It is true that, for the first seven and a half years of working together, the fact that Julian was single enabled them to function on a level playing field as friends, both at the Commission meetings and when working or simply spending time together between those meetings.

9. Tavard, "Final Report," 121.

evidence. Anglicans cannot help but be children of the Reformation, the beneficiaries of a "fundamental" difference of faith, namely, the authority of the Scriptures to reform the inherited traditions; and it has to be a question kept in view throughout this present enquiry as to whether, in breach of that Reformation principle, "tradition" has not at times acquired its own autonomous self-authenticating life, untouched by any biblical critique.

So what were the main issues to be faced in eucharistic theology, the core agenda for a revisit such as this study is undertaking? In essence there were two—two which figure across Europe in the disputes of the Reformation, and the same two which recur as the second and third headings in the first ARCIC Report and continue as the matters requiring sensitive resolution thereafter. I take them in the reverse of the ARCIC order.

First, there was the issue of the presence of Christ, in, or in association with, the bread and wine of the sacrament. The Roman doctrine of the elements being changed in their substance located that presence in a defined place, i.e., within the physical boundaries of the elements.[10] That localized presence in turn meant that Christ himself was "there"—in that defined place; and correspondingly he was to be worshipped and adored as "there," in that place (and irrespective of whether the elements were about to be consumed within the rite, or were reserved outside of any actual eucharistic celebration).[11] The reformed doctrine on the other hand viewed the sacramental elements as instrumental in conveying the benefits of Christ's passion to the recipient, rather as title deeds may "convey" a valuable property to the right recipient, without having intrinsic value of their own; and the reformers consequently rejected any notion of a "real presence" spatially within the elements or coterminous with them. The bread and wine remained bread and wine, and the instituted use of the bread and wine was the designating, delivery and consumption of them within the liturgical rite. The reformers saw reservation as superstition; they viewed the apparent Roman Catholic identification of the outward sign with the inward gift as prejudicial to the concept of a sacrament; and, because they held that the inward gift is only received by the "worthy" (i.e., the properly qualified)

10. There is a fascinating reflection by Robert Taft (in *Worship*, May 2006, 218) that until the end of the fourth century, while the eucharistic bread was viewed as (in some sacramental sense) Christ's body, that meant it was treated as a "holy object," deserving reverence, and only later became seen as "the Divine Presence," deserving of adoration.

11. Because Christ is truly present under the signs of bread and wine, the people of God "give to this sacrament in veneration the worship of *latria*, which is due to the true God" (Council of Trent, Session XIII, Chapter V).

recipient, they used as a test case of their doctrine the proposition that the "unworthy" do not receive the body and blood of Christ. This is very clearly the position of the XXXIX Articles; it is often dubbed "receptionism."[12]

"Receptionism" is best understood as operating like the "conveyancing" model suggested above—it brings the benefits of God's grace to the appropriate recipients, but brings nothing but the outward sign to the inappropriate (or, in Reformation terms, "the unworthy").

It is worth noting that there has been a tendency in modern ecumenical dialogue to observe that all Churches seem ready to affirm the "real presence" of Christ in the eucharistic celebration, and this affirmation is regularly treated as a unitive formula, promoting mutual recognition; the use of it may, however, obscure a serious polarization as to how, or even where, that real presence of Christ is to be found.[13] This difference is gently explicit in the Lima "Commentary":

> Many churches believe that . . . the bread and wine of the eucharist become, in a real though mysterious manner, the body and blood of the risen Christ, i.e., of the living Christ present in all his fullness. Under the signs of bread and wine, the deepest reality is the total being of Christ. . . . Some other churches, while affirming a real presence of Christ at the eucharist, do not link that presence so definitely with the signs of bread and wine.[14]

However, when the points above are duly noted, Anglicans today may well hold that people of different convictions do not necessarily have to be out of communion with each other. Where eucharistic rites present at least a minimum of reference to eating the body and drinking the blood of Christ, an identity of belief about God's way of operating in and through the sacrament is not a necessary prerequisite to Christians sharing in the rite with each other. Thus the Bonn agreement with the Old Catholics in

---

12. "Receptionism" gets one mention in the documents in this volume, in *Elucidation,* §3, p. 57 below. But it is there neither explained, nor excluded. It requires further sympathetic exploration. See the text of Article XXIX on p. 122 below.

13. "Real presence" recurs as a theological term regularly in use in the documents brought together here, so some warning is necessary. However, the words of Gregory Dix should be carefully considered: "It has not been necessary to use it [i.e., the term 'real presence'] at any point in this book. It would be an immense help in discussion if it could be altogether debarred from use among us for a while, and thus everyone be made to state at every stage in his arguments precisely what he does mean as to the relation of the consecrated elements to the Body and Blood of Christ" (Dix, *Shape,* 725n1).

14. Faith and Order Commission, "Commentary (13)" in WCC, *Baptism, Eucharist,*
12.

1931 inaugurated such a sharing, with a stated disavowal of seeking identity of doctrinal formulation prior to the sharing. A similar approach has been found with Lutheran Churches both in Scandinavia and in North America.[15] The implication of this Anglican outlook is that, at least in the last fifty years, issues of intercommunion have at first sight seemed to Anglicans far easier to solve than they have to Roman Catholics. But the starting point there has been the recognition of the actual practice of another church *within the action of the liturgical rite*; and it has been a somewhat different matter when, in the WCC phrase, "under the signs of bread and wine, the deepest reality is the total being of Christ" is asserted, not only as true within the rite, but also as a derivative statement about elements reserved *outside the rite*, with the corollary that adoration should be paid to that "reality" as there "under the signs."

Secondly, there was the issue of eucharistic sacrifice. None of the sixteenth-century reformers, going back to the Scriptures in order to conform their liturgies to the original teaching of the New Testament, could find any hint that the instituted Lord's Supper was of itself, or contained within itself, some sacrifice or offering to God uniquely related to the use of the bread and wine. Consequently all reformed liturgies purged any element of such offering or sacrifice from their texts. As commonly understood in the Roman Catholic Church in the sixteenth century, each celebration of the eucharist was "the sacrifice of the mass propitiatory for both the living and the dead."[16] The Reformers, however, laid their whole emphasis upon the once-and-for-all sacrifice of Christ upon the cross as the sole grounds of our forgiveness and acceptance by God; and they accordingly taught that the purpose of Christ in his command to "Do this" was that his people should, through the outward eating and drinking, "feed on him in their hearts by faith with thanksgiving." The English Reformers certainly treated the eucharist as a great occasion for "giving" alms, for "offering" intercessions, for "offering" praise and thanksgiving as a sacrifice,[17] and for the worshippers "presenting" themselves, their souls and bodies as a "living sacrifice"—but the elements were not offered to God, and none of these other oblations, offered "here," was to

15. This is without prejudice to issues of the qualifications for eucharistic presidency, which are not here in view.

16. Council of Trent, Session XXII, title of chapter II.

17. For further exploration of the meaning of "sacrifice of praise and thanksgiving" see n.13 p.11 and pp.103 and 116–19 below. See also Appendix B.

be assimilated to the sacrifice of Christ offered "there."[18] And, while the eucharist occasioned those (responsive) sacrifices by the people, there was no biblical basis whatsoever for calling it itself a "sacrifice," and each of these occasioned offerings could be offered on non-sacramental occasions, and did not of themselves earmark the eucharist as a "sacrifice." Similarly "altar" was replaced by "table" in the rubrics (and "table" continues in modern texts in England), and such phrases as "May the Lord accept the sacrifice at your hands" were wholly eliminated. Each of these reforms of 1549 and 1552 remained untouched in 1662.[19]

Such is the breadth of the gulf dividing the two positions which, if Roman Catholics and Anglicans were to agree on the eucharist, they would have to seek to reconcile. Many Anglicans might of course find themselves more or less sympathetic to the Roman Catholic side before the discussion began, but the point of principle affirmed here is that, unless the truly reformed stance of the many other Anglicans (as indeed of the original Anglican doctrinal formularies) were to be reconciled with Rome's position, then any accord registered would be inadequate and in danger of self-deception. Such Anglicans, among whom I reckon myself, have had good biblical reasons why they were not Roman Catholics, and have been well supported in that position by the historic formularies of the Church of England.

One respected correspondent has put to me that in ecumenical circles there is a "weariness" about being driven back to a Trent/Articles conflict. I respond by observing that not only does Rome at intervals insist on it (as this account will show), but that any Anglican who is today teaching confirmation candidates, or lay readers in training, or indeed ordinands, quickly encounters the students wrestling with whether, to use the terms of popular speech, the eucharistic bread and wine change their nature or, alternatively, retain their nature and change their use and significance. In one short move such a class brings the teacher back to Trent *versus* the Articles. The separate formulations may be variously illustrated, enriched, or deployed, but they are not easily denied, sidelined, or superseded.

---

18. The quotation marks reflect the occurrence of these two adverbs in the 1552–1662 eucharist—Christ "made *there* by his one oblation" and, after communion, "*here* we offer and present ourselves."

19. See Appendix B for some expansion of this paragraph on eucharistic sacrifice.

The Language of Agreements

The two ARCIC Commissions running to 2003 have from the start followed a policy of looking for new ways of expressing old positions, seeking not to fudge the issues discussed, but to reduce or eliminate differences arising solely from the traditional linguistic formulations. Whether their actual choice of wording achieves their aim or not, the actual texts must be subject to a warning which is a commonplace (though not always recognized) in ecumenical drafting, as indeed in liturgical texts or even hymnody. It is simply this: it is fruitless to ask "What did they mean by this?" To put it another way, such texts are behaviorist—that is, there is no "mind behind them," a mind that can be sought and found in different terms from those of the texts themselves. Individuals can write commentaries, perhaps commending a particular understanding of a text as being more consistent than other possibilities, or possibly drawing out the various nuances of understanding which can be elicited from a text, but such understandings remain by definition simply one person's understanding: the text itself stands immutable, the only agreed "mind" of the Commission, calling for understanding in its own terms. The only variant on this principle occurs when a Commission has itself produced more than one text on a theme (as in the present case). Then there is a *prima facie* case for understanding the two texts as consonant with each other and as both limiting and illuminating each other.

A Jurisdictional Imparity

The actual texts reproduced here and many of the individual comments and opinions disclose a problem in the dialogue between the two communions. It is that, whereas Roman Catholicism has a clear universal jurisdiction regulated through a single centralized "top-down" authority, the Anglican Communion has no comparable structure. The Pope and the Archbishop of Canterbury do not have comparable roles, and this is not always recognized. There is a corresponding tendency (discernible in both leaderships) to treat the Church of England as an entity which embraces the whole Anglican Communion. Historically, of course, it was the Church of England which broke from the Church of Rome, and established a single self-governing ecclesiastical entity; and equally the provinces of worldwide Anglicanism, thirty-nine in number at the time of writing, all have the English

Reformation somewhere in their genes if not in their formularies. However the Church of England of today cannot well speak for them formally as though they were a single jurisdiction. Even so, habits die hard—so, when Leo XIII condemns Anglican orders, the English archbishops reply; when Halifax sets up talks with Mercier, it is English friends he picks to go with him; when in December 1968 Ramsey finds himself choosing the members of the Anglican–Roman Catholic International Commission:

> He said [to John Satterthwaite] the numbers could hardly be kept down to six as had been tentatively agreed during his visit to Rome; "it would be a mistake" not to include one or two Anglicans from outside the United Kingdom.[20]

Purdy then adds in brackets "(a revealing understatement)," clearly discerning Ramsey's own half-unconscious preferences. A little later he portrays Ramsey as defying protests he had encountered in the USA about the disproportions in the membership of ARCIC I, even after ARCIC I had first met:

> Ramsey's comment when he got home was that while he enjoyed meeting the American bishops, he was of the opinion that they were light-weight theologically, keen for better relations with the Roman Catholics but ignorant of the doctrinal complexities to be cleared up first.[21]

In Ramsey's case his choice of McAdoo from the Church of Ireland for Anglican co-chair of ARCIC indicated that he was not acting as simply a little Englander. Nevertheless, the weighting of membership in the Preparatory Commission and in both ARCIC I and ARCIC II has usually meant that the nine or ten Anglican members would include four or five from the Church of England; when a co-chair was needed for ARCIC II in 1983, an English suffragan bishop was appointed; when the liturgy does come on the scene, it is the Church of England's texts which are laid under contribution[22]; when the Church of England decides to ordain women as presbyters,

---

20. Purdy, *Search for Unity*, 125.

21. Purdy, *Search for Unity*, 128.

22. The modern texts occasionally called in evidence are all from the Church of England's *Alternative Service Book 1980* (but see Appendix A for an overview of the actual liturgical diversity of the Anglican Communion). The appeal to the ASB even includes a reference to it in *Elucidation*, published in June 1979, when the eucharistic rites concerned were still engaged in their tortuous passage through General Synod, and in theory any particular feature of the rites might have perished before 1980 dawned.

that is somehow viewed as having prejudiced relationships, though other provinces had done so for many years previously; it is also in the Church of England that the most sustained and serious synodical scrutiny of the work of successive ARCICs has been conducted. This was so in the 1970s.[23] It was followed by the decisive debates recorded below in the 1980s. And "scrutiny" is particularly applicable to the back-bench campaign concerning *Clarifications* in the 1990s. Much of this anglo-centric orientation started to change as ARCIC II ran its time and was succeeded by ARCIC III; but that lies beyond the bounds of this enquiry.

Meanwhile, I write as an Englishman, acknowledging that my own context has both kept me alive over fifty years to the issues discussed here and has placed me in a privileged position to have access to firsthand sources, including peer engagement with numbers of the *personae dramatis.*

A Personal Note

Because of this element of personal history involved in the present enquiry, at this point I declare my interest. I was from 1964 to 1974 a colleague of both Michael Green and Julian Charley on the staff of St. John's College, moving with them as the College went from Northwood to Nottingham in 1970. At the very time Julian Charley was joining ARCIC I and engaging immediately in dialogue and drafting about the eucharist, I had myself been simultaneously occupied in two parallel tasks within the Church of England just a few months ahead of him. One such task was in the Autumn of 1969 writing with one other evangelical (Jim Packer) and two anglo-catholics (Eric Mascall and Graham Leonard) a book on ecclesiology to present an alternative to the Anglican-Methodist union scheme then before the two Churches in England. In this the four authors wrestled with how to answer together the question, "In what sense the eucharist may be called a sacrifice?" and provided a jointly agreed answer.[24] My other task lay in the revision of

23. Thus, there were debates in General Synod in November 1974 with a general welcome to the two Statements then available, and in February 1979 when the Authority Statement had been added and a detailed resolution was passed, commending the Statements and looking forward to closer relationships. All this was before *Elucidations* had been agreed.

24. Buchanan et al., *Growing Into Union,* 59. Part of our own answer to the question is on p.45 below. In an appendix to *Growing Into Union* entitled "Eucharistic Sacrifice— Some Interim Agreement" (186–92) Michael Green joined with Eric Mascall in a much fuller discussion of the question, and they reached some very real agreement. Julian

"Series 2" communion, the first truly experimental eucharistic rite of the Church of England.[25] Its period of currency ran until September 1971, so in 1969 and 1970 I was involved on the Liturgical Commission in working over the text in order to provide "Series 3"—a task requiring sensitive drafting, and particularly as between evangelicals and anglo-catholics, and this we were able to achieve.[26] My serious double engagement at this time with anglo-catholics about both the theology and the liturgy of the eucharist was a unique combination of opportunities which in those days came the way of no other Anglican evangelical; but, more extraordinarily, at the very time this had been happening to me on a nationwide canvas, Julian Charley was almost immediately afterwards entering into parallel debate about the eucharist on an international canvas. He faithfully kept confidentiality where that was needed, but he was well aware of the parallel character of his task, and drew upon the work in which I was involved, while my own interest in his work was being similarly deeply stirred.

There then came a day in September 1971 when he told me that ARCIC had agreed a statement on the nature of the eucharist. The news that an agreement had been reached was being released round the world, but, for reasons not wholly traceable, the Commission was not going to release the actual text of the agreement until 31 December that year. I, knowing Julian, was personally astonished, and immediately told him that evangelical Anglicans would be worried and even horrified to hear that he had agreed on the doctrine of the eucharist with a team of Roman Catholic theologians, and he would need to be prepared to explain his concurrence on the day the text was released. He assented in principle but was slow to draft anything until, halfway through that Autumn, I told him that his best hope of having a good apologia available in print on the day of publication lay with my own back-street publishing house, Grove Books. He detected that this did offer the best hope, and, as I posed him the questions he would

---

Charley reports that Jean Tillard was quoting from this volume in an article for *Nouvelle Revue Théologique* in June–July 1971 (Charley, *Anglican–Roman Catholic Agreement,* 8) and he himself similarly quotes it (18).

25. When Series 2 was produced in the years 1965–67 I initially had to dissent on my own on the Commission, being unable to support the inclusion of "We offer unto thee this bread and this cup" within the anamnesis paragraph and also being unwilling to endorse petitions for the departed within the intercessions. My dissent had been taken seriously, the texts were amended, and since then no such controversial proposals have ever won such support in the Synod as to find their way into authorized eucharistic texts. See Buchanan, "New Communion Service," 3–16.

26. For a particular significant glimpse of this process, see Jasper, *Development,* 310.

need to answer, he then did his drafting against the clock. This project happily meshed with a larger publishing plan just being formed for bringing evangelical Anglicans openly into view in a series of exploratory booklets devoted to liturgical renewal and textual revision. So Julian's explanation was published along with the ARCIC text as *The Anglican–Roman Catholic Agreement on the Eucharist: The 1971 Anglican–Roman Catholic Statement on the Eucharist with An Historical Introduction and Theological Commentary*. It formed Grove Booklet on Ministry and Worship no. 1, and was available in the shops on that New Year's Eve and sold over 10,000 copies within the first twelve months.

My own involvement with the particular dialogue was never quite as close again. I published Julian Charley's similar apologias for the Ministry and Ordination and Authority Statements; through Julian I got to know and admire Jean Tillard and published him also in this (evangelical!) booklet series;[27] and then in 1982 I published from Grove Books both John Stott's *Evangelical Anglicans and the ARCIC Final Report* and Julian's *Rome, Canterbury and the Future*. Meanwhile I was engaged in General Synod in various stages of debating ARCIC Statements, two such debates coming in the 1970s, and then in tandem with the Lima text, *Baptism, Eucharist and Ministry*, in the 1980s; I also guided the Birmingham diocesan synod through its response to *The Final Report* in 1986; and I took my part in the Lambeth Conference of 1988 where the concluding positive Anglican verdict on the Eucharist and on the Ministry and Ordination Statements was delivered. At each such stage I supported ARCIC I's findings on the eucharist.

From 1991 to 2001 I was a member of the Church of England's Council for Christian Unity (CCU), and thus I not only received *Clarifications* in 1994 (which the general run of Synod members did not), but was also in position to see the unpublished report on it from our Faith and Order Advisory Group (FOAG). In my journalistic capacity in April and May 1995 I subjected *Clarifications* to a fairly thorough scrutiny in the monthly journal I then edited, *News of Liturgy*—and in the process I conducted a fairly searching correspondence with Julian Charley, Nicholas Sagovsky, Charles Sherlock, Henry Chadwick, and others not on the Commission. Within the General Synod I was party to the unsuccessful attempts to bring *Clarifications* properly before the Synod's members, and I was present at the inconclusive "fringe" meeting about *Clarifications* in July 1998, which is reported in chapter 10 below.

27. See Tillard, *What Priesthood*.

I was unable, because of other conference responsibilities, to give any attention to ecumenical issues at the Lambeth Conference in 1998, but remained dubious about both the procedure followed in respect of *Clarifications* and the actual content of the document. In General Synod in 1999 all attention turned from previous work of ARCIC II to the Commission's astonishing Agreement, *The Gift of Authority*.[28] However, after I retired in 2004, I wrote an account from my own experience of the first thirty-five years of General Synod, and I devoted one chapter to the ARCIC issues and remaining questions.[29]

I had no plans to take the issue further, though I read the major IARCCUM report, *Growing Together in Unity and Mission* (London: SPCK, 2007) with both interest and a little apprehension. However, in 2014 I was asked to write at short notice a contribution to the *Festschrift* for Irmgard Pahl, the well-known German lay Roman Catholic liturgist, on her eightieth birthday. The brief was for me, as an Anglican, to write for my Roman Catholic friend on a liturgical or sacramental theme with ecumenical implications. Thus it was that I wrote "Can Anglicans and Roman Catholics Agree on the Eucharist?—A re-visit of the Anglican–Roman Catholic International Commission's agreed Statement of 1971 and resultant documents." The *Festschrift* was duly published in Germany (and most of the contributions are in German).[30] However, my own interest was stirred, and my sense of having done merely a sketch of what should be a larger study led me into producing a submission to publishers for that more thorough work. Hence this present volume.

Much time has gone by while the post-Vatican II events recorded here have been unfolding. As I write the only living witness from ARCIC I of whom I am aware is Christopher Hill, and he joined it as Anglican secretary in 1974, after the initial Agreement on the Eucharist had been reached. He has been unfailingly helpful over many years in closing gaps in my knowledge and providing personal angles where I might not have expected them, and I am very grateful to him. His own writings are

28. I did also write my own confrontational critique of this Agreement: *Is Papal Authority a Gift to Us?*

29. See Buchanan, *Taking the Long View*, 123–39. The chapter concerned necessarily treats Anglican–Roman Catholic relationships in a chronicling way, so that there is a synchronous treatment of all the themes that ARCIC I and ARCIC II were addressing. But on the eucharist the thrust of this present volume is there in embryo; and, where ARCIC issues bore upon General Synod, there is at some points more detail there.

30. Böntert, *Gemeinschaft im Danken*.

legion; he is open and transparent; and his grasp of information is conveyed with an undergirding of honeyed persuasiveness. So I am deeply in his debt, though still not quite in his pocket. I have had correspondence and actual meetings with more recent members of ARCIC II, including the extraordinary chance of being invited to lunch by Cardinal Cormac Murphy-O'Connor in July 2017, only a few weeks before he died. And I have been assisted by documentation and personal memories from a great number of persons, not least those in official positions. I am deeply grateful and have acknowledged them on p. ix above.

However, it is Julian Charley who has figured most strongly in my own life, as a personal friend as well as as a theologian, in relation to the Anglican–Roman Catholic dialogue. Julian has been a reluctant but principled controversialist, and the whole Anglican Communion owes him a debt of thanks for his work with Jean Tillard on behalf of ARCIC I. While I shall be found in the latter chapters here unable to applaud key aspects of *Clarifications*, which he helped draft, that hardly touches the major thanks due to him. The last survivor of the team which gathered in Windsor in January 1970, he died on September 15, 2017, while this volume was under preparation. Claire Charley, his widow (for, yes, despite Tillard's influence Julian did eventually marry), has kindly provided me with a major file of his, and a copy of the *Festschrift* for Tillard to which he had contributed.[31] Julian himself received no *Festschrift*, but I gladly dedicate this book to his memory, and I am delighted to have a very appropriate quotation from Tillard with which to embellish the dedication in the frontispiece.

---

31. Evans and Gourgues, *Communion et Réunion*. Julian's contribution is significantly entitled "Friendship—The Forgotten Factor in Ecumenism." Jean Tillard, for his part, had dedicated his *Église d'Églises* to Julian. This latter volume, however, does not in its contents touch on the Anglican–Roman Catholic Agreements or at any point mention Julian Charley or his evangelical Anglicanism. Jean Tillard died in 2000.

I

Four Centuries of Division

From the Sixteenth Century to the Nineteenth

N O ONE CAN ENTERTAIN doubts about the central place of the eucharist in the disputes and divisions of the sixteenth-century Reformation in Europe; and few other places could rival England for the intensity of the disputes and the pain of the divisions. A powerful demonstration of these is contained in the confrontation of Thomas Cranmer with Stephen Gardiner in 1550–51. It had been adumbrated in the speech of Cranmer in the debate in the House of Lords in December 1548, and it found initial expression in the communion service in the 1549 Book of Common Prayer; and this was totally confirmed by the communion service in the 1552 book. Amid a cloud of lesser difficulties, such as the use of Latin and of reception in both kinds, the storm-centres were invariably the doctrines of transubstantiation and of eucharistic sacrifice.

Against that background it is with a wholly reformed understanding of the communion service that the Church of England, freed from the power of Rome by the death of Queen Mary, emerged into the reign of Elizabeth I in November 1558. This is testified not only by the strongly protestant doctrine contained in the communion service in the 1559 Book of Common Prayer, but also by the Articles currently numbered as XXV, XXVIII, XXX, and XXXI of the XXXVIII Articles originally agreed in 1562, and then strengthened in 1571 by the addition of the very hard-edged Article XXIX to make up the full corpus of XXXIX Articles of 1571.[1] That corpus was finally endorsed that year by the Queen, and then took the canonical form it still has to this day. While the Articles wholly excluded Roman Catholic eucharistic beliefs and were actually orientated over against the

---

1. For the text of Article XXIX see p. 122 below.

Council of Trent, it is also worth noting their relationship to the puritan movement in Elizabeth's reign. The proponents of this movement sought a more thorough Reformation than the Elizabethan Settlement provided; they made particular reference to eliminating the last "popish rags" which the Settlement retained. They had little mind for compromise. Thus they objected forcefully to the imposition of a fixed form of prayers, and denounced various accoutrements to the authorized holy communion rite in the 1559 book (notably the wearing of a surplice by the presbyter and the kneeling to receive communion by the people). But, astonishingly, they never accused any of the actual text of the communion service or the wording of the XXXIX Articles as being in any way indicative of that harboring of Roman Catholic beliefs or unreformed practice which they were denouncing in the rubrics about ceremonial. This almost universal absence of protest on this great central question of the Reformation by the noisiest and most theologically embattled members of Elizabethan society speaks volumes not only about the overall teaching of the formularies, but also about the general nature of eucharistic belief and practice in the nation.[2] Nor was it different in the seventeenth century—the most determined puritans who signed the Millenary Petition, the slightly milder quartet at the Hampton Court Conference in January 1604, and the argumentative ones later at the Savoy Conference in April to July 1661, all provided a host of "exceptions" to the Book of Common Prayer and to the overall impact of the Elizabethan Settlement; but they identified virtually no problems with the text of the communion service or with the eucharistic doctrine of the XXXIX Articles. Both puritans and loyal Anglicans in the Church of England knew they were together well polarized from Roman Catholic eucharistic doctrine; and the general lack of controversy between them over the doctrine of the eucharist is all the more remarkable when it is contrasted with the virulence of such controversies both earlier, i.e., between Roman Catholics and protestants in Edward VI's reign, and later, i.e., between anglo-catholics and evangelicals in the nineteenth century; and equally remarkable when it is

---

2. Even those most adversarial documents, *An Admonition to the Parliament* and *A Second Admonition to the Parliament*, in 1572, while they object strongly to the imposed Book of Common Prayer, hardly touch on the eucharist. When they do, it is to complain either about the sheer fact of the rite being imposed, or in detail against the lack of preaching, or the use of wafer bread, or bishops giving unwelcome directions about the placing of the communion table, complaints that lie against misuse of the BCP rite, not against its central teachings on the Lord's Supper.

contrasted with the actual controversies in which the two sides were themselves engaged at the time concerning other liturgical matters.

There is little need to carry the story through to the nineteenth century in any depth. After the debacle of the Glorious Revolution (1688–89), monarchs were required to deny the doctrine of transubstantiation at their coronations.[3] Individual clergy may have veered towards Roman Catholic beliefs; but the general suspicion of the aims, methods and influence of the Church of Rome kept the nation at large and the Church of England's leaders in particular well to the reformed side of any line that could be drawn. William Purdy, in tracing the background to the dialogue in the eighteenth and nineteenth centuries, sees little but antagonism.[4] During the nineteenth century, however, a different picture within the Church of England itself began to emerge. Here the rise of anglo-catholicism led, among the most "advanced" exemplars of the cult, to their formulating eucharistic doctrine in Roman terms; first teaching about the eucharist in those terms, then larding over the Anglican liturgy with Roman ceremonial, and then changing it for Roman or semi-Roman texts; and they began also to reserve the consecrated species outside the times of celebration of the liturgy not only for communicating the sick, but also for the use of the reserved wafer in adoration and for the liturgical exercise known as Benediction. This affirmation of the Church of England as truly "Catholic" naturally led to pressure from the Anglican side for overtures to be made towards Rome; and even if such overtures received rebuffs (as with promulgation of the doctrine of papal infallibility) or a fairly cold shoulder in relation to doctrinal concerns, yet, if conversations ever were to come, anglo-catholics would press for it, but it would have to be a very mixed picture to be presented from the Anglican side.

Apostolicae curae

In 1896–97 a cool official interchange between Rome and Canterbury indirectly bore upon their respective doctrines of the eucharist. The presenting issue was the question of Anglican orders, a question pressed heavily from the Anglican side. Anglo-catholics had treasured the preservation of an unbroken succession of bishops and of those ordained by them as the

3. George V in 1911 was the first not to do so (Parliament had amended the requirement at his request).

4. Purdy, *Search for Unity*, 1–2.

hallmark of validity, and thus of the true standing of the Church of England as an integral part of the Western Catholic Church. It was, however, not seen that way by English Roman Catholics (who viewed themselves as the only true Catholics in England) nor by Leo XIII. In his encyclical, *Apostolicae curae,* in 1896 he suspended a major part of his rejection of Anglican orders upon the actual text of the Reformation ordinal, and particularly its omissions in relation to the office and work of a priest in respect of the eucharist.[5] The vital parts read as follows:

Table 1

Apostolicae curae —Latin Part of §§7 & 8	*Apostolicae curae* —English Part of §§7 & 8
Iamvero verba quae ad proximam usque aetatem habentur passim ab Anglicanis tamquam forma propria ordinationis presbyteralis, videlicet, *Accipe Spiritum Sanctum,* minime sane significant definite ordinem sacerdotii vel eius gratiam, et potestatem, quae praecipue est potestas *consecrandi et offerendi verum corpus et sanguinem Domini* (Trid. Sess. XXIII, de sacr. Ord.,can.1), eo sacrificio, quod non est *nuda commemoratio sacrificii in Cruci peracti* Forma huiusmodi aucta quidem est postea iis verbis, *ad officium et opus presbyteri*: sed hoc potius convincit, Anglicanos vidisse ipsos primam eam formam fuisse mancam neque idoneam rei.	[In §7] But the words used which until recently were commonly held by Anglicans to constitute the proper form of priestly Ordination—namely, "*Receive the Holy Ghost*" certainly do not in the least definitely express the Sacred Order of Priesthood, or its grace and power, which is chiefly the power "*of consecrating and of offering the true body and blood of the Lord*" (Council of Trent, Sess. XXIII. *De Sacr. Ord.,* Can.1) in that sacrifice which is no "*nude commemoration of the sacrifice offered on the Cross*"*(Ibid.,* Sess. XXII, *de Sacrif. Missae. Can.3).* This form had indeed afterwards added to it the words "*for the office and work of a priest,*" etc.; but this rather shows that the Anglicans themselves perceived that the first form was defective and inadequate. . . .

5. A full survey of the original documents and the division of opinion among the eight Roman Catholic theologians on the Papal Commission that advised Leo XIII is to be found in Hill and Yarnold, *Anglican Orders,* 5–22.

Apostolicae curae —Latin Part of §§7 & 8	*Apostolicae curae* —English Part of §§7 & 8
. . . eius namque aetatis memoria satis diserte loquitur, cuius animi essent in Ecclesiam catholicam auctores Ordinalis, . . . liturgiae ordinem, specie quidem redintegrandae eius formae primaevae, ad errores Novatorum multis modis deformarunt. Quamobrem toto Ordinali non modo nulla est aperta mentio sacrificii, consecrationis, sacerdotii, potestatisque consecrandi et sacrificii offerendi; sed immo omnia huiusmodi rerum vestigia, quae superessent in precationibus ritus catholici non plane reiectis, sublata et deleta sunt de industria, quod supra attigimus. Ita per se apparet nativa Ordinalis indoles ac spiritus, uti loquuntur.	[In §8] . . . the history of that time is sufficiently eloquent as to the animus of the authors of the Ordinal against the Catholic Church . . . they corrupted the liturgical order in many ways to suit the errors of the reformers, For this reason in the whole Ordinal not only is there no clear mention of the sacrifice, of consecration, of the sacerdotium, and of the power of consecrating and offering sacrifice, but, as we have just stated, every trace of these things, which had been in such prayers of the Catholic rite as they had not entirely rejected, was deliberately removed and struck out. In this way the native character—or spirit as it is called—of the Ordinal clearly manifests itself.

Leo XIII may have got the basic components of an ordinal wrong (and it is that which undermines his whole condemnation), but, as a matter of history, he had read the ordinals of 1550 and 1552 aright. Whereas the medieval ordination rites had concentrated almost entirely on the eucharistic role of the priest (including the injunction "Receive power to offer sacrifice on behalf of the living and the dead"), this was now entirely excised. In Cranmer's first ordinal in 1550 there remained the *porrectio* of the paten and cup alongside the (new) donation of the Bible, but in 1552 the delivery of the eucharistic vessels had been eliminated, and only the Bible was given. The eucharist was not even named in the rite, and the only remaining reference to it within the whole provision for ordination was in the unspecific reference to ministering the sacraments, once in the interrogation before ordination, once at the laying on of hands, and once at the *porrectio* of the Bible. In even greater contrast with the pre-Reformation rite the rite exhibited a long—very long—exhortation by the bishop setting out the nature of the presbyteral office, with a vision of a pastoral, learned and self-disciplined ministry, ministering the word and the grace of God *without any mention of sacraments whatsoever*. No one could derive from the 1552 ordinal (nor indeed from its 1662 successor) any hint that the presbyter's chief task was to consecrate the eucharist or to offer the eucharistic sacrifice.[6] Leo XIII did not go on from the ordinal to refer to the 1552 communion service, but, had he chosen to do so, he could have made his point even more strongly: the text of 1552 is wholly receptionist, there was no objective consecration of the elements (any bread or wine left over unconsumed at the end of the service could go home to the presbyter's table), and there was no hint of offering the elements (let alone offering the sacrifice of Christ) to the Father.[7]

In 1897 the two English archbishops made a joint reply to *Apostolicae curae* with their own statement, *Saepius officio*. In it they defended the 1552 ordinal (and thus the 1662 one) on the very proper grounds that the laying on of hands with prayer was the central necessity for ordination; and to require the other features on which the Pope was insisting was not only wrong, but would also call in question the validity of ordinations in Rome itself in earlier centuries. However, they also chose to advert to his criteria that presbyters had to be ordained explicitly to consecrate the elements and offer to God the eucharistic sacrifice. One can see that for the archbishops to want the Pope to recognize Anglican orders by his own criteria might be viewed as some gain, but it is arguable that they were thereby lured onto false ground (perhaps by Bishop Wordsworth who did the drafting), and driven to a false exposition of their own rites. Accepting the papal criteria, they defended the 1662 communion rite, the official text of their time, as actually meeting those criteria. In doing so, they went considerably—and controversially—beyond the text of 1662, as the table below demonstrates.

6. The 1662 ordinal, with which I was myself ordained, retains these features of 1552, and within today's Declaration of Assent it remains a part of the Church of England's historic formularies by which the Church gives witness to its biblical foundations.

7. The fully protestant character of the 1552/1662 communion rite was constantly reaffirmed by evangelical Anglicans in the nineteenth century—see, e.g., William Goode, J. C. Ryle, J. T. Tomlinson, Nathaniel Dimock, T. P. Boultbee, etc. It was strongly attested also in a weighty Roman Catholic work that we may presume was known in the Vatican, namely, Gasquet and Bishop, *Edward VI*. These expositions were in contradistinction to the regular anglo-catholic apologia that even the 1552 rite retained the basic character of a "catholic" liturgy, with the further fall-back that Cranmer was really a reforming catholic, though he was pushed somewhat in an unwelcome direction by somewhat more extreme colleagues. Such a catholic view prevailed through the first half of the twentieth century, and it can be seen here in the expositions of both the two archbishops in 1897 (see p. 7 opposite) and Lord Halifax in 1921 (see p. 11), when they later came to cite the 1662 rite. Gregory Dix finally called the bluff in 1945, and was largely supported by Edward Ratcliff (see, e.g., his 1935 article "Communion Service of the Prayer Book") and Arthur Couratin. This was not, however, to the forefront of ARCIC minds.

Table 2

Saepius officio ch. XI re the 1662 rite	Critical analysis of the passage
But we think it sufficient in the Liturgy which we use in celebrating the holy Eucharist,—while lifting up our hearts to the Lord, and when now consecrating the gifts already offered that they may become to us the Body and Blood of our Lord Jesus Christ, to signify the sacrifice which is offered at that point in the service in such terms as these. We continue a perpetual memory of the precious death of Christ, who is our advocate with the Father and the propitiation of our sins, according to His precept until His coming again. For first we offer the sacrifice of praise and thanksgiving; then next we plead and represent before the Father the sacrifice of the cross and by it we confidently entreat remission of sins and all other benefits of the Lord's Passion for all the whole Church; and lastly we offer the sacrifice of ourselves to the Creator of all things which we have already signified by the oblation of His creatures. This whole action, in which the people has necessarily to take its part with the Priest, we are accustomed to call the Eucharistic sacrifice.	There is no reference in the 1662 rite to the gifts having been "already offered"—they had merely been placed on the table. The elements are indeed to signify to us Christ's sacrifice made once for all upon the cross, but there is no hint that this "is offered at that point in the service," and no mention of "terms such as these." If the next sentences are intended to follow the order of themes within the 1662 rite, then— a. "the sacrifice of praise and thanksgiving" comes in *gratias agamus* ("Let us give thanks") b. There is no hint in the rite that our citing "the sacrifice of the cross" is in order to "plead and represent" (*"proponimus et praesentamus"*) it before the Father—terminology apparently chosen to suggest a Godward offering by us. c. entreating remission of sins and offering ourselves in self-sacrifice come within one of two alternative responsive post-communion prayers and may therefore in any celebration of the rite not be spoken at all, and in any case are simply responsive to God's gift. d. there is nowhere in the rite an "oblation of his creatures" (unless it irrelevantly refers to alms).[8] e. neither the rite, nor other formularies, nor a large proportion of Anglican worshippers then or now, have been "accustomed" to calling the rite or any part of it the "eucharistic sacrifice."

8. If this is intended to refer to the preparation of the elements upon the table, then any suggestion that use of "oblations" in the phrase in the Prayer for Christ's Church Militant here in Earth asking God "to accept our alms and oblations" has any reference to offering the elements to God (rather than to offering financial gifts in categories other than alms) must be dismissed. It was authoritatively refuted in Dowden, *Further Studies*, 176–223. See also Buchanan, *The End of the Offertory*. "Offertory theology" lies beyond the purview of this present volume.

The whole of the Reply's reference to the eucharist is orientated to make the 1662 rite conform to the Pope's criteria, at whatever cost to the visible meaning of the rite's actual wording. There is, for instance, no part of the rite which can plausibly carry the title "eucharistic sacrifice." Nevertheless the Reply of the archbishops has been frequently taken up and treated as an authoritative exposition of the Church of England rite.[9] However, from a strictly Church of England standpoint, the Reply was never, for instance, debated in Convocation, as it could have been and in a later generation would have been; and so the Reply actually stood on its own unsupported. It is more than possible that the death of Archbishop Benson in October 1896, and the succession to the see of Canterbury of Frederick Temple in December, delivered rather more responsibility than had been intended into the hands of the drafters, led by Bishop John Wordsworth.[10]

We may add that this present enquiry concerns an international agreement involving two worldwide Communions. Yet, although the Pope's verdict also affected Anglican orders throughout the world, it does not look as though the archbishops took wide international soundings before the Reply was agreed. So the question is appropriately asked as to whether or not, once the archbishops had made their Reply, the Anglican Communion internationally approved that Reply. Happily, as the 1897 Lambeth Conference met only a few months after *Saepius officio* was published, we can discover how the bishops viewed it on that worldwide basis. Sure enough, the Conference report included the findings of the "Committee appointed to consider and report upon the subject of church unity in its relation (a) to

9. Two major books greeted the centenary of *Apostolicae curae* in 1996, namely, Franklin, *Anglican Orders*; and Hill and Yarnold, *Anglican Orders*. In the hundreds of pages written there is virtually no attention paid to the statements about the eucharist on either side. To be fair, Hugh Montefiore does, in introducing the Franklin volume, say "*Saepius officio* receives only a passing mention in the papers that follow. In a systematic study of the matter it would require as much extended study as *Apostolicae curae* itself" (Franklin, *Anglican Orders*, 3). My impression is that Anglican authors touching on *Saepius officio* have generally treated it as a properly robust refutation of Leo XIII without considering critically how skewed is its defence of the 1662 eucharist.

10. John Wordsworth's own account of his cooperation with Stubbs and Creighton suggests very strongly that, whatever submissions may have come his way, there was no attempt on the drafters' part to seek a wider agreement. The idea of the two English archbishops replying on their own on behalf of Anglican orders worldwide seems to have held the field from to start. Temple, inheriting this situation, made his own contribution to the tone of the Wordsworth draft, but does not seem to have retouched the main contents (see Sandford, *Memoirs of Archbishop Temple*, 261–62, for the brief description of Temple's part, and 388–97 for Wordsworth's own account of his part).

the Churches of the East; (b) to the Latin Church; (c) to other bodies." They reported in respect of (b):

(b) ON THE LATIN COMMUNION

As regards the Church of Rome, a series of documents has been issued by Pope Leo XIII, expressing his desire for the union of Christendom, but unfortunately asserting as its only basis the recognition of the papal supremacy as of divine right. In the last of these documents the Pope proceeded to an examination of the position of the Church of England, and thus called forth an answer from the Archbishops of the English Church. Though controversy is rarely a method of promoting unity, there are grounds for thankfulness in the courteous tone in which much of this controversy has been conducted; in the abandonment by the Pope of much irrelevant and spurious matter which previously rendered discussion hopeless; in the limitation of the sphere of controversy to definite points; in a large amount of subsidiary literature, embodying the results of much research; and in the desire shown on both sides to understand and not consciously to misrepresent one another. If this spirit eases, even controversy will not have been in vain; and we await the issue of such controversy with entire confidence.

The Committee do not propose to submit any resolution to the Conference on this branch of their subject. They desire to adopt, as the substantial expression of their own opinion, the words of a Committee on Home Reunion of the Lambeth Conference of 1888.

> The Committee with deep regret felt that, under present conditions, it was useless to consider the question of Reunion with our brethren of the Roman Church, being painfully aware that any proposal for reunion would be entertained by the authorities of that Church only on condition of a complete submission on our part to those claims of absolute authority, and the acceptance of those other errors, both in doctrine and in discipline, against which, in faithfulness to God's Holy Word, and to the true principles of His Church, we have been for three centuries bound to protest.[11]

---

11. A modern reader, aware of 120 years of reflection and debate since 1897, not all of it measured or urbane, cannot but be amazed that the Lambeth sub-committee both thought the Bull irenic and declined to refute it in their own names. Thus, no reflection on the eucharistic implications of either *Apostolicae curae* or *Saepius officio* was registered.

It is of some interest (and surely also of some significance) that the Lambeth bishops gave thanks for the tone of the controversy, but neither gave thanks to the archbishops for making their Reply nor at any point endorsed or even discussed the content of *Saepius officio;* and the committee members concerned were apparently reluctant in their own persons either to discuss the issues involved or to say anything about either Anglican orders or the Prayer Book eucharist. In the absence of the endorsement one might have expected, it is reasonable to say that the Lambeth bishops gave no indication that they viewed the two archbishops as having spoken representatively on their behalf.

The Early Twentieth Century—Conversations at Malines 1921–25

The Malines Conversations were organized by Lord Halifax in co-operation with Cardinal Mercier, the Archbishop of Malines, initially on a personal friendship basis. They were occasioned by the 1920 Lambeth Appeal "To all Christian People," not least because the bishops were saying they were ready to receive whatever another denomination could give them to rectify any shortcomings in their orders. The Conversations gained a guarded recognition from Archbishop Davidson, guarded because not only had no Church of England authoritative commission been given for such talks, but also Halifax's personal choice of Anglican theologians was heavily loaded towards anglo-catholicism—his initial threesome being Walter Frere, Armitage Robinson and Halifax himself. The conversations could not but be informal, but Davidson was more or less kept in the picture, and he himself nominated Charles Gore and A. J. Kidd to join the team in 1923.

So was this an opportunity for the two sides to engage with each other over eucharistic doctrine? In the event this was an issue not discussed at Malines; and it does not look as though it were ever intended on either side that it should be discussed. The large weight of the Conversations fell upon papal primacy and kindred questions concerning how far the Church of England could go to share in a common Communion. But it is worth noting that the participants tackled these subjects after having already judged, at least in an interim way, that they had no need of a close doctrinal scrutiny of the eucharist, because, as they told themselves, they were already in substantial agreement. Mercier's opening address in 1921 included an affirmation that the XXXIX Articles were compatible with the Council of

Trent, and, as he responded to the "Memoire" submitted by Halifax, he ran quickly through a survey of the sacraments, i.e., of the seven sacraments asserted by Rome, and said:

> On passe au sacrement de l'Eucharistie. Le Mémoire dit: l'Eglise anglicane ensigne que le corps et le sang de N. S. Jésus-Christ sont vraiment donnés, pris et reçus dans le saint sacrement. Ce sont les termes mêmes du cathéchisme.
>
> Sur la doctrine de la Transubstantiation, les Anglicans déclarent admitter le changement du pain et du vin en le corps et le sang du Christ par la Consécration. Aux yeux des catholiques, le mot Transubstantiation ne signifie pas autre chose.
>
> *Sacrifice.*—Le Mémoire dit: "que l'Eucharistie est le même sacrifice que celui de la croix offert par N. S. Jésus-Christ à Son Père d'maniére mystique et sacramentelle." Les anglicans font la lecture de deux documents sur le sacrifice.
>
> a. L'oraison dite priére d'oblation, dans le service Eucharistique, *Domine Pater caelestis nos humiles famuli tui rogamus etc.*
>
> b. Dans la réponse que firent les archevêques de Cantorbèry et d'York à la Bulle *Apostolicae curae* (n° XI) il est dit *Further, we truly teach the doctrine of Eucharistic sacrifice* etc.
>
> Les deux passages ont paru suffisamment exprimer la notion du sacrifice eucharistique.[12]

A critic must query whether the "prayer of oblation" (not actually a title used in the Book of Common Prayer) taught or implied anything about eucharistic sacrifice;[13] and might equally query whether *Saepius officio*, which certainly did speak of eucharistic sacrifice, should have had any credible standing as an authoritative Anglican statement. In this connection the reticence of the 1897 Lambeth Conference in respect of *Saepius officio* has already been noted. Clearly the Anglicans at Malines were content to be thus recognized in the eyes of Rome as orthodox on the main eucharistic issues;

12. Halifax, *Conversations*, 13–15.

13. The title originated in the Scottish Liturgy of 1637, where it was in a rubric ensuring the "prayer of consecration" ran on after the narrative of institution instead of ending with the narrative as in the 1604 book. Later, Scottish use was to indent the title "*The Oblation*" within the prayer, where it accompanied a stated offering of the "gifts" to God within the text, and thus it passed also into American usage. It cannot well carry the same meaning in its post-communion position. See the examination of the meaning of this "prayer of oblation" on p. 103 and pp. 116–19 below.

and they contented themselves with instead putting down markers to register existing differences on secondary issues about the use of the vernacular and reception in both kinds.[14] The Roman Catholics, in their own final report in 1927, recorded within Halifax's edition, again cited *Saepius officio* as evidence that the Anglicans held the same doctrine as they did.

Whether or not such a verdict would carry weight with the Anglican Communion at large never came to the test. Mercier died in 1926, and then the whole procedure came under a ban from Rome, as in January 1928 Pope Pius XI issued *Mortalium animos*, forbidding Roman Catholics from participating in conferences seeking the union of other Churches with Rome.

14. These two issues had virtually no doctrinal (and therefore probably no non-negotiable) character to the Roman authorities: the issues were clearly disciplinary and were both already conceded by Rome in its relationship with Uniat Churches of the East. So the Conversationalists virtually swallowed a camel while showing unnecessary concern about assimilating a gnat.

2

Historical Background to the ARCIC Texts

The Run-Up to Vatican II

AFTER WORLD WAR II the times were not immediately conducive to the resumption of any theological dialogue on the European scene. Perhaps 1948, the year of the founding of the World Council of Churches in Amsterdam, provides a plausible new starting point, though the Roman Catholic Church took no part in the process or in the actual Council. The 1948 Lambeth Conference, in its section on "The Unity of the Church," had a report on "Relations with Episcopal Churches," and this referred to the "unyielding attitude of the Roman Catholic Church in regard to reunion and matters of faith." It also noted that Roman Catholics were forbidden "to hold mixed meetings with other Christians in which matters of faith are dealt with without previous permission of the Holy See." There were no resolutions on relationships with Rome. On that front the times did not look very promising.

In 1950 there came the Apostolic Constitution making the bodily assumption of Mary an article of faith, a move by Pius XII which polarized Rome further from the churches of the Reformation, and made the idea of dialogue that much harder to focus. Nevertheless William Purdy records that informal explorations by notable theologians in 1949–50 led to a first meeting of eight Anglicans and eight Roman Catholics in Paris in April 1950, followed by a four-a-side conversation in Strasbourg in September that year. The 1950s are then punctuated with further gatherings, with some minimal continuity of membership, through until the death of Pius XII in 1958. Then the surprising election of John XXIII led quickly to a somewhat changed climate.[1] The

1. See Purdy, *Search for Unity*, 9–23.

present purposes are sufficiently served by noting that the agenda for these early meetings did not touch on the eucharist, but started much further back, with issues of revelation and authority.

There followed Pope John's announcement in 1959 of a forthcoming General Council, the formation in 1960 of the Secretariat for Promoting Christian Unity (SPCU), and the untrumpeted visit of Archbishop Geoffrey Fisher to see the Pope in December 1960. In an atmosphere that was clearly changing, in April 1961 the meetings for conversations were resumed at Assisi; and in 1962 a major Roman Catholic national conference on ecumenism was planned at Heythrop in England, and Cardinal Bea, the president of the SPCU, was invited to speak at it. He, being in England, called on Archbishop Michael Ramsey and opened the question of Anglican observers at the Council. The Heythrop Conference on "Education" was followed that Summer by two inter-church meetings, one at Oxford, one at Worth Abbey, the first on "Eucharistic Sacrifice" and the second on "The Eucharist"—topics which had not appeared in any earlier talks. The agenda were to explain and compare positions rather than engage in either assimilation or polemics. But the eucharist and differences between the two Communions about the eucharist were apparently now well above the horizon.

Vatican II and Post-Vatican Preliminaries

The next stages of slow convergence towards serious theological encounter are well charted. There were appointed Anglican observers for Vatican II, as the Council started in Autumn 1962; and at the Council there emerged the much-quoted kind passing mention "Among those [other Churches] in which some Catholic traditions and institutions continue to exist, the Anglican Communion occupies a special place."[2] Then at the end of the Council's last session in November 1965, the Anglican observers were received by Pope Paul VI prior to their departure. There was a forward-looking conversation, exploring the possibilities of a change in relationships that might spring from the projected official visit to Rome of Archbishop Michael Ramsey. In England in early 1966 Cardinal Heenan said in public that Roman Catholics ought to be in conversation with evangelicals, and the Church of England Evangelical Council (CEEC) convened a theological team who met for some years with a comparable

2. Decree on Ecumenism (*Unitatis Redintegratio*) 13, promulged November 1964.

Roman Catholic team. One of the points on which they agreed was that the Reformation was about real issues.

Archbishop Michael Ramsey duly visited Rome in March 1966 and made with Pope Paul a "Common Declaration," at the heart of which was a stated intention of setting up a serious dialogue ("*Colloquia*" in the Latin text) between the two Communions, a dialogue to include scripture, tradition, liturgy, and practical difficulties.

TEXT A

The Common Declaration by Pope Paul VI and the Archbishop of Canterbury

ROME, SAINT PAUL WITHOUT-THE-WALLS, 24 MARCH 1966

In this city of Rome, from which Saint Augustine was sent by Pope Gregory to England and there founded the cathedral see of Canterbury, towards which the eyes of all Anglicans now turn as the centre of their Christian Communion, His Holiness Pope Paul VI and His Grace Michael Ramsey, Archbishop of Canterbury, representing the Anglican Communion, have met to exchange fraternal greetings.

At the conclusion of their meeting they give thanks to Almighty God Who by the action of the Holy Spirit has in these latter years created a new atmosphere of Christian fellowship between the Roman Catholic Church and the Churches of the Anglican Communion.

This encounter of the 23 March 1966 marks a new stage in the development of fraternal relations, based upon Christian charity, and of sincere efforts to remove the causes of conflict and to re-establish unity.

In willing obedience to the command of Christ who bade His disciples love one another, they declare that, with His help, they wish to leave in the hands of the God of mercy all that in the past has been opposed by this precept of charity, and that they make their own the mind of the Apostle which he expressed in these words: "Forgetting those things that are behind, and reaching forth unto those things which are before, I press towards the mark for the prize of the high calling of God in Christ Jesus" (Phil.3:13–14).

They affirm their desire that all those Christians who belong to these two Communions may be animated by these same sentiments of respect, esteem and fraternal love, and in order to help these develop to the full, they intend to inaugurate between the Roman Catholic Church and the Anglican Communion a serious dialogue which, founded on the Gospels and on the ancient common traditions, may lead to that unity in truth, for which Christ prayed.

The dialogue should include not only theological matters such as Scripture, Tradition and Liturgy, but also matters of practical difficulty felt on either side. His Holiness the Pope and His Grace the Archbishop of Canterbury are, indeed, aware that serious obstacles stand in the way of a restoration of complete communion of faith and sacramental life; nevertheless, they are of one mind in their determination to promote responsible contacts between their Communion in all those spheres of Church life where collaboration is likely to lead to greater understanding and a deeper charity, and to strive in common to find solutions for all the great problems that face those who believe in Christ in the world of today.

Through such collaboration, by the Grace of God the Father and in the light of the Holy Spirit, may the prayer of Our Lord Jesus Christ for unity among His disciples be brought nearer to fulfilment, and with progress towards unity may there be a strengthening of peace in the world, the peace that only He can grant who gives "the peace that passeth all understanding," together with the blessing of Almighty God, Father, Son and Holy Spirit, that it may abide with all men for ever.

+MICHAEL CANTUARIENSIS   PAULUS PP.VI

For our present purposes, it is worth noting that neither sacramental theology nor, more specifically, the eucharist is mentioned. On the other hand "liturgy" is there, set alongside Scripture and Tradition as a major exemplar of theological dialogue. One wonders whether either signatory was defining mentally what limits he would set to "liturgy." Was the appropriate door being left invitingly open?

3

The Malta Report (1968)

T HE PLANNED DIALOGUE WAS to come to pass in two stages. In May 1966 Bishop Willebrands, the secretary of the SPCU, visited Lambeth and agreed with Michael Ramsey about the appointment of the Joint Preparatory Commission. On the Anglican side John Moorman, Bishop of Ripon, was the chairman, and the nine members included four from the Church of England, plus Edward Knapp-Fisher, an Englishman in South Africa, and one from Wales, and three from the rest of the Anglican Communion. At the second meeting of the Commission there were added one American and Henry McAdoo from the Church of Ireland. The two secretaries were also from England. This particular loading of the membership marched alongside a different loading—among the eleven members only James Atkinson of Hull University would have made any claims to be a protestant; and four or five were overtly anglo-catholic.[1] The Commission met in January and September 1967, and completed its work at Malta across the new year into January 1968.[2] Its report, normally known as "The Malta Report," was not published immediately, but was provided

---

1. A latterday evangelical can but smile at the confusion recorded by Purdy, where other Anglicans suggested Atkinson was not representative of Anglican evangelicalism (presumably because he was too conservative). When Fairweather approached Ramsey about this he apparently thought Massey Shepherd, already on the Commission, might qualify as a "liberal evangelical" (an attribution that the Commission members summarily dismissed), and finally A. T. Mollegen, a member of faculty from Virginia Theological Seminary was added to the team (see Purdy, *Search for Unity*, 107). Evangelicals were obviously strange people who did not regularly come within the purview of "normal" Anglicans, and, so it seems, were therefore the harder to identify accurately when the need arose.

2. The Commission's work is written up in full detail in Clark and Davey, *Anglican/Roman Catholic Dialogue*. It is also the subject of a chapter in the first person singular by the Roman Catholic secretary in Purdy, *Search for Unity*, 99–114.

in confidence to the bishops meeting for the Lambeth Conference in July-August 1968, and was later leaked to the press and published in various church journals in November 1968.[3]

TEXT B

THE MALTA REPORT (1968)

Report of the Anglican–Roman Catholic Joint Preparatory Commission

I

[Paras 1–6 report that the Joint Preparatory Commission has met three times in the period 1967–68; the members have had a sense of urgency as well as charity and frankness; they have been bonded by a common faith and common baptism, and "our common Christian inheritance for many centuries with its living traditions of liturgy, theology, spirituality, Church order, and mission." They have been aware of the differences between them and the need for close study of those differences, and for the need to recognize "the Anglican distinction of fundamentals from non-fundamentals and the distinction implied by the Vatican Council's reference to a 'hierarchy of truths' (*Decree on Ecumenism*, 11)," and also to recognize "the difference between 'revealed truths' and 'the manner in which they are formulated' (*Pastoral Constitution on the Church in the Modern World*, 62)"].

II

7. We recommend that the second stage in our growing together begin with an official and explicit affirmation of mutual recognition from the highest authorities of each Communion. It would acknowledge that both

---

3. "Leaked" is the Clark and Davey wording (see *Anglican/Roman Catholic Dialogue*, 25). How any document given to six hundred people could ever have been thought to be "confidential" escapes credibility. Nor, on inspection of its contents, does any reason for confidentiality emerge.

Communions are at one in the faith that the Church is founded upon the revelation of God the Father, made known to us in the person and work of Jesus Christ, who is present through the Holy Spirit in the Scriptures and his Church, and is the only Mediator between God and Man, the ultimate Authority for all our doctrine. Each accepts the basic truths set forth in the ecumenical Creeds and the common tradition of the ancient Church, although neither Communion is tied to a positive acceptance of all the beliefs and devotional practices of the other.

8. In every region where each Communion has a hierarchy, we propose an annual joint meeting of either the whole or some reasonable representation of the two hierarchies.

9. In the same circumstances we further recommend:

    a. Constant consultation between committees concerned with pastoral and evangelistic problems including, where appropriate, the appointment of joint committee.

    b. Agreements for joint use of churches and other ecclesiastical buildings, both existing and to be built, wherever such use is helpful for one or other of the two Communions.

    c. Agreements to share facilities for theological education, with the hope that all future priests of each Communion should have attended some course taught by a professor of the other Communion. Arrangements should also be made where possible for temporary exchange of students.

    d. Collaboration in projects and institutions of theological scholarship to be warmly encouraged.

10. Prayer in common has been recommended by the Decree on Ecumenism and provisions for this common worship are to be found in the *Directory* (para. 56). We urge that they be implemented.

11. Our similar liturgical and spiritual traditions make extensive sharing possible and desirable; for example, in non-eucharistic services, the exploration of new forms of worship, and retreats in common. Religious orders of similar aspiration in the two Communions are urged to develop a special relationship.

12. Our closeness in the field of sacramental belief leads us further to recommend that on occasion the exchange of preachers for the homily during the celebration of the Eucharist be also permitted, without prejudice to the more general regulations contained in the *Directory*.

13. Since our liturgies are closely related by reason of their common source, the ferment of liturgical renewal and reform now engaging both our Communions provides an unprecedented opportunity for collaboration. We should co-operate, and not take unilateral action, in any significant changes in the seasons and major holy days of the Christian Year; and we should experiment together in the development of a common eucharistic lectionary. A matter of special urgency in view of the advanced stage of liturgical revision in both Communions is that we reach vernacular forms of those prayers, hymns and responses which our people share in common with their respective liturgies. We recommend that this be taken up without delay.

    We are gratified that collaboration in this work has been initiated by the exchange of observers and consultants in many of our respective liturgical commissions. Especially in matters concerning the vernacular, we recommend that representatives of our two Communions (not excluding other Christian bodies with similar liturgical concerns) be associated on a basis of equality both in international and in national and regional committees assigned for this responsibility.

[14–16 Recommendations about co-operation between church leaders on urgent human issues, in the field of missionary strategy and activity, and in the implications of mixed marriages.]

III

17. We cannot envisage in detail what may be the issues and demands of the final stage in our quest for the full, organic unity of our two Communions. We know only that we must be constant in prayer for the grace of the Holy Spirit in order that we may be open to his guidance and judgment, and receptive to each other's faith and understanding. There remain fundamental theological and moral questions between us where we need immediately to seek together for reconciling answers. In this search we cannot escape the witness of our history; but we cannot resolve our difference by mere reconsideration of, and judgment upon, the past. We must press on in confident faith that new light will be given us to lead us to our goal.

18. The fulfilment of our aim is far from imminent. In these circumstances the question of accepting some measure of sacramental intercommunion apart from full unity is being raised on every side. In the minds of many Christians no issue is today more urgent. We cannot ignore this, but equally we cannot sanction changes touching the very heart of Church life, eucharistic communion, without being certain that such changes would be truly Christian. Such certainty cannot be reached without more and careful study of the theology implied.

19. We are agreed that among the conditions required for intercommunion are both a true sharing in faith and the mutual recognition of ministry. The latter presents a particular difficulty in regard to Anglican Orders according to the traditional judgment of the Roman Church. We believe that the present growing together of our two Communions and the needs of the future require of us a very serious consideration of this question in the light of modern theology. The theology of the ministry forms part of the theology of the Church and must be considered as such.

It is only when sufficient agreement has been reached as to the nature of the priesthood and the meaning to be attached in this context to the word "validity" that we could proceed, working always jointly, to the application of this doctrine to the Anglican ministry of today. We would wish to re-examine historical events and past documents only to the extent that they can throw light upon the facts of the present situation.

20. In addition, a serious theological examination should be jointly undertaken on the nature of authority with particular reference to its bearing on the interpretation of the historic faith to which both our Communions are committed. Real or apparent differences between us come to the surface in such matters as the unity and indefectibility of the Church and its teaching authority, the Petrine primacy, infallibility, and Mariological definitions.

21. In continuation of the work done by our Commission, we recommend that it be replaced by a Permanent Joint Commission responsible (in co-operation with the Secretariat for Promoting Christian Unity and the Church of England Council on Foreign Relations in Association with the Anglican Executive Officer) for the oversight of Roman Catholic-Anglican relations, and the co-ordination of future work undertaken together by our two Communions.

22. We also recommend the constitution of two joint sub-commissions, responsible to the Permanent Commission, to undertake two urgent and important tasks:

> ONE to examine the question of intercommunion, and the related matters of Church and Ministry;

> THE OTHER to examine the question of authority, its nature, exercise, and implications.

We consider it important that adequate money, secretarial assistance, and research facilities should be given to the Commission and its sub-commissions in order that their

members may do their work recommend with thorough-
ness and efficiency.

23. We also recommend joint study of moral theology to de-
termine similarities and differences in our teaching and
practice in this field.

24. In concluding our Report, we cannot do better than quote
the words of those by whom we were commissioned, and
to whom, with respect, we now submit it:

> In willing obedience to the command of Christ who
> bade His disciples love one another, they declare that,
> with His help, they wish to leave in the hands of the
> God of mercy all that in the past has been opposed by
> this precept of charity, and that they make their own
> the mind of the Apostle which he expressed in these
> words: "Forgetting those things that are behind, and
> reaching forth unto those things which are before, I
> press towards the mark for the prize of the high calling
> of God in Christ Jesus" (Phil.3:13–14).

The Common Declaration by Pope Paul VI
and the Archbishop of Canterbury
24 March 1966

Malta, 2 January 1968

The central thrust of the Report lies in the recommendation in §22 towards the establishment of the "Permanent Joint Commission," and it was
to such a Commission that it was envisaged all theological issues would be
steered; and it was clear that plenty of such issues were calling for attention.
The eucharist as such was only lightly mentioned, but for the purposes of
the present enquiry three relevant issues are discernible.

First comes the issue of intercommunion or shared communion
(§§18–19). Clearly this was felt in quite personal terms as a high priority
on the Commission.

Next there is the fairly full list of tasks to be addressed jointly in the
liturgical field (§11). This was being drafted just three years since the first
use of the vernacular in Roman Catholic Churches had occurred (in the
light of *Sacrosanctum Concilium*, the Constitution on the Liturgy, the first

product of Vatican II in December 1963). By 1967 all the Latin texts were undergoing revision and the exploration of how best to achieve common English-language translations was also under way. The common texts would necessarily include elements traditionally embedded in the eucharistic rites, such as Gloria in Excelsis, Creeds, Sursum Corda, Sanctus, the Lord's Prayer, etc. So joint work would be fuelling common texts. This would have some direct application to the eucharistic rites, though would probably not be touching the most sensitive issues of eucharistic doctrine.[4]

Thirdly, there is in §12 a bold assertion of "closeness in the field of sacramental belief." Yet, with that said, the report's recommendations provide only a tinkering with the edges of eucharistic rites over and above the common texts. There are suggestions of joint action re preachers, re calendar and lectionary, and re hymnody. In the light of later history, we can but marvel at the sheer timidity of these suggestions. There is not a hint that a serious permanent Commission might address the doctrine of the eucharist. The Malta participants clearly steered their path away from such a dialogue, possibly because the idea was so remote that it never rose above their horizon, or possibly because they feared that, on close approach, it would prove to be sinking sands.

The Lambeth Conference, 1968

In the Lambeth Conference, which was held in July and August 1968, the section addressing "Renewal in Unity" had a strong sub-committee on "Relations with the Roman Catholic Church," chaired by J. R. H. Moorman, who, as noted above, had been both the official Anglican observer at the Vatican Council and the Anglican chair of the Preparatory Commission. The sub-committee report quoted the "Common Declaration" of the

---

4. It is extraordinary to revert fifty years later to this almost prophetic call by the Commission. The story is told elsewhere how for many years some approximation to this outlined programme was pursued by the English-speaking churches. It is also a matter of history that in 2001 for Roman Catholics the encyclical *Liturgiam authenticam* forbade any ecumenical drafting of translations, and insisted that Roman texts must be clearly distanced (not least by a Latinate style) from English texts used in other churches; and this was duly followed up by the wholly new, deliberately unecumenical, authorized Roman translations newly imposed in 2011. This lies beyond the purview of this present volume, but revisiting the Malta Report shows what a thorough and ill-advised *volte-face* the Roman Catholic English-speaking liturgists were in 2001 forced by authority to adopt. Note how the Malta Report was saying, "We should cooperate, and not take unilateral action."

Pope and Archbishop, and in quiet tones welcomed the (confidential!) Malta Report. The members then gave a major place in their report to the issue of intercommunion. This included half a page on "Consensus on the Eucharist" (p.158), and the first paragraph registered "the need . . . for sharing in the present renewal of eucharistic thinking and practice now taking place amongst the Churches." The second paragraph then welcomed "the inclusion of members of the Roman Catholic Church within the membership of the [WCC] Faith and Order Commission." Finally the third paragraph ran as follows:

> Whenever intercommunion is proposed between Churches we believe that there should first be found a basic agreement on the meaning of the Eucharist. Any consensus between Churches should include mention of those essential elements to be found in any service of the Eucharist.

Sure enough, the sub-committee *was* interested in intercommunion with the Roman Catholic Church. It then listed a common faith and a whole series of areas of progress in co-operation between the two Communions, before coming to a section with the sub-heading "A Permanent Joint Commission." Now came this clear aim of intercommunion with the Roman Catholics:

> We recommend the setting up of a Permanent Joint Commission, our delegation to be chosen by the Lambeth Consultative Council or its successor[5] and to be representative of the Anglican Communion as a whole. This commission or its subcommissions should consider the question of intercommunion in the context of a true sharing in faith and the mutual recognition of ministry, and should also consider . . . the orders of both Churches.

So although the sub-committee thought agreement on doctrine went with practicing intercommunion, and although it aimed for intercommunion with Rome, somehow it was as silent on eucharistic doctrine as part of the agenda with Rome as the Malta Report itself had been. Then when it came to drafting resolutions, even intercommunion disappeared from

5. Editorial footnote: the reference here to "the Lambeth Consultative Body or its successor" reflects the fact that the bishops knew they would soon be voting in plenary to create an "Anglican Consultative Council." So they repeated the same wording in Resolution 53 (see above). The proposals for the ACC in Resolution 69 of the Conference included (in §5) as one of its functions "to make arrangements for the conduct of pan-Anglican conversations with the Roman Catholic Church, the Orthodox Churches, and other Churches." The Resolution was duly adopted and the ACC was correspondingly inaugurated, holding its first meeting in 1971.

sight. Instead the Section brought the following uncontroversial resolutions to the plenary meetings of the Conference and carried them there without dissent being registered.

TEXT C

The Resolutions on the Roman Catholic Church of the 1968 Lambeth Conference

The Roman Catholic Church

52. The Conference welcomes the proposals made in the report of Section III which concern Anglican relations with the Roman Catholic Church.

53. The Conference recommends the setting up of a permanent Joint Commission, for which the Anglican delegation should be chosen by the Lambeth Consultative Body (or its successor) and be representative of the Anglican Communion as a whole.

54. [A resolution on mixed marriages and the work of the Joint Commission on the Theology of Marriage.]

There must, however, have been individuals who saw the Section Report as saying rather more than the resolutions; yet even so, as noted, the Section Report had itself not quite proposed a joint study of eucharistic doctrine.

4

The Windsor Agreed Statement
on Eucharistic Doctrine (1971)

T HE WAY WAS NOW open for action, save that on the Anglican side there existed no constitutional body to appoint the Commission's members. The Lambeth Consultative Body was being replaced, but the replacement-in-waiting, the ACC, could not exist until the provinces had all separately voted for it. So Purdy reports Michael Ramsey as saying in September 1968 that "the Lambeth Consultative Body had 'unfortunately' left the appointment . . . in his hands."[1] Although he was circulating the metropolitans of all the provinces, he clearly started with a notion of at least a core of membership from the United Kingdom. Henry McAdoo, Bishop of Ossory in the Republic of Ireland, who had joined the JPC at its second meeting, became the Anglican chairman. John Moorman was there again; Edward Knapp-Fisher, an English College principal who was now a bishop in South Africa, was there; Harry Smythe and Howard Root, the previous and the current Directors of the Anglican Centre in Rome, were there; Henry Chadwick brought his vast learning; and Julian Charley was there, as recorded earlier in the Introduction.[2] Dr. J. Kelly of St. Edmund Hall, Oxford, came to one meeting only. John Halliburton, the Principal of Chichester Theological College, was there (like Smythe, technically as a "consultant"). Alongside these eight were Felix Arnott, Archbishop of Brisbane, Arthur Vogel from Nashotah House, USA (and later Bishop of West Missouri), and Professor Eugene Fairweather of Trinity College, Toronto, who replaced Dr. Kelly at the second meeting. The team still looked not only very English, but also strongly anglo-catholic. The Roman Catholics also had a core from

---

1. Purdy, *Search for Unity*, 125.
2. See pp. xviii–xix above.

England, but were marginally more international, and were spiced by the inclusion of two French-speaking members, both theologically creative, Jean Tillard from Ottawa and Pierre Duprey from the Vatican SPCU. Their chair was Alan Clark, Bishop of East Anglia.

McAdoo records that a preliminary meeting of the chairman and two others from each side was held in Dublin in April 1969. They planned for preliminary papers to be commissioned and to be ready in advance for when the full Commission first met at Windsor in January 1970.[3] One of the four topics was "Church, Intercommunion and the Ministry" and that was the nearest the titles of the papers came at that stage to suggesting that the eucharist should be strongly focused as a lead title in the doctrinal enquiry.[4] Nevertheless in the first days of that week in residence the early discussions led the Commission to three key-areas—"The Church and Authority," "The Ministry," and "The Eucharist." The sub-commission to work on "The Eucharist" was to be convened by Knapp-Fisher (from South Africa) with Julian Charley and Jean Tillard as "correspondent members." It looks as though they did much work in closer concert with each other than with their convenor.

At the Commission's second meeting, in Venice in September 1970, the new draft reports were discussed, and were "further elaborated and amended."[5] But the resultant crowding of the agenda led to a decision thereafter to take the three themes one at a time rather than simultaneously, in order to give maximum time, with maximum involvement by all, to each theme. Meanwhile they would publish the three drafts, as "working papers," intended to show the directions in which they were heading, but in no sense to claim more than an interim agreement about the actual wording. And the first theme was to be the eucharist, perhaps because the drafting seemed to be at a more mature stage than was the case with other two themes. The Commission was meanwhile planning to reach the point of a definitive agreed Statement a year later.

3. See McAdoo, "Anglican/Roman Catholic," 224–26.

4. The record of the "Meetings of the Commission" (*The Final Report*, 102) states about this first meeting that "Anglican and Roman Catholic position papers had been prepared in advance on all three subjects," but that is a little distant from how McAdoo describes the "position papers" as shown above.

5. The words quoted are from the "Introduction" to the texts published as shown in the next footnote and they mirror Purdy's account.

The three texts were published as "The Venice Conversations" with a single Introduction in three journals.[6] Features of the "Church and Eucharist" paper which touch on controversial areas are of some significance as background to the later Agreements made by the Commission.

TEXT D

The Venice Draft Texts[7]

I Church and Authority

[This section for the present purposes raised no controversial matters]

II Church and Eucharist

I CHURCH

[1–4 handle ecclesiological issues, touching briefly in §3 on the lack of complete communion between the two Churches, arising partly from different understandings of the nature of the church.]

5. The characteristic service (*leitourgia*) of the Church is the Eucharist in which, with thanksgiving for all God's mercies in creation and redemption, Christ's members joyfully celebrate their unity and community with Him in this saving work, until He comes again. Church is *Eucharistic community*.

6. In *Theology* (February 1971), *The Clergy Review* (February 1971) and *One in Christ* (2–3 1971). Purdy provides some background to the publishing of these drafts. Julian Charley, conscious of his exposed position as (in Purdy's words) "the evangelical member of the Commission" and aware that much of the content would raise disquiet in his "constituency," had at Venice got the Commission to agree that Jean Tillard and he would write a joint introduction to any publication, carefully indicating its very interim status. However, he learned at a late stage that this had been overlooked in the releasing of the texts to the journals, and he wrote to the co-chairmen in some alarm. They took the point and, as Tillard was away in Canada, the secretary, Michael Mayne, wrote an introduction that met Charley's need. Some relevant parts of that introduction are quoted after the main text "D" on p.35 below.

7. Care should be taken over the "Venice" provenance, as the first Authority Statement of ARCIC I in 1976 was sometimes known as the "Venice Statement." The "drafts" published here from "conversations" at Venice were distinctly *not* a "Statement."

II THE EUCHARIST

1. It is through the life, death and resurrection of Jesus Christ that God reconciled men to Himself, and, in Him, offers unity to all mankind. Our relationship with one another as children of God is inaugurated by baptism into Christ through the Holy Spirit, and is expressed and deepened through the Eucharist.

2. The Eucharist is central in the obedience and worship of the people of God. It was instituted by our Lord in the context of the Passover. The Passover was the celebration of Israel's deliverance from slavery and of the constitution as God's people sealed by the Covenant of Sinai. It foreshadowed the universal deliverance from sin offered for the reconciliation of all men by Christ through the New Covenant sealed with His blood.

3. Christ's whole life, culminating in his death on the Cross, was the one true perfect and sufficient sacrifice for the sins of the whole world. He was raised from the dead and entered into His glory. He is the head of His body, the Church, who through the Holy Spirit in the Eucharist deepened the union of His members with Himself in His death and resurrection.

4. God so loved the world that He gave his only begotten Son to the end that all who believe in Him should not perish, but have everlasting life. It is God the Father who in Christ is reconciling all men to Himself.

   When the Church gathers for the Eucharist it is Christ the Lord, crucified and risen, who gives thanks and unites us with His thanksgiving for all God's mercies in creation and redemption.

   It is Christ the Lord who offers to the Father the total self-surrender which found its supreme expression in his death, and unites us with his perfect obedience to the Father.

   It is Christ the Lord who brings us to repentance, forgives our sins and gives us grace to amend.

It is Christ the Lord who unites us with Himself in His intercession for ourselves and for all mankind.

It is from Christ the Lord that we receive the bread of life and the cup of salvation, and in Him that we are offered anew to the Father's service.

In the eucharist therefore it is the whole Church which shares Christ's priesthood and is associated with His sacrifice, although the ordained minister who presides has particular liturgical functions as the representative of Christ and His people.

5. When His people gather for the Eucharist to commemorate His saving acts for our redemption, Christ, sacramentally present, makes effective among us the eternal benefits of His victory on the Cross and elicits and renews our response of faith, thanksgiving and self-surrender. It is by Christ's activity through the Holy Spirit in the Eucharist that the life of the Church is built up, its fellowship strengthened and its mission furthered. It is in the Eucharist that the Church becomes most intensely itself. The identity of the Church as the Body of Christ is both expressed and effectively proclaimed by its being gathered around, and partaking of, His body and blood. In the whole action of the Eucharist, and in his sacramental presence in the bread and wine, the crucified and risen Lord according to His promises offers himself to all His people.

6. In the Eucharist we proclaim the Lord's death until He comes. Receiving a foretaste of the kingdom to come, we are spurred to hasten its realization on earth. We look back with thanksgiving to what Christ has done for us; we greet Him present among us; we look forward to His final coming in the fullness of His kingdom when "the Son Himself will be subjected to Him who put all things under Him, that God may be everything to everybody" (1 Cor. 15.28).

7. [A listing of different names for the sacrament used in history.] Perhaps *the Eucharist* has become the most

universally acceptable term. Underneath the use of differing terms lie the real problems of belief and practice.

8. Christ and the early Church, in expressing the meaning of His death and resurrection, found the language of sacrifice indispensable. For the Hebrew, sacrifice was a traditional means of communication with God. This involved a wide range of expression, for example, the Passover, which was essentially a communal feast; the Day of Atonement, which was essentially expiatory; the Covenant, which was essentially the establishing of communion between God and man. In the mind of the early Church there was a close nexus between the Cross as a sacrifice and the Eucharist. It was around this point that controversy was later to rage. Some parties took any sacrificial content in the Eucharist to detract from the "once and for all" nature of Christ's self-offering on the Cross, because they thought it meant regarding the Eucharist as a repeatable sacrifice on its own right. Others insisted on the sacrificial character of the Eucharist and by their language and practices appeared to lend colour to these suspicions. We believe that this conflict can be transcended by a fresh understanding of the Passover. We all accept Christ's death as having taken place once and for all in history. As the events of the Exodus were accepted as having happened once for all, as the annual Passover sacrifice was seen by them as the *memorial* (i.e., the making effective in the present) of this event in the continuing life of Israel, so we see the Eucharist as the memorial of Christ's self-offering in the continuing life of the Christian church. Against this background it is possible to think of the eucharist in sacrificial terms, but when a phrase like "the Sacrifice of the Mass" is used, this raises in the minds of many Anglicans historical objections which stem from past controversies. We suggest that the whole language of sacrifice, and the relevance of sacral terms when used in the modern Western situation, be reconsidered in the light of the Old and New Testaments.

9. Another recovered insight of recent years has been the sense of the Eucharist as the community meal. This goes back to the practice of the early Church where the Eucharist took place in the context of the agape. This communal meal—the breaking of bread—which establishes fellowship between God and man and between men and men is a cardinal aspect of the Eucharist. By partaking of the one loaf and gathering round the same table at the invitation of the same Lord, we are one not only in commitment to Christ and to one another but also to the mission of the Church in the world.

10. The mode of the presence of Christ in the eucharist has often been a cause of discord in the Western Church. This has led to arguments focussed too narrowly on the way in which Christ is present in the consecrated bread and wine. The real presence of the Risen Christ in the elements, as understood by the Western Catholic tradition, should be seen as a dynamic presence,* finding its fulfilment in the unity of the body of Christ and in the sanctification of the believer. The doctrinal explanation of *transubstantiation* has been linked with a specific philosophical system which is now open to question and need not necessarily continue to be an obstacle to unity. The meaning of the term *real presence* which is also subject to many different interpretations is in great need of serious reconsideration.

III [This section is on "Eucharistic Practice" and is largely descriptive.]

IV [This section is on "Eucharist and Ministry in a Divided Church" and considered difficulties of intercommunion.]

NOTE: FUTURE WORK

[This Note recommended further work on matters already tackled, and concluded.]

In addition we have not yet been able to give adequate consideration to three important matters:

* The term "dynamic presence" is not intended to restrict the presence of Christ to His power alone.

1. Eucharist as great Thanksgiving.

2. Real Presence.

3. Reservation.

III Church and Ministry

[While there is reference to the presidency of the ordained ministers at the eucharist, a large part of this section deals with the role of Peter in the church, and the issue of the validity of Anglican orders.]

These Venice documents have to be read in the light of the disclaimers provided (by agreement) in the Introduction which was added in early 1971 in the light of Julian Charley's concern:

> No member of the commission would wish to identify himself with every statement in any of the documents. They are not joint statements, nor statements of a doctrinal consensus, but they express work done in hard and serious collaboration and discussion. Their aim is to focus more precisely where that collaboration and discussion may continue. . . .
>
> How far the Commission is from thinking it has reached satisfactory conclusions in these three fields may be gauged from the fact that it proposes to devote the whole of its next meeting, later in this present year, to examining work now being done by sub-commissions on three themes arising out of the document on "Church and Eucharist" here published. These three are: "The notion of sacrifice in the Eucharist in Anglican and Roman Catholic Theology"; "The real presence in Anglican and Roman Catholic Theology"; "An examination in depth of our various Eucharistic rites."[8]

The text on "The Eucharist" was clearly still at an early stage of drafting.[9] There is an untidiness of thought at some points, and an acknowledgment that more study is needed on the other. Among other details, the defini-

---

8. Slightly comically, in *Theology* this introduction provides the third sub-commission's task as being to examine "eucharistic *rules*" (sic)—and the mistake (arising from someone's misleading handwriting?) would actually be plausible, in that intercommunion had been prominent among the Commission's themes. The correction "rites" is attested by McAdoo, "Anglican/Roman Catholic," 231.

9. Purdy says it drew heavily upon the paper submitted at Venice by the South African Anglican–Roman Catholic Commission.

tion of Christ's sacrifice in §3 of chapter II is one-sided. Oddly, the three highlighted features at the end of the paper do not mention eucharistic sacrifice, whereas that theme appears as the task of the first of the three ongoing sub-commissions mentioned in the Introduction. Clearly the Commission would have to cover issues of eucharistic sacrifice and eucharistic presence (including reservation) with enormous care and sensitivity. It is good at this point to read a reference to the actual liturgies in both Communions, apparently following up the references to liturgy in the Malta Report, and the contemporary authorization of various new eucharistic texts in both Communions.

The sub-commission on eucharistic sacrifice met at Poringland, Norwich, in April 1971. Reading between the lines, it was there that Julian Charley and Jean Tillard picked up again their friendly partnership, and, unhappy (as noted earlier) with the Venice text, they were trusted by the other members to do the major drafting together on eucharistic sacrifice.[10]

The full Commission met at Windsor in the first week of September 1971 to complete the task. The Poringland drafting was available, and there were papers from Canada on eucharistic presence, including one by Tillard, who thus contributed on two fronts. We hear nothing at this point about any report from South Africa on eucharistic rites. If there was one, it did not figure within the agenda or affect the drafting.

At the end of the week the Commission had agreed a "Statement on Eucharistic Doctrine," and a press release put this news into the public arena. However, the actual text of the agreement was not going to be published until 31 December. This on the one hand raised speculation and even, in some places, alarm; but on the other hand gave Julian Charley time to write his apologia and have it published at Nottingham on the (somewhat oddly chosen) day when the text of the Statement was released.[11]

---

10. McAdoo says that the full Commission received "a collection of ten papers from the sub-commission on eucharistic sacrifice" ("Anglican/Roman Catholic," 232), whereas Charley refers only to one, saying, with regard to the Venice text, "Large areas of the document were excised, other parts re-written, and fresh matter incorporated. This new statement became the working basis for . . . September 1971 at Windsor" (see Charley, *Anglican–Roman Catholic*, 7). Curiously, McAdoo, "Anglican/Roman Catholic," 231, does not mention Tillard as present at the sub-commission at all.

11. See pp. xxvii–xxviii above.

The Agreement on the Eucharist (1971)

TEXT E

The Windsor Statement (1971)

Eucharistic Doctrine [12]

Co-Chairmen's Preface

The following Agreed Statement evolved from the thinking and the discussion of the Anglican-Roman Catholic International Commission over the past two years. The result has been a conviction among members of the Commission that we have reached agreement on essential points of eucharistic doctrine. We are equally convinced that nothing essential has been omitted. The document, agreed upon at our third meeting, at Windsor, on 7 September 1971, has been presented to our official authorities, but obviously it cannot be ratified by them until such time as our respective Churches can evaluate its conclusions.

We would want to point out that the members of the Commission who subscribed to this Statement have been officially appointed and come from many countries, representing a wide variety of theological background. Our intention was to reach a consensus at the level of faith, so that all of us might be able to say, within the limits of the Statement; this is the Christian faith of the Eucharist.

September 1971   H. R. McADOO
                                                 ALAN C. CLARK

The Statement (1971)

Introduction

1. In the course of the Church's history several traditions have developed in expressing Christian understanding of

---

12. This title "*Eucharistic Doctrine*" is used in most discussion in these pages; sometimes, when the context makes the reference clear, it is called the "Statement."

the eucharist. (For example, various names have become customary as descriptions of the eucharist: Lord's supper, liturgy, holy mysteries, synaxis, mass, holy communion. The eucharist has become the most universally accepted term.) An important stage in progress towards organic unity is a substantial consensus on the purpose and meaning of the eucharist. Our intention has been to seek a deeper understanding of the reality of the eucharist which is consonant with biblical teaching and with the tradition of our common inheritance, and to express in this document the consensus we have reached.

2. Through the life, death and resurrection of Jesus Christ God has reconciled men to himself, and in Christ he offers unity to all mankind. By his word God calls us into a new relationship with himself as our Father and with one another as his children—a relationship inaugurated by baptism into Christ through the Holy Spirit, nurtured and deepened through the eucharist, and expressed in a confession of one faith and a common life of loving service.

I The Mystery of the Eucharist

3. When his people are gathered at the eucharist to commemorate his saving acts for our redemption, Christ makes effective among us the eternal benefits of his victory and elicits and renews our response of faith, thanksgiving and self-surrender. Christ through the Holy Spirit in the eucharist builds up the life of the Church, strengthens its fellowship and furthers its mission. The identity of the Church as the body of Christ is both expressed and effectively proclaimed by its being centred in, and partaking of, his body and blood. In the whole action of the eucharist, and in and by his sacramental presence given through bread and wine, the crucified and risen Lord, according to his promise, offers himself to his people.

4. In the eucharist we proclaim the Lord's death until he comes. Receiving a foretaste of the kingdom to come, we look back with thanksgiving to what Christ has done for

us, we greet him present among us, we look forward to his final appearing in the fullness of his kingdom when "The Son also himself (shall) be subject unto him that put all things under him, that God may be all in all" (1Cor. 15.28). When we gather around the same table in this communal meal at the invitation of the same Lord and when we "partake of the one loaf," we are one in commitment not only to Christ and one another, but also in the mission of the Church in the world.

II The Eucharist and the Sacrifice of Christ

5. Christ's redeeming death and resurrection took place once for all in history. Christ's death on the cross, the culmination of his whole life of obedience, was the one, perfect and sufficient sacrifice for the sins of the world. There can be no repetition of or addition to what was then accomplished once for all by Christ. Any attempt to express a nexus between the sacrifice of Christ and the eucharist must not obscure this fundamental fact of the Christian faith.* Yet God has given the eucharist to his Church as a means through which the atoning work of Christ on the cross is proclaimed and made effective in the life of the Church. The notion of *memorial* as understood in the Passover celebration at the time of Christ—i.e., the making effective in the present of an event from the past—has opened the way to a clearer understanding of the relationship between Christ's sacrifice and the eucharist. The eucharistic memorial is no mere calling to mind of a past event or its significance, but the Church's effectual proclamation of God's mighty acts. Christ instituted the eucharist as a memorial (*anamnesis*) of the totality of God's reconciling action in him. In the eucharistic prayer the church continues to make a perpetual memorial of Christ's death, and his members, united with God and

---

* The early Church in expressing the meaning of Christ's death and resurrection often used the language of sacrifice. For the Hebrew *sacrifice* was a traditional means of communication with God. The Passover, for example, was a communal meal; the day of atonement was essentially expiatory; and the covenant established communion between God and man.

one another, give thanks for all his mercies, entreat the benefits of his passion on behalf of the whole Church, participate in these benefits and enter into the movement of his self-offering.

III *The Presence of Christ*

6. Communion with Christ in the eucharist presupposes his true presence, effectually signified by the bread and wine which, in this mystery, become his body and blood.** The real presence of his body and blood can, however, only be understood within the context of the redemptive activity whereby he gives himself, and in himself reconciliation, peace and life to his own. On the one hand, the eucharistic gift springs out of the paschal mystery of Christ's death and resurrection, in which God's saving purpose has already been definitively realized. On the other hand, its purpose is to transmit the life of the crucified and risen Christ to his body, the Church, so that its members may be more fully united with Christ and with one another.

7. Christ is present and active, in various ways, in the entire eucharistic celebration. It is the same Lord who through the proclaimed word invites his people to his table, who through his minister presides at that table, and who gives himself sacramentally in the body and blood of his paschal sacrifice. It is the Lord present at the right hand of the Father, and therefore transcending the sacramental order, who thus offers himself to his Church, in the eucharistic signs, the special gift of himself.

8. The sacramental body and blood of the Saviour are present as an offering to the believer awaiting his welcome. When this offering is met by faith, a lifegiving encounter results. Through faith Christ's presence—which does not depend on the individual's faith in order to be the Lord's

** The word *transubstantiation* is commonly used in the Roman Catholic Church to indicate that God acting in the eucharist effects a change in the inner reality of the elements. The term should be seen as affirming the *fact* of Christ's presence and of the mysterious and radical change which takes place. In contemporary Roman Catholic theology it is not understood as explaining *how* the change takes place.

real gift of himself to his Church—becomes no longer just a presence *for* the believer, but also a presence *with* him. Thus, in considering the mystery of the eucharistic presence, we must recognize both the sacramental sign of God's presence and the personal relationship between Christ and the faithful which arises from that presence.

9. The Lord's words at the last supper, "Take and eat; this is my body," do not allow us to dissociate the gift of the presence and the act of sacramental eating. The elements are not mere signs; Christ's body and blood become really present and are really given. But they are really present and given in order that, receiving them, believers may be united in communion with Christ the Lord.

10. According to the traditional order of the liturgy the consecratory prayer (*anaphora*) leads to the communion of the faithful. Through this prayer of thanksgiving, a word of faith addressed to the Father, the bread and wine become the body and blood of Christ by the action of the Holy Spirit, so that in communion we eat the flesh of Christ and drink his blood.

11. The Lord who thus comes to his people in the power of the Holy Spirit is the Lord of glory. In the eucharistic celebration we anticipate the joys of the age to come. By the transforming action of the Spirit of God, earthly bread and wine become the heavenly manna and the new wine, the eschatological banquet for the new man: elements of the first creation become pledges and first fruits of the new heaven and the new earth.

Conclusion

12. We believe that we have reached substantial agreement on the doctrine of the eucharist. Although we are all conditioned by the traditional ways in which we have expressed and practised our eucharistic faith, we are convinced that if there are remaining points of disagreement they can be resolved on the principles here established. We acknowledge a variety of theological approaches within both our

communions. But we have seen it as our task to find a way of advancing together beyond the doctrinal disagreements of the past. It is our hope that, in view of the agreement which we have reached on eucharistic faith, this doctrine will no longer constitute an obstacle to the unity we seek.

The Statement requires some comment on minor or background issues; then serious treatment of the themes of eucharistic sacrifice and eucharistic presence in Sections II and III; and finally a hard look at a major omission.

Preliminaries

Firstly, I note the title in the heading to Section I: "The Mystery . . . " This is a term which has had great currency in Roman Catholic eucharistic theology for the last hundred years or so. It was greatly favoured by Dom Odo Casel, with one eye on mystery religions.[13] It is used with different shades of meaning, but frequently indicates that the saving acts of Christ are in some way present in and through sacramental ministrations. Its use here looks to be close to that meaning. However, it remains a title, and there is no point of explanation as to why it is so used. It recurs later in §6, where it is used as an almost exact equivalent to "sacrament."

The opening of the treatment of the eucharist and the sacrifice of Christ in §5 states: "Christ's death on the cross, the culmination of his whole life of obedience, was the one, perfect and sufficient sacrifice for the sins of the world." These words, quoted almost *verbatim* from Cranmer's eucharistic liturgy, reverse the emphasis in the Venice document. In Julian Charley's words,

> The Venice Paper makes Christ's death merely the high point of obedience and it is the obedience which is the sacrifice. The Statement makes Christ's obedience the necessary qualification and pre-condition for his death, and it is his death which is the sacrifice.[14]

13. 1662 did retain from Cranmer within the second post-communion prayer, "who have duly received these holy mysteries," and there is also use of the term in the long exhortations in the rite. Modern Anglican texts have brought in a cue line "Great is [*or* Let us proclaim] the mystery of faith" from Roman Catholic usage. The *Final Report* refers to "the mystery of Christ" on p. 70 in the *Elucidation* of the Authority report.

14. Charley, *Anglican–Roman Catholic*, 17.

It is important to both this Statement and later documents that this understanding of the sacrifice is well registered. It is not without challenges in the contemporary church (and the Venice text must have arisen from such), but it proved to be agreed on all sides, papal or protestant alike, that this is the authentic Christian understanding of Christ's sacrifice, and all further debate, drafting and definition throughout the processes recorded here have treated this as foundational to an understanding of the sacrament.

Eucharistic Sacrifice

Perhaps the most notable feature of this §5 is that it does not at any point state that the eucharist is, in itself and by some mode, a sacrifice. The paragraph does lay weight upon *anamnesis*, and it translates it as "memorial," a word which comes three times. However, neither the Greek word nor the English has to bear the weight of meaning of the word "sacrifice," and, although Gregory Dix in particular attempted to interpret Jesus' use of εἰς τὴν ἐμὴν ἀνάμνησιν as meaning "present this reminder of me [to the Father]," the Roman Catholic development of eucharistic sacrifice has not historically been seen as rooted in such a specialized meaning of "remembrance"; and Anglicans have not only used the word at the distribution of the elements ("take and eat this *in remembrance . . .* "), but have also written anamnesis paragraphs for their eucharistic prayers without implying much more to "remembrance" than "calling to mind."[15] (Remembering is an exercise which even in ordinary speech includes our "remembering" the living who are out of sight, as well as the dead and events of the past, and certainly in liturgy is intended to bond us to the living Christ as we recall his saving deeds.) Just as "body" and "blood" present a problem of interpretation in the biblical accounts, so does "remembrance" in the original—it ranks with "body" and "blood" as posing a problem, not as solving it.

The explanation of "memorial" as having meant in the Passover "the making effective in the present of an event in the past" looks portentous, but that phrase is actually saying no more than has properly to be said about any means of grace—our dependence upon the historic acts of God

---

15. While "calling to mind" is in this §5 treated as an inadequate understanding of *anamnesis*, it is the term that was used in the translation of "Memores igitur" in the official English language text of the Roman Catholic Eucharistic Prayer III just then coming into use. However, the 2011 translation has changed this to "we celebrate the memorial." See Appendix A for an overview of "memorial" in Anglican texts.

in Christ means we invoke God on that basis and look for his grace to be correspondingly "effective" in our lives today.[16]

Finally we come to the clause that says we "enter into the movement of his [Christ's] self-offering." Here the language used has to be read very carefully. My own reading of it suggests that an actual sequence of events in the eucharist is triggered by the opening mention of "In the eucharistic prayer" but it is a sequence which by its clear wording in logic runs beyond the eucharistic prayer. This is best illustrated by a brief table:

Table 3

ARCIC-I TEXT §5	COMMENTARY
In the eucharistic prayer the church continues to make a perpetual memorial of Christ's death,	*In meam commemorationem* is a central theme of Christ's work articulated in the eucharistic prayer;
and his members, united with God and with one another, give thanks for all his mercies,	thanksgiving for Christ's work is the central theme of our response articulated in the prayer
entreat the benefits of his passion on behalf of the whole Church,	but we also go on to ask for the benefits of his work for the communicants present and for the whole church
participate in these benefits	and then we participate (or communicate—both words in English translate *koinonia*), by receiving the elements
and enter into the movement of his self-offering.	and, through communicating, the members offer themselves to God, doing so as the members of Christ as he offers himself to the Father.

While this is a very specific allocating a particular point of reference in the liturgical action to each clause in the long original sentence, a less exact commentary on similar lines is offered by Julian Charley:

> The participation in the benefits and "the entry into the movement of his self-offering" are not in this sentence narrowly related to the eucharistic *prayer* (as is the memorial of Christ's death), but they

16. Roger Beckwith bluntly stated that "the idea (expressed in the *Agreed Statement*) that this is how the passover 'memorial' was understood in the first century is simply a fashionable fancy, without historical basis" ("Agreed Statement," 21). The biblical use of *anamnesis* and its cognates certainly appears to differ from the ARCIC usage.

THE WINDSOR AGREED STATEMENT ON EUCHARISTIC DOCTRINE (1971)

are simply two among several universally acknowledged features of the whole eucharistic celebration.[17]

For the present purposes, we note that the only reference to "offering" in §5, i.e., in the one section dealing with eucharistic sacrifice, is in no visible way connected to the use of the bread and wine prior to reception. The sentence *may* have been devised to enable some members of the Commission to hear the word they treasure, *viz* "offering," (a tokenist kind of drafting not unknown in Anglican liturgical revision), but in the upshot the wording does not necessarily refer to a uniquely eucharistic action, but, having no necessary overt connection with the bread and wine, may also well describe the church's approach to God through Christ in many varied non-sacramental contexts and is in no way determinative of eucharistic *doctrine*.

As a slightly varied way of coming at this, Julian Charley cites a passage from *Growing into Union*, which had been published some months before he and Tillard were drafting the Statement for ARCIC, and we know to have been welcomed by Tillard, as running close to his own emphasis upon the given purpose of communion:

> What *can* we offer at the eucharist? Not mere bread and wine— even the term "offertory" sounds an odd note; not merely the "fruit of our lips"; not merely undefined 'spiritual sacrifices"; not merely ourselves considered apart from Christ; not even ourselves in Christ, if that is seen in separation from our feeding on Christ; but ourselves as reappropriated by Christ. If the sacrament is to communicate to us afresh the benefits of Christ's passion, then we must reaffirm quickly that it also communicates to us the demands of it.[18]

Thus our self-offering is understood as Christ's reappropriation of us through our receiving the sacrament.

However, Nicholas Sagovsky has proposed a source for the "movement of his self-offering" language in Gregory Dix:

> Dix's view of eucharistic sacrifice, summed up in the phrase, "we enter into the movement of his self-offering," has been

17. Charley, *Anglican–Roman Catholic Agreement*, 18n2. He later quotes the same pattern of understanding as in my table above from Buchanan, Lloyd, and Miller, *Anglican Worship Today*, 124; see Charley, *Rome, Canterbury*, 18.

18. Buchanan et al, *Growing Into Union*, 58, quoted in Charley, *Anglican–Roman Catholic Agreement*, 18. The Tillard citing of it is noted in n. 24 on pp. xxvi–xxvii.

widely welcomed. The phrase itself is quoted—without acknowledgment—in the ARCIC Joint Agreed Statement on the
Eucharist.[19]

Was this in mind by the drafters? It should be noted that the emphasis in
Dix upon what we "do" at the eucharist is related to the action of the rite
independently of whether the worshippers are to receive communion or
not. The actual phrase "enter into the movement of his self-offering" does
not *verbatim* occur in Dix; and, as can be seen by the interest of Charley
and Tillard in the *Growing into Union* emphasis on the significance of
reception, their choice of wording, even if it was influenced by echoes of
Dix's alluring turns of phrase, does not have to carry the significance he
gave to it. We return to my initial axiom that the wording of agreed statements can only mean what the words in it mean—the quest for a different
"mind" behind it is in vain.

The Presence of Christ

It is axiomatic that in a dominical sacrament the Lord's own words should
be used—the people of God eat Christ's body and drink his blood. But we
need to go to the full wording of Jesus's commands to his original disciples.
He says not simply "This is my body," but places those words within the
command "Take, eat: this is my body." It is in the context of eating and
drinking that the bread and wine are to us the body and blood of Christ.
And with a view to such eating and drinking it is entirely appropriate to
speak of "the bread and wine which, in this mystery, become his body and
blood." "Become" in this context has always sounded dangerous to protestants, but it does not necessarily imply a change of nature. The Statement is
concerned here with the significance of the elements, and so we can spell
it out—the eucharistic prayer provides the context in which the bread and
wine are designated as Christ's body and blood (a process we call "consecration") but designation does imply that the elements "become" what they are
designated to be. Consecration changes not the nature but the use of the
bread and wine—they are to "convey" the benefits of Christ's death to us,
and the verb "become" has its immediate purpose in view, namely that the
communicants eat and drink Christ's body and blood as he commanded.
Julian Charley floats the term "trans-signification," a term which has been

19. Sagovsky "Gregory Dix," 120. Sagovsky's footnoted reference says Dix "speaks
several times" with these words but only gives a reference of p. 153.

tentatively used in Roman Catholic circles. The strongest thrust in this direction comes with a context-setting sentence at the beginning of §9 "The Lord's words . . . do not allow us to dissociate the gift of the presence and the act of sacramental eating." *Prima facie* this seems to preclude all extra-liturgical devotions that are in "dissociation" from eating and drinking. At the very least it lays the onus of proof upon those who wish to practice such devotions in relation to the reserved elements. However, there is no discussion of reservation in this Statement, despite the recommendation of the Venice text.

What then of transubstantiation? It was perhaps inevitable that transubstantiation should be mentioned, though it was credibly affirmed at the time that the footnote about it was included through Anglican insistence, and that it was an Anglican who actually drafted it.[20] In 1971 the Roman Catholics were saying they were not going to lay any emphasis on precisely *how* Jesus is present in or at the eucharist, and that read to the Anglicans as helpfully reticent in itself, and as indicative of a relaxed way of handling historic formulae.

The Omission

The Venice paper on the eucharist had concluded that more work was needed on:

1. Eucharist as great Thanksgiving

2. Real Presence

3. Reservation[21]

If we take these in reverse order, then *Eucharistic Doctrine*, by both what it said and what did not say, had almost taken reservation off the agenda. It certainly gave no favorable weight to it. On "real presence" it made various general remarks, but was not very specific, and probably differing understandings could live with the result.

However, the phrase "Eucharist as great Thanksgiving" inevitably takes us into the sphere of liturgy (indeed the phrase arose at just the time

---

20. Julian Charley's later account confirms that an Anglican drafted it (apparently because the Roman Catholics "simply could not agree upon it"), but does not confirm that Anglicans had asked for it (see Charley, *Rome, Canterbury*, 15).

21. See p. 35 above.

in liturgical history when "Great Thanksgiving" was passing into common currency to denote the eucharistic prayer). §10 refers to the "consecratory prayer (*anaphora*)" which "leads to the communion of the faithful." But liturgy as a serious source (and shopwindow) for the two Churches' beliefs remained off-limits. It is the case that the Commission had at one time reckoned to get reports on the Churches' respective eucharistic rites, and had entrusted to Knapp-Fisher to compile such a report in South Africa. Sure enough, McAdoo reports that at Windsor "an examination and comparison of the Anglican and Roman Catholic eucharistic rites was presented by the South African sub-commission."[22] However, although it has not been possible to trace that report, it is not difficult to reconstruct what should have been in it that touched on the doctrine of the eucharist:

> (a) On the Anglican side: 1662 was the parent of virtually all developments within the Anglican Communion. In itself this was a wholly protestant document.[23] The recensions that dated from the (semi-underground) Episcopal Church in Scotland in the eighteenth century, notably as then developed in the Episcopal Church in the USA, had both reverted to a "long prayer" of consecration, with some echoes of 1549. While retaining the "one oblation of himself once offered" in the lead-in to the narrative, they had omitted the quasi-epiclesis "Grant that we receiving . . . may be partakers," and instead, following Eastern models, had inserted a consecratory epiclesis within the post-narrative section of the prayer, following immediately after the anamnesis paragraph. They had also inserted an actual offering of the bread and cup to God within the anamnesis. The 1929/1954 South African rite reproduced these characteristics, but with the offering embellished from a well-known source as "we offer . . . this holy Bread of eternal life and this Cup of everlasting salvation." However, only 1662 could have stood as in any way typical of the Anglican Communion as a whole, and, while a minority of revised provincial rites certainly indicated catholicizing influences, those phrases could not be evidence for more than the tendencies of their own provinces. In the second half of the 1960s some new liturgiography was occurring, partly prompted by the Church of South India's initiative from 1950 onwards. Such, for instance, were the rites in the American *Prayer Book Studies* XVII and the Church of England's Hippolytus-based Series 2 communion,

22. McAdoo, "Anglican/Roman Catholic," 234.
23. See pp. xxi–xxii and pp. 1–2 above.

both in 1967—but again such experimental alternative rites would have not have been credible as typifying the Communion's eucharistic practice overall. Even later on, in the texts of *Elucidation* (1979) and *Clarifications* (1994), when ARCIC I and II came to cite an Anglican liturgical text, it was 1662 to which they both referred as the major text with the claim to be the classical rite of Anglicanism. And even in the twentieth-century rites there was little more anywhere referring to reservation than a rubric or two introducing extended communion.[24]

(b) On the Roman Catholic side, the situation was much clearer. On the one hand the "Tridentine" Liturgy (i.e., of Pius IV in 1570, but minimally retouched by John XXIII in 1962) handed on its historic canon into the new *Missa Normativa* (of Paul VI in 1967). On the other hand three new canons had been added, and the title "eucharistic prayer" adopted. The "Preparation of the gifts" included offering the bread and cup to God in the prayers which have become known as the "offertory prayers"; but the striking bidding and response followed:

Celebrant: Pray, brethren that my sacrifice and yours may be acceptable to God, the almighty Father.

People: May the Lord accept the sacrifice at your hands. . . .

The Tridentine Canon remained, hardly amended, as Eucharistic Prayer I, and the offering of a holy victim (*offerimus . . . hostiam puram, hostiam sanctam, hostiam immaculatam*) remained in its anamnesis. In Prayer II the anamnesis (from supposed Hippolytus) was "we offer this life-giving bread, this saving cup" (*tibi, Domine, panem vitae et calicem salutis offerimus*). In Prayer III it was "Look with favor on your Church's offering, and see the Victim whose death has reconciled us to yourself" (*Respice, quaesumus, in oblationem Ecclesiae tuae et, agnoscens Hostiam, cuius voluisti immolatione placari*). And in Prayer IV it was even franker "We offer you his body and blood, the acceptable sacrifice . . . " (*offerimus tibi cius corpus ct sanguinem*).[25]

We may leave aside other flanking sacramental provision, such as for requiem masses, for "Benediction with the blessed sacrament," and for Corpus

24. See Appendix C.

25. The English texts of the mass are taken here from the 1969 approved ICEL translation, which may or may not have been available to Knapp-Fisher's sub-committee in 1970, but must have been before ARCIC I itself at Windsor in 1971. English-language texts have been changed since 2011 in accordance with *Liturgiam authenticam*.

Christi devotions. Here was embedded in the Roman Catholic liturgies, new as well as traditional, at a very central point a very explicit doctrine of eucharistic sacrifice. It mirrored the text of the Council of Trent, but, whether it was reported at Windsor or not, astonishingly it found no mention in the Windsor Statement.

We may conclude from this that, in forming the Agreement, ARCIC I seems to have left the eucharistic rites of both Communions somewhere over the horizon. Paradoxically, the omission may well have lightened their task, for bringing them into sight would certainly have made agreement harder to achieve.

Overall Judgment

The surprising feature of the Statement was that, although it required evangelicals to do some rethinking, they were by 1971 largely ready for this, and the Statement's total impact was that it was far more acceptable to them than they could ever have forecast.[26] The commensurate surprise was that Roman Catholics were also acknowledging (in §12) that the Statement presented "substantial agreement on the doctrine of eucharist," that is, they saw their own eucharistic faith reasonably fairly displayed in the Statement. When it was first published, a fair reading of the text where it handles the two controversial areas suggested that the Roman Catholics had not insisted on the formulations which for hundreds of years had been viewed as non-negotiable by their Church. Re-reading the text today rather confirms that judgment. The Commission had sought different terminology, but had reckoned within that choice of new language to retain their faith uncompromised; and the Roman Catholic Commission members made this very clear when interviewed or when writing their own commentaries on the Agreement. All this was surprising, though it was obviously welcome, and was indeed

---

26. As noted in the Introduction, Julian Charley wrote his apologia, *Anglican–Roman Catholic Agreement*, in anticipation of serious distrust of the Statement being articulated among evangelical Anglicans, and he went a long way to disarming them. He led a section on the Roman Catholic Church at the second National Evangelical Anglican Congress at Nottingham in 1977, and the section's statement, while concerned with other areas of historic disagreement, included: "we welcome the progress made towards doctrinal agreement such as is evidenced in the ARCIC . . . statements" (National Evangelical Anglican Congress 2, *Nottingham Statement*, 44).

unlike the pictures of vast polarization which had been handed down from the Reformation era, or indeed from the nineteenth century.[27]

So the Statement was now in the public arena, was widely welcomed, and was open to comment. Plenty was to be expected; and plenty came. But the overall impression of a jointly agreed undefensive positive statement about the eucharist made a widespread favourable impression. A happy word to quote here came in a casual conversation with Archbishop Michael Ramsey soon after its publication. He spoke to this effect: "I like the Statement particularly because its style is pastoral, and it would be an easy document from which to teach."

27. Perhaps I might quote myself here: "[the fact that both Cranmer and Gardiner used 'memorial' to mean 'remembrance' without sacrificial overtones] . . . does give rise to the interesting speculation that Cranmer could probably have signed up to the 1971 Anglican–Roman Catholic Agreement on the Eucharist, whereas his adversaries probably could not have." *What Did Cranmer Think,* 7n1; reprinted in *An Evangelical Among,* 77n22.

5

Elucidation of the Statement on Eucharistic Doctrine (1979)[1]

I T IS HARDLY SURPRISING that the 1971 Statement evoked comment and criticism from round the world. The coming of the agreed Statement on Ministry and Ordination in 1973 prompted a debate in the Church of England General Synod on the Eucharist and Ministry agreements in November 1974, without much more then than a broad welcome and a commendation of them for study. The coming of the First Statement on Authority (1976) thereafter overtook much of the debate on the eucharist, and started also to invite across-the-board evaluation of the total work of ARCIC I at large.

Three points of special historical relevance here then arose. First, in April 1977 Archbishop Donald Coggan visited Pope Paul VI; and in their 1,000-word "Common Declaration" they said:

> The Anglican/Roman Catholic International Commission has produced three documents: on the Eucharist, on Ministry and Ordination, and on Church and Authority. We now recommend that this work it has begun be pursued, through the procedures appropriate to our respective Communions, so that both of them may be led along the path towards unity.[2]

It is tempting to read this somewhat colorless mention of work that was apparently breaking wholly new ground as almost the most minimal commendation available to the two leaders to offer.[3] Anything much less

1. Both the Statement and its *Elucidation* were published in *The Final Report*, a volume that includes all the agreed documents of ARCIC I, and also the original Declaration of Pope Paul VI and Michael Ramsey and the Malta Report.

2. The full text of the Declaration is in *Final Report*, 119–22.

3. Purdy's account confirms this analysis, and tells us nothing of the final content of

would have been a cancellation. But the historian has to recall that the most recent ARCIC Statement had been that on Authority in 1976, and it may well have been that which was leading one or both of the two sides to harbor reservations.

Next, in July 1977 in England, on the initiative of Latimer House, Oxford, an *Open Letter on Relations between the Anglican Churches & the Roman Catholic, Eastern Orthodox, Old Catholic and Ancient Oriental Churches* was sent by one hundred and thirty evangelical Anglicans to "The Archbishops and Diocesan Bishops of the Anglican Communion."[4] Not all signatories were from England, but about seventy-five percent were, and their names were very representative of English evangelical Anglicans.[5] The Open Letter covers a great width of doctrinal concerns, and does so in very irenic spirit, but it touches on ARCIC on the eucharist when it says in its §5:

> We think it necessary, for the gospel's sake, to detect and oppose any views of eucharistic sacrifice which obscure the sufficiency, finality, and historical completeness of Christ's one sacrifice for sins on the cross.

Evangelical Anglicans had no doubt been in view in the insistence in *Eucharistic Doctrine* "There can be no repetition of or addition to what was then accomplished once for all in Christ."[6] But as long as the term "eucharistic sacrifice" hung in the atmosphere, it was likely that evangelical cautions would be uttered.

The Lambeth Conference met at Canterbury the following year. No section of the Conference was specifically given to ecumenism, though Section 3 was on "The Anglican Communion in the Worldwide Church." This did include groups on ecumenical subjects, and that on "the Anglican Communion and the Roman Catholic Church," was chaired by Archbishop McAdoo, co-chair of the Commission.[7] The introductory chapter to the

---

the Declaration—see Purdy, *Search for Unity*, 189–92.

4. My own copy is contained within a larger "exposition" of the *Open Letter*, Beckwith, Duffield and Packer, *Across the Divide*.

5. I was not myself a signatory, simply, I think, because I was out of the country and travelling when it was put together.

6. ARCIC I, *Eucharistic Doctrine*, §5.

7. Other bishops on the Commission were not allocated to this group at Canterbury. Two other members of the Commission—Henry Chadwick and the Roman Catholic secretary, William Purdy—were present at the Conference. Chadwick was a consultant, Purdy was an ecumenical Observer. They were free to roam, so whether and how far they participated in this group is a matter of guesswork. Henry Chadwick did introduce the

report pointed out that the participants had been sent an advance volume of Preparatory Essays, so were well equipped to contribute to their group; but in fact the volume concerned contained only three pages on ecumenism, and they did not mention ARCIC at all.[8] The report of the group was cautious in the extreme:

> The Lambeth Conference of 1968 recommended the setting up of a joint theological commission by the Anglican and Roman Catholic Communions. We therefore believe that Lambeth 1978 should evaluate the fruits of the Anglican–Roman Catholic Commission's work, as found in the three Agreed Statements [then listed].
>
> Most of us assent fully to the Agreed Statements, but some would prefer to regard them as simply as a basis for further discussion. Additional explications from ARCIC (at present under consideration by ARCIC) have helped remove many of the doubts expressed. Areas of disagreement await further study between and within the two Churches, as well as by ARCIC itself.[9]

Between the lines, it is likely that it was the Statement on Authority (which recorded divided convictions as between the two Communions) which was inculcating caution. But how Lambeth 1978 could itself "evaluate the fruits" of ARCIC as this report came with dozens of others to the final plenary meetings escapes imagination. The group itself, containing about eight bishops, obviously reckoned itself unable to do so, though presumably the "explications" to come were being leaked to them by Henry McAdoo, even before they were agreed by ARCIC itself. The Section took to the plenary meetings of the Conference this Resolution:

33. The Anglican–Roman Catholic International Commission

The Conference:

1. welcomes the work of the Anglican–Roman Catholic International Commission which was set up jointly by the Lambeth Conference of 1968 and by the Vatican Secretariat for Promoting Christian Unity;

2. recognizes in the three Agreed Statements of this Commission a solid achievement, one in which we can recognize the faith of our Church, and hopes that they will provide a basis

work of ARCIC to a plenary "hearing," and William Purdy also spoke at that.
8. *Lambeth Conference 1978*, 287–90.
9. *Report of the Lambeth Conference 1978*, 107.

for sacramental sharing between our two Communions if and when the finished Statements are approved by the respective authorities of our Communions;

3. invites ARCIC to provide further explication of the Agreed Statements in consideration of responses received by them;

4. commends to the appropriate authorities in each Communion further consideration of the implications of the Agreed Statements in the light of the report of the Joint Preparatory Commission (the Malta Report received by the Lambeth Conference 1968—see p. 134 of its report), with a view to bringing about a closer sharing between our two Communions in life, worship, and mission;

5. asks the Secretary-General of the Anglican Consultative Council to bring this resolution to the attention of the various synods of the Anglican Communion for discussion and action;

6. asks that in any continuing Commission, the Church of the South and the East be adequately represented.[10]

The call in the Section report for "further explications" accompanies a "leak" (presumably from Henry McAdoo) that such explications are in preparation.

The Lambeth resolution had reinforced the call to the Commission, and, although public attention was probably at that stage more interested in the Authority issues, the Commission duly agreed its *Eucharistic Doctrine: Elucidation* in January 1979, and published it on June 7 1979. Meanwhile, in the General Synod of the Church of England in February 1979, in a major debate on all the documents then available, the coming of "elucidations" was adumbrated, and a lengthy resolution took note of difficulties but sought that "the Anglican Communion should now proceed to the implementation of the stage-by-stage progress to full communion recommended by the 1968 Malta Report " The *Elucidation* when published contained its own summary of the places where readers had been unhappy or puzzled by issues in the original 1971 text.

10. *Report of the Lambeth Conference 1978*, 47–48.

TEXT F

Eucharistic Doctrine: Elucidation

1. When each of the Agreed Statements was published, the Commission invited and has received comment and criticism. This *Elucidation* is an attempt to expand and explain to those who have responded some points raised in connection with *Eucharistic Doctrine* (Windsor 1971).

Substantial Agreement

2. The Commission was not asked to produce a comprehensive treatise on the eucharist, but only to examine differences which in the controversies of the past divided our two communions. The aim of the Commission has been to see whether we can today discover substantial agreement in faith on the eucharist. Questions have been asked about the meaning of *substantial* agreement. It means that the document represents not only the judgment of all its members—i.e., it is an agreement—but their unanimous agreement "on essential matters where it considers that doctrine admits no divergence" (Ministry, para 17)—i.e., it is a substantial agreement. Members of the Commission are united in their conviction "that if there are any remaining points of disagreement they can be resolved on the principles here established" (Eucharist, para 12).

Comments and Criticisms

3. The following comments and criticism are representative of the many received and are considered by the Commission to be of particular importance.

    In spite of the firm assertion made in the Agreed Statement of the "once for all" nature of Christ's sacrifice, some have still been anxious that the term *anamnesis* may conceal the reintroduction of the theory of a repeated immolation. Others have suspected that the word refers not only to the historical events of salvation but also to an eternal sacrifice in heaven. Others again have doubted whether *anamnesis* sufficiently implies the reality indicated by traditional sacrificial language concerning the eucharist. Moreover, the accuracy and adequacy of the Commission's exegesis of *anamnesis* have been questioned.

Some critics have been unhappy about the realistic language used in this Agreed Statement, and have questioned such words as *become* and *change*. Others have wondered whether the permanence of Christ's eucharistic presence has been sufficiently acknowledged, with a consequent request for a discussion of the reserved sacrament and devotions associated with it. Similarly there have been requests for clarification of the Commission's attitude to receptionism.

4. Behind these criticisms there lies a profound but often unarticulated anxiety that the Commission has been using new theological language which evades unresolved differences. Related to this anxiety is the further question as to the nature of the agreement claimed by the Commission. Does the language of the Commission conceal an ambiguity (either intentional or unintentional) in language which enables members of the two churches to see their own faith in the Agreed Statement without having in fact reached a genuine consensus?

Anamnesis and Sacrifice

5. The Commission has been criticized for its use of the term *anamnesis*. It chose the word used in New Testament accounts of the institution of the eucharist at the last supper:

> "Do this as a memorial (*anamnesin*) of me"
> (1 Cor.11:24–25; Luke 22:19: JB, NEB).

The word is also to be found in Justin Martyr in the second century. Recalling the last supper he writes:

> "Jesus, taking bread and having given thanks, said 'Do this for my memorial (*anamnesin*): This is my body'; and likewise, taking the cup and giving thanks, he said, 'This is my blood'" (*First Apology* 66; cf *Dialogue with Trypho* 117).

From this time onwards the term is found at the very heart of the eucharistic prayers of both East and West not only in the institution narrative but also in the prayer which follows and elsewhere: cf. e.g., The Liturgy of St John Chrysostom; Eucharistic Prayer 1—The Roman Missal; The Order of the Administration of the Lord's Supper or Holy Communion—The Book of Common Prayer (1662); and Rites A and B of the Church of England Alternative Service Book (1980).

The word is also found in patristic and later theology. The Council of Trent in explaining the relation between the sacrifice of the cross and the eucharist uses the words *commemoratio* and *memoria* (Session 22, ch. 1); and in the Book of Common Prayer (1662), the Catechism states that the sacrament of the Lord's Supper was ordained "for the continual *remembrance* of the sacrifice of Christ, and of the benefits which we receive thereby." The frequent use of the term in contemporary theology is illustrated by *One Baptism One Eucharist and a Mutually Recognized Ministry* (Faith and Order Commission Paper No. 73), as well as by the *General Instruction on the Roman Missal* (1970).

The Commission believes that the traditional understanding of sacramental reality, in which the once-for-all event of salvation becomes effective in the present through the action of the Holy Spirit, is well expressed by the word *anamnesis*. We accept this use of the word which seems to do full justice to the semitic background. Furthermore it enables us to affirm a strong conviction of sacramental realism and to reject mere symbolism. However the selection of this word by the Commission does not mean our common eucharistic faith may not be expressed in other terms.

In the exposition of the Christian doctrine of redemption the word *sacrifice* has been used in two intimately associated ways. In the New Testament, sacrificial language refers primarily to the historical events of Christ's saving works for us. The tradition of the Church, as evidenced for example in its liturgies, used similar language to designate in the eucharistic celebration the *anamnesis* of this historical event. Therefore it is possible to say at the same time that there is only one unrepeatable sacrifice in the historical sense, but that the eucharist is a sacrifice in the sacramental sense, provided that it is clear that this is not a repetition of the historical sacrifice.

There is therefore one historical, unrepeatable sacrifice, offered once for all by Christ and accepted once for all by the Father. In the celebration of the memorial, Christ in the Holy Spirit unites his people with himself in a sacramental way so that the Church enters into the movement of his self-offering. In consequence, even though the Church is active in this celebration, this adds nothing to the efficacy of Christ's sacrifice upon the cross, because the action is itself the fruit of this sacrifice. The Church in celebrating the eucharist gives thanks for the gift of Christ's sacrifice and identifies itself with the will of Christ who has offered himself to the Father on behalf of all mankind.

Christ's Presence in the Eucharist

6. Criticism has been evoked by the statement that the bread and wine become the body and blood of Christ in the eucharist (para. 10). The word *become* has been suspected of expressing a materialistic conception of Christ's presence, and this has seemed to some to be confirmed in the footnote on the word *transubstantiation* which also speaks of *change*. It is feared that this suggests that Christ's presence in the eucharist is confined to the elements, and that the Real Presence involves a physical change in them.

   In order to respond to these comments the Commission recalls that the Statement affirmed that:

   a. It is the glorified Lord himself whom the community encounters in the eucharistic celebration through the preaching of the word, in the fellowship of the Lord's supper, in the heart of the believer, and, in a sacramental way, through the gifts of his body and blood, already given on the cross for their salvation.

b. His body and blood are given through the action of the Holy Spirit, appropriating bread and wine so that they become the food of the new creation already inaugurated by the coming of Christ (cf. paras. 7, 10, 11).

Becoming does not here imply material change. Nor does the liturgical use of the word imply that the bread and wine become Christ's body in such a way that in the eucharistic celebration his presence is limited to the consecrated elements. It does not imply that Christ becomes present in the eucharist in the same manner that he was present in his earthly life. It does not imply that this *becoming* follows the physical laws of this world. What is here affirmed is a sacramental presence in which God uses realities of this world to convey the realities of the new creation: bread for this life becomes the bread of eternal life. Before the eucharistic prayer, to the question "What is that?" the believer answers: "It is bread." After the eucharistic prayer, to the same question he answers: "It is truly the body of Christ, the Bread of Life."

In the sacramental order the realities of faith become present in visible and tangible signs, enabling Christians to avail themselves of the fruits of the once-for-all redemption. In the eucharist the human person encounters in faith the person of Christ in his sacramental body and blood. This is the sense in which the community, the body of Christ, by partaking of the sacramental body of the risen Lord, grows into the unity God intends for his Church. The ultimate change intended by God is the transformation of human beings into the likeness of Christ. The bread and wine *become* the sacramental body and blood of Christ in order that the Christian community may *become* more truly what it already is, the body of Christ.

Gift and Reception

7. This transformation into the likeness of Christ requires that the eucharistic gifts be received in faith. In the mystery of the eucharist we discern not one but two complementary movements within an indissoluble unity: Christ giving his

body and blood, and communicants feeding upon them in their hearts by faith. Some traditions have placed a special emphasis on the association of Christ's presence with the consecrated elements; others have emphasized Christ's presence in the heart of the believer through reception by faith. In the past, acute difficulties have arisen when one or other of these emphases has become almost exclusive. In the opinion of the Commission neither emphasis is incompatible with eucharistic faith, provided that the complementary movement emphasized by the other position is not denied. Eucharistic doctrine must hold together these two movements since in the eucharist, the sacrament of the New Covenant, Christ gives himself to his people so that they may receive him through faith.

Reservation

8. The practice of reserving the sacrament for reception after the congregation has dispersed is known to date back to the second century (cf. Justin Martyr, *First Apology*, 65 and 67). In so far as it maintains the complementary movements already referred to (as for example, when communion is taken to the sick) this practice clearly accords with the purpose of the institution of the eucharist. But later there developed a tendency to stress the veneration of Christ's presence in the consecrated elements. In some places this tendency became so pronounced that the original purpose of reservation was in danger of becoming totally obscured. If veneration is wholly dissociated from the eucharistic celebration of the community it contradicts the true doctrine of the eucharist.

Consideration of this question requires clarification of the understanding of the eucharist. Adoration in the celebration of the eucharist is first and foremost offered to the Father. It is to lead us to the Father that Christ unites us to himself through our receiving of his body and blood. The Christ whom we adore in the eucharist is Christ glorifying his Father. The movement of all our adoration is to the Father, through, with, and in Christ, in the power of the Spirit.

The whole eucharistic action is a continuous movement in which Christ offers himself in his sacramental body and blood to his people and in which they receive him in faith and thanksgiving. Consequently communion administered from the reserved sacrament to those unable to attend the eucharistic celebration is rightly understood as an extension of that celebration. Differences arise between those who would practice reservation for this reason only, and those who would also regard it as a means of eucharistic devotion. For the latter, adoration of Christ in the reserved sacrament should be regarded as an extension of eucharistic worship, even though it does not include immediate sacramental reception, which remains the primary purpose of reservation (cf. the Instruction *Eucharisticum Mysterium*, para. 49, of the Sacred Congregation of Rites (AAS 59, 1967)). Any dissociation of such devotion from this primary purpose, which is communion in Christ of all his members, is a distortion in eucharistic practice.

9. In spite of this clarification, others still find any kind of adoration of Christ in the reserved sacrament unacceptable. They believe that it is in fact impossible in such a practice truly to hold together the two movements of which we have spoken: and that this devotion can hardly fail to produce such an emphasis upon the association of Christ's sacramental presence with the consecrated bread and wine as to suggest too static and localized a presence that disrupts the movement as well as the balance of the whole eucharistic action (cf. Article 28 of the Articles of Religion).

   That there can be a divergence in matters of practice and in theological judgments relating to them, without destroying a common eucharistic faith, illustrates what we mean by *substantial* agreement. Differences of theology and practice may well coexist with a real consensus on the essentials of eucharistic faith—as in fact they do within each of our communions.

Other Issues

10. Concern has been expressed that we have said nothing about intercommunion, though claiming to have attained substantial agreement on eucharistic faith. The reason is that we are agreed that a responsible judgement on this matter cannot be made on the basis of this Statement alone, because intercommunion also involves issues relating to authority and to the mutual recognition of ministry. There are other important issues, such as the eschatological dimension of the eucharist and its relation to contemporary questions of human liberation and social justice, which we have either not fully developed or not explicitly treated. These are matters which call for the common attention of our churches, but they are not a source of division between us and are therefore outside our mandate.

The *Elucidation* never received the same worldwide attention that the initial Agreed Statement, *Eucharistic Doctrine*, had gained, not least, as noted above, because other issues in the Anglican–Roman Catholic dialogue were by then jostling with the eucharist for that attention. However, the Commission itself thereafter urged that the Statement and the *Elucidation* had to be taken together, and no treatment of the Statement on its own would now have an independent validity. This in turn gives an urgency to revisiting some of the language of the Statement.

In the sphere of eucharistic sacrifice the *Elucidation* says, what *Eucharistic Doctrine* had not said, that the eucharist itself constitutes "a sacrifice in the sacramental sense" (§5). This is suspended upon a particular (and arguably partisan) interpretation of *anamnesis*, though it is perhaps lightened by the lead-in that "it is possible to say," which, to a careful reading, presumably allows that it is also possible "not to say." This, if pressed, would mean the statement about the eucharist being a sacrifice was simply one opinion that could be uttered, hardly a statement of agreed doctrine. In addition the very phrase of being "a sacrifice in the sacramental sense" is wholly opaque, totally without scriptural foundation (save by a very loaded interpretation of *anamnesis*), and open to the suspicion that, under pressure from critics, the Commission had reckoned it necessary to make *some* affirmation of the eucharist as a sacrifice, even if the origins, purpose and character of that sacrifice were not here explained. "In the sacramental sense" is capable of bearing several highly flexible meanings and is consequently almost irrefutable. Furthermore §5 says, "The tradition of the Church, as evidenced for example in its liturgies, used similar language to designate in the eucharistic celebration the *anamnesis* of this historical event." The "similar language" would appear to be asserting that the eucharist is called a "sacrifice" in the liturgies, but that is actually quite hard to establish in the "tradition" of Anglican rites.[11] Indeed, the liturgical texts of both Communions which are quoted do not consistently provide the evidence which is being asserted about "memorial"—as, for instance, 1662 does not use the word "memorial" at all and the Church of England's 1980 Rite A abandoned it for its First Eucharistic Prayer.[12]

In *Eucharistic Doctrine* the Commission had simply said that Christ's sacrifice did not admit of any repetition or addition. Now in *Elucidation* the Commission both acknowledged in §3 that they had aroused fears of "repeated immolation" and of an "eternal sacrifice in heaven," and had also in this §5 stated that "the eucharist is a sacrifice in a sacramental sense." They had therefore needed to emphasize a few words later "this is not a repetition of the historical sacrifice."

On the issue of the presence of Christ, the Commission now offered

> Before the eucharistic prayer, to the question "What is that?" the believer answers: "It is bread." After the eucharistic prayer, to the same question he answers: "It is truly the body of Christ, the Bread of Life."

It is at the very least interesting that the Commission was now beginning to dabble with liturgical texts. Just out of sight here is the question of

11. What of the Roman missal? In the *General Instruction of the Roman Missal*, both in the original text of 1964 and also in the 2005 revision for the new translation of the liturgical texts, under "The Eucharistic Prayer" the "Anamnesis" (section (e)) is stated as the place where the church "keeps the memorial" of "recalling" Christ's saving work; and the "Offering" (section (f)) is where "in this very memorial" the church "offers in the Holy Spirit the Victim to the Father." This therefore half-distinguishes between anamnesis and offering! See further on "sacrifice" in Appendix B.

12. It is rather odd that the ASB is being quoted at all. *The Final Report* states (104) that *Elucidation* was finished in January 1979, and was published on June 7, 1979. Rite A had completed its Revision Committee stage halfway through January 1979, and was going to General Synod for what proved to be nineteen hours of the Revision Stage in Synod, lasting on and off through both the February and the July Sessions of Synod in that year. Amendments were being made to the texts throughout. So no one in January 1979 could actually know what texts would be in the 1980 book. See the discussion of "memorial" in Appendix A.

consecration, a term which the Commission generally avoids. And it has to be acknowledged that Anglican desires to say that the whole eucharistic prayer consecrates were being carefully met by avoiding discussion of whether a particular formula (as, e.g., within the narrative of institution) consecrates, or whether it is the whole prayer—and thus we have simply to say that "after" the prayer we know that the elements have been duly consecrated, and that we are ready to call them the "body" and "blood" of Christ.[13] The issue of "become" is handled above. There is a curious contrast drawn in this §5 between "sacramental realism" and "mere symbolism."[14] And it will prove significant for the future that the Commission was now stepping so firmly onto liturgical ground in those references in §5 to both Eastern and Roman rites and twice to the 1662 BCP.[15]

§8 and §9 raise the question of reservation, which *Eucharistic Doctrine* had not addressed (save with the caution that the words of Jesus "do not allow us to dissociate the gift of the presence and the act of sacramental eating"). Certainly there appears wide (though far from universal) support in Anglicanism for taking the consecrated elements from the liturgical celebration to minister them by extension to the sick and shut-in, in which the "act of sacramental eating" expresses the very purpose of the reservation.[16] But the *Elucidation* is raising the far more controversial question of adoration and kindred activities which, the Commission admits, seem to many Anglicans to assert "too static and localized a presence" (§9), for they entail a form of worship which, except by special pleading, is wholly unrelated to

13. This modern Anglican reasoning about consecration (publicized through the section report on liturgy at the 1958 Lambeth Conference) is undeniably modern (though adumbrated in, e.g., Justin Martyr, *First Apology*, 66). It cannot be applied to the 1552 rite (where Cranmer had no objective consecration at all), nor to the 1662 rite, where rubrics and manual acts had been so grafted onto Cranmer's rite that a very clear objective consecration was now located in the dominical words in the narrative of institution. However, a clear distinction has to be kept between the issue of what effects consecration (an issue avoided by ARCIC), and the issue of what consecration effects, the issue with which ARCIC was wrestling.

14. Why "curious"? It is simply that the Catholic tradition has tended to treat "symbol" as a rich and positive concept, even as containing within itself that which it signifies, and it is surprising to find symbolism here lightly dismissed with a "mere," presumably as being near to a *nuda commemoratio* (see also on pp. 119–122 below).

15. The first of these references in §5 seems to be saying that *anamnesis* is found "in the prayer which follows" the institution narrative (i.e., the "anamnesis" paragraph)—but 1662 has no such prayer. It does retain "remembrance" in its words of distribution, which follow immediately after the institution narrative.

16. See the evidence in Appendix C.

the eating and drinking which Jesus had commanded. The special pleading does occur in §8; but even a limited experience of, say, the rite of Benediction with the Blessed Sacrament, or of Corpus Christi processions, or of "exposition" for devotional purposes, demonstrates to the unconvinced a use of the reserved element so far "dissociated" from any act of communion as to qualify for the term used in §8, namely "distortion."[17]

From an Anglican point of view, those who do not practice "adoration of Christ in the reserved sacrament" can usually live in communion with those who do, simply not wanting to join in the latters' extra-liturgical devotions. The *Elucidation* very clearly acknowledges that these two views exist in Anglicanism and can live with each other. It is indeed likely that, round the whole Communion, those who do practice adoration in this way are vastly outnumbered by those who do not. And, because the *Elucidation* is still affirming "substantial" agreement, it seems to be saying that Roman Catholics too ought to accept and respect this "divergence" within Anglicanism. Nevertheless it is not difficult at this point to foresee that there might well lie trouble ahead.

ACC-4 met in London, Ontario, near to the time *Elucidation* was published. Its report on Anglican–Roman Catholic relations welcomed *Elucidation*, and interestingly said "It is not of the same status as the Agreed Statement which it interprets." But its main contribution to the developing narrative came from its expectation that there would soon be an ARCIC "final report." So the Council passed this resolution:

Resolution 4: Response to ARCIC Statements

The Council requests the Secretary General to initiate an enquiry of the member Churches concerning the most appropriate way in which the Communion as a whole should be able to respond to the three Agreed Statements of the ARCIC, and to the results of international dialogues in general, and to report to ACC-5.[18]

ARCIC I had still further work to do, formulating their second Statement on Authority. When this was complete in 1981, all the ARCIC documents which up to that point had been published as separate pamphlets were brought together in *The Final Report* (London: CTS/SPCK, 1982). This was introduced by both a Preface, setting out the history, and an Introduction

---

17. See Appendix C for an overview of where provision for reservation has reached in the Anglican Communion.

18. ACC-4, 7–8.

addressing the theological issues handled. The Introduction says the "theme of *koinonia* runs through our Statements" and then lists the eucharist "as the effectual sign of *koinonia*." Within this large theme, the Introduction refers only briefly to the documents on the eucharist:

> In the Statement *Eucharistic Doctrine* the eucharist is seen as the sacrament of Christ, by which he builds up and nurtures his people in the *koinonia* of his body. By the eucharist all the baptized are brought into communion with the source of *koinonia*. He is the one who destroyed the walls dividing humanity (Eph.2:14); he is the one who died to gather into unity all the children of God his Father (cf. John 11:52; 17:20ff).[19]

For what a three-sentence summary is worth, it should perhaps be noted that the thrust of the eucharist is, according to this summary, wholly directed towards the building up and perfecting of the people of God. Does this, one might ask, set other more controversial issues into perspective?

Thus *The Final Report* was published in 1982, almost coinciding in time with the WCC publication of the Faith and Order "Lima" statement, *Baptism, Eucharist and Ministry.* ARCIC I was disbanded, but its published work now invited a major response from both worldwide Communions.

19. *Final Report*, 6–7.

6

The Anglican Response

THE ANGLICAN RESPONSE TO *The Final Report* was instigated even before the book had been published. ACC-5, meeting at Newcastle upon Tyne in September 1981, was informed that ARCIC I had completed its work, and it was due to go shortly to publication. The co-chairmen had suggested to the Archbishop of Canterbury and the Pope the form of the questions to be asked of their Communions; and the ACC took up the suggestion and passed the following resolution:

Resolution 4: ARCIC

The Council:

a. Expresses its gratitude [to all on ARCIC I]

b. Commends to the Churches of the Anglican Communion the two questions proposed by the co-chairmen in their letter of 2 September 1981 to the Archbishop of Canterbury, *viz.:* -

"Whether the Agreed Statements on Eucharistic Doctrine, Ministry and Ordination, and Authority in the Church (I and II), together with Elucidations are consonant in substance with the faith of Anglicans"

and

"Whether the Final Report offers a sufficient basis for taking the next concrete step towards the reconciliation of our Churches grounded in agreement in faith":

a. Endorses the further proposal that a new Commission be set up.[1]

1. ACC-5, 39–40.

Thus the key phrase which would echo for many years ahead, "consonant in substance," passed into the Anglican–Roman Catholic discourse.

Then in 1982 it all happened. *The Final Report* was published in January. Pope John Paul II visited England in May (and met primates from elsewhere in the Communion), and steps were taken to appoint a new Commission. ARCIC II began in 1983 with Bishop Mark Santer as the Anglican co-chair and Bishop Cormack Murphy-O'Connor as the Roman Catholic one. This meant that the official responses of the two Communions to ARCIC I's work would only emerge during the period of ARCIC II. The questions had been asked as early as possible, as above, and were reinforced from the ACC secretariat. But what form would those responses take?

This chapter is headed "The Anglican Response," and it comes before the Roman Catholic response because the Anglican process (called in some quarters "reception") in fact reached its conclusion in 1988, whereas the Vatican's concluding *Response* was not issued until 1991. However, if the Vatican was slow to reach its concluding word (covered here in the next chapter), it was by no means slow with its first ones. Within 1982, soon after the publication of *The Final Report*, the Congregation for the Doctrine of the Faith (CDF), prompted by the Pope, produced its *Observations*.[2] These were not intended to be definitive, but in effect they fired a warning shot across the ARCIC bows; at the same time their concluding "remarks" on "the next concrete step to be taken" began with recommending "that the dialogue be continued," thus clearing the way for the appointment of ARCIC II noted above. Within the thirteen pages, the eucharistic questions take just two pages, and they predictably handle "Eucharist as Sacrifice" and "Real Presence." About the sacrifice question they want assurance that the church participates "in the sacrificial act of her Lord, so that she offers sacramentally in him and with him his sacrifice"; and they also complain of the absence of the "propitiatory value that Catholic dogma attributes to the Eucharist," citing the Council of Trent. About the real presence question they not only say (once again citing Trent) that transubstantiation has not been presented "adequately," but go on to say that, as the Commission goes on referring to "bread and wine" after consecration, they may well therefore be unacceptably affirming that the elements retain their "ontological

2. These are reprinted in Hill and Yarnold, *Anglicans and Roman Catholics,* under "Official Comments," 79–91.

substance" at that point. In short, the CDF *Observations* amounted to a strong warning that there did indeed lie trouble ahead.

Two short publications by Anglican evangelicals responded quickly to the *Final Report* and the CDF *Observations*. They were the Church of England Evangelical Council pamphlet, drafted by John Stott, *Evangelical Anglicans and the ARCIC Final Report* and Julian Charley, *Rome, Canterbury, and the Future* (both published by Grove Books, Bramcote, 1982). Both are measured, both are deeply troubled by *Observations*, and CEEC has continued problems with the ARCIC Statements, while Julian Charley has a carefully argued defense of them. A slightly more embattled booklet came from Ireland, Dermot O'Callaghan, *Rome, Canterbury and Armagh* (Church of Ireland Evangelical Fellowship, 1984). While strongly opposing the controversial treatment of the eucharist, this also echoed both the English pamphlets in submitting that the doctrine of justification should have preceded the other subjects which ARCIC had been addressing. The common evangelical protest was that responding to ARCIC's Statements included an element of frustration at being asked the wrong question.

Anglicans in England officially addressed *The Final Report* initially in connection with the Lima text, *Baptism, Eucharist and Ministry* from the WCC, which was also published in 1982. General Synod debated them both together in a preliminary way in July 1983. The range of themes took the debate in several directions. Decision-taking was inaugurated by further debates in February 1985, and then in respect of ARCIC's two documents on the eucharist the Synod referred the issue of "consonant in substance with the faith of the Church of England" to the dioceses. The dioceses duly reported back in 1986, broadly in favour, and in November General Synod voted definitively on the same motion. It was passed by over 75% in favour, though with a vote of 141–65 among members of the House of Laity, those voting against the motion being largely evangelicals.

However, the alerting of the whole Communion came through ACC-6 meeting in July 1984 at Badagry in Nigeria. The Council adopted this resolution:

Resolution 28 ARCIC FINAL REPORT

The Council requests:

a. Provinces which have not already done so to prepare a response to the ARCIC Final Report for ACC-7 in preparation for the Lambeth Conference 1988;

b. The Secretary General and his staff to consider how provinces can be assisted in the study and interpretation of the ARCIC Final Report, especially in churches where English is not spoken as a first language;

c. That there should be further meeting of ecumenical officers before ACC-7 to begin the task of collating the responses of the provinces to ARCIC and other ecumenical dialogues.[3]

The call in (a) followed up the 1981 resolution, urging the provinces to evaluate the ARCIC I documents. Steps were also taken to implement (c); the two bishops who had been nominated to be chair and vice-chair for the "Ecumenical Relations" Section of the forthcoming 1988 Lambeth Conference convened a conference from round the Communion at the Emmaus Centre in Kent. This was to meet in January 1987 with a view to reporting to ACC-7 meeting in Singapore in April that year, and in due time to the 1988 Lambeth Conference, and the provinces of the Communion were alerted accordingly.

The *Emmaus Report* duly came to ACC-7 in Singapore in April.[4] The Preface states that the report is prepared "primarily for Lambeth 1988 to pronounce the consensus of the Anglican Communion." It records that nineteen out of then twenty-nine separate provinces had responded to the call, and in the Preface it requested "Can the members of ACC-7 whose Provinces have not yet issued their Response manage to elicit one as soon as possible?" There is, however, no record of further responses. Of the nineteen who had responded only five reported specific hesitations or doubts about whether the eucharistic statements in particular were "consonant" with their beliefs: namely, Australia, Ireland, Kenya, New Zealand, Tanzania. The Church of England was reported as having a strong majority in favour of "consonance." Of the five who hesitated, the Australians said they were divided; the Church of Ireland agreed a report noted below; in Kenya the Provincial Board for Theological Education had reservations about "the concept of the Real Presence of Christ in the eucharistic elements, and the ambiguity of the word *anamnesis* (memorial)"; the New Zealanders noted "difficulties such as the range of meanings of anamnesis and the problem of a precise or generalized presence of Christ"; in Tanzania they simply noted "there were still some points of ambiguity about the eucharist."

3. ACC-6, 102.
4. *Emmaus Report.*

In the Church of Ireland the General Synod in 1983 asked its Standing Committee to assess *The Final Report*. The Standing Committee provided a very thorough forty-eight-page booklet, and the General Synod adopted the booklet entire in May 1986 as the response of the whole Synod.[5] The report raised serious objections to ambiguities in the text and in particular thought the teaching ran near to transubstantiation and to mass-sacrifice.[6] As Christians in constant contact with the Roman Catholic Church, the Irish also noted that "contemporary Roman Catholic theology" often differed from "official Roman Catholic doctrine," but it was inevitably from the latter they had to distance themselves. The Synod asked for further consideration of that distinction, and also of "the teaching of the Epistle to the Hebrews in relation to the all-sufficient sacrifice of Christ."

At Singapore in April 1987 ACC-7 simply thanked the Emmaus team for their work, asked for the report to be published, and passed on the preparation for Lambeth 1988 to the St. Augustine's Seminar due in August that year. Those preparing for the Lambeth Conference clearly took the view that they had little basis for querying whether the Statement on the Eucharist and its *Elucidation* were to be viewed as "consonant" with Anglican doctrine.

The 1988 Lambeth Conference section on "Ecumenical Relations" had a lengthy report on general principles but it contained virtually no mention of ARCIC. Instead the section brought to the Conference plenary session a resolution with its own "Explanatory Note" subjoined to it. The Conference then passed without measurable dissent the following resolution:

---

5. Church of Ireland, *Response of the General Synod.*

6. The critique is significant particularly because Henry McAdoo was still in post as Archbishop of Dublin, and presumably threw his weight into defending the Statements, yet was unsuccessful against a strong tide of disquiet.

TEXT G

The 1988 Lambeth Conference Resolution

8 ANGLICAN–ROMAN CATHOLIC INTERNATIONAL COMMISSION (ARCIC)

This Conference:

1. Recognizes the Agreed Statements of ARCIC I on *Eucharistic Doctrine, Ministry and Ordination*, and their *Elucidations*, as consonant in substance with the faith of Anglicans and believes that this agreement offers a sufficient basis for taking the next step forward towards the reconciliation of our Churches grounded in agreement in faith.

2–5. [Welcoming work started and in prospect by ARCIC II, discussing Statements on authority, and touching on the ordination of women.]

EXPLANATORY NOTE

This Conference has received the official responses to the *Final Report* of the Anglican–Roman Catholic International Commission (ARCIC I) from the member provinces of the Anglican Communion. We note the considerable measure of consensus and convergence which the *Agreed Statements* represent. We wish to record our grateful thanks to Almighty God for the very significant advances in understanding and unity thereby expressed.

In considering the *Final Report*, the Conference bore two questions in mind:

i. Are the *Agreed Statements* consonant with Anglican faith?

ii. If so, do they enable us to take further steps forward?

Eucharistic Doctrine

The Provinces gave a very clear "yes" to the statement on *Eucharistic Doctrine*.

Comments have been made that the style and language used in the statement are inappropriate for certain cultures. Some Provinces asked for clarification about the meaning of *anamnesis* and bread and wine "becoming" the body and blood of Christ. But no Province rejected the Statement and many were extremely positive.

While we recognize that there are hurts to be healed and doubts to be overcome, we encourage Anglicans to look forward with new hope which the Holy Spirit is giving to the Church as we move away from past mistrust, division and polarization. While we respect continuing anxieties of some Anglicans in the area of "sacrifice" and "presence," they do not appear to reflect the common mind of the Provincial responses, in which it was generally felt that the *Elucidation* of *Eucharistic Doctrine* was a helpful clarification and reassurance. Both are areas of "mystery" which ultimately defy definition. But the Agreed Statement on the Eucharist *sufficiently* expresses Anglican understanding.

Thus spoke Lambeth 1988. Anglican interest would now pass to the works of ARCIC II which were just becoming public. The next meeting of the ACC, ACC-8 at Cardiff in Wales in 1990, did not have an ecumenical section. But on the eucharist, as on *The Final Report* generally, Rome had not yet officially spoken.

7

The Official Roman Catholic
Response (1991)

F ROM ROME, THE INITIAL, almost instant, *Observations* of the SCDF in
1982 have already been reported above. Julian Charley commented then:

> My immediate reaction on reading an advance copy of *Observa-*
> *tions* was that, if this represented official Roman Catholicism,
> then our Commission had wasted its eleven years. Its attitude is
> so utterly inflexible, with nothing of the true spirit of Vatican II. It
> displays a rigid conciliar fundamentalism.[1]

Observations was not, however, the definitive response of Rome. The possibility that the Commission had not "wasted its eleven years" could be kept
alive. And a more measured and emollient appraisal of the *Final Report*
came in 1985 from the (Roman Catholic) Bishops' Conference of England
and Wales.[2] They wrote very positive paragraphs about the Statement's presentation of both eucharistic sacrifice and "real presence," seeing each as a
true "expression of Catholic faith." They did want the Statement to go a little
further in their direction, but, for instance, their treatment of the reservation question (and the division of Anglicans over that issue) was marked
more by regret than confrontation. They wrote as friends. They also spoke
from local knowledge when their recommendations included two para
graphs about the "importance of the Anglican Evangelical Voice," and in
them they asked for "strong representation and consideration of Anglican
evangelical concerns." Were they suspecting they were not always meeting
properly balanced Anglican teams? Soon after they had published their appraisal, Rome decreed that Bishops' Conferences round the world should

---

1. Charley, *Rome, Canterbury,* 25.

2. Bishops' Conference of England and Wales, *Response.*

not make their own responses. This question was going to be addressed by Rome's own authority.

The official "Response" of the Roman Catholic Church took longer to emerge, and it ultimately came in December 1991. It came from the Pontifical Council for Promoting Christian Unity (PCPCU), which had succeeded the SPCU but like it operated under the aegis of the CDF. It was far less positive than the Lambeth Conference had been about the Statement, but contained many echoes of *Observations*.[3] The PCPCU on behalf of Pope John Paul II included polite enthusiasms for the project, but doubted whether "substantial agreement" had been reached, and raised specific issues which "would need greater clarification from the Catholic point of view." Pending such clarification the Vatican obviously would not and did not agree or endorse *The Final Report*. An editorial in the English Roman Catholic journal, *The Tablet*, recognizing that the *Response* would fall hard on Anglican ears, commented diplomatically, "There are here hard things which each Communion should not hesitate to say to the other."[4] Whether the Anglicans would ever venture upon saying "hard things" remained an open question.

TEXT H

THE CATHOLIC CHURCH'S *RESPONSE* TO THE FINAL REPORT OF ARCIC I (1991)

General Evaluation

1. The Catholic Church gives a warm welcome to the Final Report of ARCIC I and expresses its gratitude to the members of the International Commission responsible for drawing up this document. The Report is a result of an in-depth study of certain questions of faith by partners in dialogue and witnesses to the achievement of points of convergence and even of agreement which many would

---

3. It is entitled "*The Catholic Church's Response to The Final Report of ARCIC I.*" Its text was not included in ARCIC II's reply, *Clarifications*, but is published in Hill and Yarnold, *Anglicans and Roman Catholics*, 156–66, and is accessible online. The original (online) version has no numbering of the paragraphs, but they are added here, as included by Hill and Yarnold, who cite earlier precedents.

4. *The Tablet*, editorial, December 7, 1991.

not have thought possible before the Commission began its work. As such, it constitutes a significant milestone not only in relations between the Catholic Church and the Anglican Communion but in the ecumenical movement as a whole.

2. The Catholic Church judges, however, that it is not yet possible to state that substantial agreement has been reached on all the questions studied by the Commission. There still remain between Anglicans and Catholics important differences regarding essential matters of Catholic doctrine.

3. The following Explanatory Note is intended to give a detailed summary of the areas where differences or ambiguities remain which seriously hinder the restoration of full communion in faith and in the sacramental life. This Note is the fruit of a close collaboration between the Congregation for the Doctrine of the Faith and the Pontifical Council for Promoting Christian Unity, which is directly responsible for the dialogue—a dialogue which, as is well known, continues within the framework of ARCIC II.

4. It is the Catholic Church's hope that its definitive response to the results achieved by ARCIC I will serve as an impetus to further study, in the same fraternal spirit that has characterized this dialogue in the past, of the points of divergence remaining, as well as of those other questions which must be taken into account if the unity willed by Christ for His disciples is to be restored.

Explanatory Note

5. Before setting forth for further study those areas of the Final Report which do not satisfy fully certain elements of Catholic doctrine and which thereby prevent our speaking of the attainment of substantial agreement, it seems only right and just to mention some other areas in which notable progress has been achieved by those responsible for the redaction of the Report. The members of the Commission have obviously given a great deal of time, prayer, and reflection to the themes which they were asked to

study together and they are owed an expression of gratitude and appreciation for the manner in which they carried out their mandate.

6. It is in respect of *Eucharistic Doctrine* that the members
of the Commission were able to achieve the most notable
progress toward a consensus. Together they affirm "that
the eucharist is a sacrifice in the sacramental sense, provided that it is made clear that this is not a repetition of
the historical sacrifice" (*Eucharistic Doctrine: Elucidation,*
para 5); and areas of agreement are also evident in respect
of the real presence of Christ: "Before the eucharistic
prayer to the question 'what is it?,' the believer answers
'it is bread.' After the eucharistic prayer to the same question he answers: 'it is truly the body of Christ, the bread
of life'" (*Eucharistic Doctrine: Elucidation,* para 6). The
Catholic Church rejoices that such common affirmations
have become possible. Still, as will be indicated further
on, it looks for certain clarifications which will assure that
these affirmations are understood in a way that conforms
to Catholic doctrine.

7. With regard to *Ministry and Ordination,* the distinction
between the priesthood common to all the baptized
and the ordained priesthood is explicitly acknowledged:
"These are two distinct realities which relate each in its
own way to the high priesthood of Christ" (*Ministry and
Ordination: Elucidation,* para 2). The ordained ministry
"is not an extension of the common Christian priesthood
but belongs to another realm of the gifts of the Spirit"
(*Ministry and Ordination: Elucidation,* para 13). Ordination is described as a "sacramental act" (*Ministry and Ordination: Elucidation,* para 15) and the ordained ministry
as being an essential element of the Church: "The New
Testament shows that the ministerial office played an essential part in the life of the Church in the first century
and we believe that a ministry of this kind is part of God's
design for his people" (*Ministry and Ordination* para 4).
Moreover, "it is only the ordained minister who presides

at the eucharist" (*Ministry and Ordination: Elucidation*, para 2). These are all matters of significant consensus and of particular importance for the future development of Anglican–Roman Catholic dialogue.

8. On both the eucharist and the ordained ministry, the sacramental understanding of the Church is affirmed, to the exclusion of any purely "congregational" presentation of Christianity. The members of the Commission are seen as speaking together out of a continuum of faith and practice which has its roots in the New Testament and has developed under the guidance of the Holy Spirit throughout Christian history.

[paras 9–19: *1500 words on Authority in the Church.*]

20. It is clear, as already affirmed, that on the questions of eucharist and the ordained ministry, greater progress has been made. There are, however, certain statements and formulations in respect of these doctrines that would need greater clarification from the Catholic point of view.

21. With regard to the Eucharist, the faith of the Catholic Church would be even more clearly reflected in the *Final Report* if the following points were to be explicitly affirmed:

— that in the Eucharist, the Church, doing what Christ commanded His Apostles to do at the Last Supper, makes present the sacrifice of Calvary. This would complete, without contradicting it, the statement made in the Final Report, affirming that the Eucharist does not repeat the sacrifice of Christ, nor add to it (*EucharisticDoctrine*, para 5: *Elucidation*, para 5);

— that the sacrifice of Christ is made present with all its effects, thus affirming the propitiatory nature of the eucharistic sacrifice, which can be applied also to the deceased. For Catholics "the whole Church" must include the dead. The prayer for the dead is to be found in all the Canons of the Mass, and the propitiatory character of the Mass as the sacrifice of Christ that may be offered for the living and the dead, including a particular dead person, is part of the Catholic faith.

22. The affirmations that the Eucharist is "the Lord's real gift of himself to his Church" (*Eucharistic Doctrine*, para 8) and that the bread and wine "become" the body and blood of Christ (*Eucharistic Doctrine: Elucidation*, para 6) can certainly be interpreted in conformity with Catholic faith. They are insufficient, however, to remove all ambiguity regarding the mode of the real presence which is due to a substantial change in the elements. The Catholic Church holds that Christ in the Eucharist makes himself present sacramentally and substantially when under the species of bread and wine these earthly realities are changed into the reality of his Body and Blood, Soul and Divinity.

23. On the question of the reservation of the Eucharist, the statement that there are those who "find any kind of adoration of Christ in the reserved sacrament unacceptable" (*Eucharistic Doctrine: Elucidation*, para 9), creates concern from the Roman Catholic point of view. This section of *Eucharistic Doctrine: Elucidation*, seeks to allay any such doubts, but one remains with the conviction that this is an area in which real consensus between Anglicans and Roman Catholics is lacking.

24. Similarly, in respect of the Ordained Ministry, the Final Report would be helped if the following were made clearer:

— that only a validly ordained priest can be the minister who, in the person of Christ, brings into being the sacrament of the Eucharist. He not only recites the narrative of the institution of the Last Supper, pronouncing the words of consecration and imploring the Father to send the Holy Spirit to effect through them the transformation of the gifts, but in so doing offers sacramentally the redemptive sacrifice of Christ;

— that it was Christ himself who instituted the sacrament of Orders as the rite which confers the priesthood of the New Covenant. This would complete the significant statement made in *Ministry and Ordination* 13, that In the Eucharist the ordained minister "is seen to stand in sacramental relation to what Christ himself did in offering his own sacrifice." This clarification would seem all the more important in view of the fact that the ARCIC document does not refer to the character of priestly ordination which implies a configuration to the priesthood of Christ. The character of priestly ordination is central to the Catholic understanding of the distinction between the ministerial priesthood and the common priesthood of the baptized. It is moreover important for the recognition of Holy Orders as a sacrament instituted by Christ, and not therefore a simple ecclesiastical institution.

[paras 25–29: *736 words on the ordination of women and on Authority in the Church.*]

Conclusion

30. The above observations are not intended in any way to diminish appreciation for the important work done by ARCIC I, but rather to illustrate areas within the matters dealt with by the Final Report about which further clarification or study is required before it can be said that the statements made in the Final Report correspond fully to Catholic doctrine on the Eucharist and on Ordained Ministry.

31. The quite remarkable progress that has been made in respect of Authority in the Church indicates just how essential this question is for the future of the Roman Catholic-Anglican dialogue.

32. The value of any consensus reached in regard to other matters will to a large extent depend on the authority of the body which eventually endorses them.

33. The objection may be made that this reply does not sufficiently follow the ecumenical method, by which agreement

is sought step by step, rather than in full agreement at the first attempt. It must, however, be remembered that the Roman Catholic Church was asked to give a clear answer to the question: are the agreements contained in this Report consonant with the faith of the Catholic Church? What was asked for was not a simple evaluation of an ecumenical study, but an official response as to the identity of the various statements with the faith of the Church.

34. It is sincerely hoped that this reply will contribute to the continued dialogue between Anglicans and Catholics in the spirit of the Common Declaration made between Pope John Paul II and Archbishop Robert Runcie during the visit of the latter to Rome in 1989. There it is stated: "We here solemnly recommit ourselves and those we represent to the restoration of visible unity and full ecclesial communion in the confidence that to seek anything else would be to betray Our Lord's intention for the unity of his people."

Along with appreciation, which appears not as mere conventional ecumenical politeness, but also as having substance, this *Response* contains clear criticism of ARCIC I's work, and with respect to the Statements on the eucharist it is quite specific. There is little sign of the co-chairmen's original phrase "consonant with" (the words are used in §33, but the sense appears to be tightly bounded), but instead we find "correspond fully to" (§30) and "identity . . . with the faith" (§33). Against this demanding criterion the three themes originally identified in the Venice conversations in 1970–71 are each subjected to a rigorous examination; and in their treatment in *Eucharistic Doctrine* and its *Elucidation* they are found wanting in the following respects.

Concerning eucharistic sacrifice, in §21 there is desired to be "explicitly affirmed":

"—that in the Eucharist, the Church, doing what Christ commanded His Apostles to do at the Last Supper, makes present the sacrifice of Calvary . . . "

and

"—that the sacrifice of Christ is made present with all its effects, thus affirming the propitiatory nature of the eucharistic sacrifice, which can be applied also to the deceased."

Concerning the presence of Christ in or under the species of bread and wine, in §22 it is stated that the affirmation in *Elucidation* §6 that the bread and wine "become" the body and blood of Christ is insufficient to "remove all ambiguity regarding the mode of the real presence"; and in §23 there is concern expressed because the same document in its §9 acknowledged that among Anglicans there are those who "find any kind of adoration of Christ in the reserved sacrament unacceptable."

Those are the bald objections to the texts forwarded to Rome by ARCIC I. What was now to be done? §34 clearly anticipates "continued dialogue"; the *Response* was not to be the end of the road, but a pointer towards what from Rome's standpoint would be expressive of Roman Catholic sacramental theology, without, as we might say, remainder. Could it be done? Should it be done? And how could it be done?

There is no doubt that the *Response* cast some gloom upon those Roman Catholics and Anglicans who had stood close to the initial Statements and had waited over three years since the 1988 Lambeth Conference for Rome to deliver a verdict. Despite previous cautions from Rome, there had been good hopes that the eminent Roman Catholic theologians on the Commission would have carried the day. Some of the disappointment related to the general tone of reproof for ARCIC I's failure to express Roman Catholic teaching; and some of this of course referred to the Statements on Authority which are beyond the present purview. But for the present purposes the *Response* had, as noted, included substantial criticism of the Statements on the Eucharist, and the impact of that provoked widespread baffled and even hurt comment.

The Roman Catholic Reactions

The Hill and Yarnold volume printed two quasi-official comments by Roman Catholic bodies.

First was the very brief Statement of the Roman Catholic Bishops' Conference of England and Wales.[5] This politely accepted the *Response* of the Holy See, and in conformity with it acknowledged further work

5. Hill and Yarnold, *Anglicans and Roman Catholics*, 166–67.

was to be done, gently indicating that clarifications (the word was growing in currency) were particularly needed in the work on authority, where
ARCIC I itself had forwarded its work unfinished. There is perhaps one
tiny hint of dismay where the Statement quotes and endorses what the
Holy Father had himself said back in 1980, as he had then commended the
ARCIC method of "going behind the habit of thought and expression, born
and nourished in enmity and controversy, to scrutinize *together* the great
common treasure."[6] Was this quotation giving just a hint that they did not
discern the same supportiveness of the ARCIC I method in the immediate
Response? They not only made no specific reference to eucharistic doctrine,
but, by underlining the need of "clarifications" (that word again) "particularly regarding the subject of Authority," they perhaps gently downplayed
any asserted shortcomings in the Statements on the eucharist.

In the Hill and Yarnold volume there then followed an astonishing
comment, thirteen pages long, from the French Roman Catholic Episcopal Commission for Christian Unity. They viewed themselves as existing in
France alongside Anglicans, and therefore as immediately engaged ecumen-
ically with them. After a somewhat cosmetic appreciation of the *Response*,
this Commission then appraised it with "regret." They cited considerable
Roman Catholic approval of the work of ARCIC I from a variety of Roman
Catholic sources; they repeated the favorable findings they themselves had
published seven years before[7]; and they quoted pronouncements by Pope
John Paul II himself as setting out a far more positive approach to ecumenical relationships. The bishops said, "It is no business of ours to pass judgment
on the final version published by the Holy See," and then concluded that
sentence with the blunt but perceptive "we are astonished at the demands
for an identity of formulations in an age when we live in a society which has
become conscious of its multicultural character."[8]

The French comment is general in character, concentrating on methodology rather than content, and, like the comment in 1985 of the Bishops' Conference of England and Wales, it makes no specific reference to
the eucharist. It is significant that they picked up the words "identity of

6. Hill and Yarnold, *Anglicans and Roman Catholics*, 167. The italic [*or* emphasis] is
original.

7. These had been published in tandem with the comments of the Bishops' Conference of England and Wales in 1985.

8. Hill and Yarnold, *Anglicans and Roman Catholics*, 173.

formulations"—were they reading the *Response* as asking for the Anglican Communion to sign up to the decrees of Trent?

Anglican Reactions

The *Response* provoked much Anglican reaction. Much was inevitably reflecting on the processes discernible in its drafting and form, and was not immediately addressing its eucharistic *desiderata*. These reactions provide a context for evaluating here both the *Response* and the further work done by ARCIC II in the light of it.

First came George Carey, the Archbishop of Canterbury. He issued a statement on the day the *Response* was officially delivered to him, and he too struck conventional polite notes of gratitude for the evident progress made. However, as he was forwarding the *Response* to the churches of the Anglican Communion, he accompanied it by "a personal reflection." He noted that the 1988 Lambeth Conference had overwhelmingly agreed that the ARCIC I documents on the Eucharist and on Ministry and Ordination were "consonant" with the faith of the Anglican Churches. He continued:

> In the case of the Roman Catholic *Response*, however, the question to our two Communions appears to have been understood instead as asking: "Is the Final Report *identical* with the teachings of the Roman Catholic Church?" The argument of the *Response* suggests that a difference in methodology may have led to this approach.[9]

A measured personal reaction came from Christopher Hill, who had served sixteen years on ARCIC I and ARCIC II until 1990. In a lengthy critique for the Church of England's Council for Christian Unity (CCU) in 1992, he began by saying "Anglicans, of no matter what school, will at best be able to raise only one cheer out of three at the long awaited [Vatican *Response*]."[10] In a trenchant and compelling contribution he then distinguished carefully between the PCPCU's methodology ("going behind definitions") and the CDF's ("any document is scrutinized for identity with the official teaching").[11] Then "Overall I have an uneasy feeling that

---

9. Hill and Yarnold, *Anglicans and Roman Catholics*, 169–70.

10. CCU, *Anglican and Roman Catholic Response*, 29.

11. CCU, *Anglican and Roman Catholic Response*, 31.

the drafters of much of the *Response* have forgotten the agreed basis for Anglican–Roman Catholic Dialogue."[12]

A more confrontational angle was provided by Howard Root, who had been a member of both the Preparatory Commission and ARCIC I:

> Generally, when it [the *Response*] is negative, it takes the form of saying that in this or that matter the Report is lacking in its conformity to or understanding of "Catholic doctrine." As one goes through the *Response* one is repeatedly conscious that criticisms of inadequacy in "Catholic doctrine" must be criticisms of the Roman Catholic members of the Commission.[13]

This is breathtaking stuff: the Holy See had appointed top-class theologians to the Commission, but then, if we follow Howard Root's logic, had in effect accused them of betraying the faith.

There was then the Anglican Consultative Council. ACC-9 met jointly with primates of the Anglican Communion at Cape Town in January 1993. Curiously, there was no report on ecumenical relationships on the agenda, and no hint of any discussion of the *Response* in the documents. Nevertheless, the ACC was the *locus* of care and co-ordination for the Anglican Communion; and in their meeting with the primates there must have been considerable informal (presumably off-the-record table-talk) discussion, somewhat dismayed discussion, within the members, as is visible from the plenary resolution which the joint meeting passed:

Resolution 3—Relations with the Roman Catholic Church

Resolved, that this Joint Meeting of the Primates of the Anglican Communion and the Anglican Consultative Council, while acknowledging that there has been widespread Anglican disappointment with the Roman Catholic response to the ARCIC I Final Report, issued in December 1991, nevertheless gives thanks to God that . . . [there follows a long list of the kinds of local co-operation to be found around the world between the two Communions].

Encourages the development of local initiatives.

Recommends that ARCIC II proceed as a matter of priority with its mandate to give attention to the official responses of both

---

12. CCU, *Anglican and Roman Catholic Response*, 35.

13. Howard Root in a detailed and magisterial examination of the *Response* in "Some Remarks," 165.

Churches as well as the issue of methodology raised by the Archbishop of Canterbury.[14]

While the Roman Catholic *Response* had anticipated and virtually
commissioned further work, and in §3 had named ARCIC II as the place
for that dialogue to occur, so now these two international Anglican "instru-
ments of communion" in the light of "widespread disappointment" jointly
confirmed that mandate, and urged "attention to the official responses" as a
"matter of priority." ARCIC II were receiving their orders.

Joint Anglican and Roman Catholic Reactions

On the other hand, there were authorities who addressed the actual theological points made in the *Response*.

First for our purposes comes a gallery of distinguished theologians
paraded by Christopher Hill and Edward Yarnold in *Anglicans and Roman
Catholics: The Search for Unity* in 1994. Curiously, however, although the
volume was published in 1994 and contained the actual documents from
what is the next chapter here, *viz* both *Clarifications* and the Letter of Cardinal Cassidy, all the individual contributions they published addressing
the *Response* dated from before *Clarifications*, and do not therefore offer
comment on it. The key commentators on the *Response* are Henry Chadwick and Christopher Hill (Anglicans), and Edward Yarnold, Francis Sullivan, and John McHugh (Roman Catholics).

These, however, were commenting as individuals. More interesting
perhaps are the three separate agreed findings of the Anglican Roman
Catholic Consultation USA (ARC-USA). On June 17 1992 they issued a
short document, *A Recommitment to Full Communion*, in which "We here
acknowledge that there has been a widespread disappointment with the
official Roman Catholic *Response to The Final Report*, and we note the concern of some theologians about the language and methodology of the *Response*." The document then continued with a pledge to work at the tasks.[15]
It did not include any specific discussion of the eucharist.

14. ACC-9, 139–40.

15. There is here a slightly misleading presentation in the Hill and Yarnold volume,
Anglicans and Roman Catholics; the second of the three Statements reviewed here is the
only one printed in that volume, and it appears with the date "1992," suggesting it is
the first, and it is published without its title. All three are available online, and the third
follows here as Text K.

Then on April 5 1993 they issued a lengthy document, *How can we recognize "substantial agreement"?* They were largely concerned with the methodology of the *Response*, and were not attempting at this point to meet the Holy See's call for "clarification" at several points. A typical quotation from the document reads as follows:

> 17 . . . The Vatican response seems to urge that clarification be given through the use of language that is closer to and even identical with traditional Roman Catholic theological formulations. (For example, the response identifies a number of points it would like to have "explicitly affirmed." One of these is "the propitiatory character of the Mass as the sacrifice of Christ." The *Response* also asks that clarification be given on a number of matters and cites "the fact that the ARCIC document does not refer to the character of priestly ordination, which implies a configuration to the priesthood of Christ.")

Whereas these two statements suggested hesitation about the Vatican's *Response*, the third statement from ARC-USA was quite different. It attempted to meet outright the stated need of clarification on Rome's terms, and, unlike most of the other documents concerning Anglican–Roman Catholic doctrinal agreement, it did address the eucharist alone. Curiously, the Consultation was meeting well after ARCIC II had already agreed its own "clarifications," which form the next chapter here, but the Americans answered the *Response* seemingly without any awareness of ARCIC II's work (which was still awaiting Cardinal Cassidy's reply, and had presumably not been in any way leaked to the Americans). Here is their statement in full:

TEXT J

The Statement on the Eucharist of ARC/USA

At the forty-first meeting of the Anglican–Roman Catholic Dialogue in the United States of America (ARC/USA), on January 6, 1994, having in mind the significant agreement on the eucharist represented by *The Final Report* of the Anglican Roman Catholic International Commission and responding to the request in the *Vatican Response to the ARCIC I Final Report* for clarification, we wish as the official representatives of our two Churches in the United States to make together the following affirmations.

1. We affirm that in the eucharist the Church, doing what Christ commanded his apostles to do at the Last Supper, makes present the sacrifice of Calvary. We understand this to mean that when the Church is gathered in worship, it is empowered by the Holy Spirit to make Christ present and to receive all the benefits of his sacrifice.

2. We affirm that God has given the eucharist to the Churches as a means through which all the atoning work of Christ on the cross is proclaimed and made present with all its effects in the life of the Church. His work includes "that perfect redemption, propitiation, and satisfaction, for all the sins of the whole world" (Cf. Art. 31 BCP [USA], p.874). Thus the propitiatory effect of Christ's one sacrifice applies in the eucharistic celebration to both the living and the dead, including a particular dead person.

3. We affirm that Christ in the eucharist makes himself present sacramentally and truly when under the species of bread and wine these earthy realities are changed into the reality of his body and blood. In English the terms *substance, substantial,* and *substantially* have such physical and material overtones that we, adhering to *The Final Report*, have substituted the word *truly* for the word *substantially* in the clarification request by the Vatican *Response*. However, we affirm the reality of the change by consecration as being independent of the subjective disposition of the worshipers.

4. Both our Churches affirm that after the eucharistic celebration the body and blood of Christ may be reserved for the communion of the sick, "or of others who for weighty cause could not be present at the celebration" (BCP, pp.408–409). Although the American *Book of Common Prayer* directs that any consecrated bread and wine not reserved for this purpose should be consumed at the end of the service, American Episcopalians recognize that

many of their own Church members practice the adoration of Christ in the reserved sacrament. We acknowledge this practice as an extension of the worship of Jesus Christ present at the eucharistic celebration.

5. We affirm that only a validly ordained priest can be the minister who, in the person of Christ, brings into being the sacrament of the eucharist and offers sacramentally the redemptive sacrifice of Christ which God offers us.

As the Vatican *Response* had already recorded the notable progress toward consensus represented by *The Final Report* in respect of eucharistic doctrine, in the light of these five affirmations ARC/USA records its conclusions that the eucharist as sacrifice is not an issue that divides our two Churches.

These affirmations, which the two sides of the dialogue in the USA agreed together, would go a long way to meeting the requirements of the PCPCU in the *Response*. They are, however, somewhat breathtaking to an evangelical Anglican; and part of the reason why the participants could agree it is because the Episcopal Church in the USA has very few evangelicals, and almost certainly none representing it in inter-Church dialogue. Any hesitations about methodology were now laid aside, and the statement appears almost without exception to mirror a strictly Roman Catholic understanding of the eucharist. The only point where a wedge might be driven between the doctrine and practices of the two Communions is where in §4 the Episcopalians "recognize that many of their own Church members practice the adoration of Christ in the reserved sacrament"—a report which hardly commits the Episcopal Church as a body to that practice.

Robert Wright, the American Episcopalian scholar who had himself been a member of ARCIC II until 1990, wrote a little later in 1994 to introduce this USA Statement under the title of "The Reception of ARCIC I in the USA."[16] By this time he had seen the text of *Clarifications*. Nevertheless, in the essay he asked of the US Statement "what place it may have in the process of reception," though he recognized that it was a "local (i.e., national) statement." He interestingly commented that "It certainly seems to come closer to meeting the Vatican's objections than the *Clarifications* later issued by the new ARCIC," and he went on to say that he would have

16. Wright, "Reception," 228–30.

been ready to sign it himself, though "The language of this statement is not what I actively teach, but . . . I know I already do live in full communion with many who use such language and think in such ways." If, as it appears, this last sentence is a reason for being ready to affirm the Statement, it reads suspiciously like a *non sequitur*: for it is fully possible for an Anglican to "live in full communion" with people, whether Anglicans in different parts of the world or, say, Old Catholics, without thereby endorsing the language they use about the eucharist. So was Robert Wright perhaps stretching charity somewhat beyond logic? Presumably he would *a fortiori* have been ready to align himself with *Clarifications*.

There was more to come on the ARC-USA "Five Affirmations." In September 1995 three scholarly Americans contributed essays on eucharistic sacrifice as addressed within their Anglican–Roman Catholic Dialogue in the international journal of liturgy, *Worship*.[17] These were R. William Franklin, Charles P. Price and Joanne M. Pierce, the first two being Anglicans, the third a Roman Catholic. Franklin's essay contained the whole text of the "Five Affirmations." This September 1995 issue came a full year after *Clarifications* had been published, and yet, most oddly, all three contributors delivered carefully worded essays in the light of the 1991 *Response* without any mention of the ARCIC reply in *Clarifications* at all. Had they never seen *Clarifications*, or did they consider it beneath notice, or did they think they had themselves answered the *Response* better? We do not know, as they say nothing which would inform us.

If we then return to the Hill and Yarnold volume, the individual contributors there wrote in 1992–93, without knowledge of *Clarifications*, though, as noted in the Introduction here, the text of *Clarifications* was then added within the actual volume to nestle alongside their essays.[18] Each contributor was, however, considering the whole range of the *Response* as it covers all the themes of the *Final Report*, and the eucharist, as such, received correspondingly less attention.

Henry Chadwick's chapter, eleven pages long but covering all the topics of *The Final Report*, is entitled "Unfinished Business." It is typically

---

17. Franklin, "ARC-USA," 380–90; Price, "Anamnesis," 391–93; Pierce, "Eucharist as Sacrifice," 394–405. Similarly in 1995 David Bird's *Receiving the Vision* shows no knowledge of *Clarifications*.

18. The Introduction does, on p.5, refer to the inclusion of *Clarifications* and the Cassidy Letter within the collection, but it does not discuss their contents, save smoothly to state that the "reception" of ecumenical agreements "is indeed a continuing process." "Reception" is in this case an interesting choice of terminology.

pacific, and is concerned with methodology, not least with the ambiguity inherent in the phrase "substantial agreement." He reads the Vatican as saying that the statements on the eucharist are acceptable as far as they go, but that they do not sufficiently define Roman Catholic belief, and that from the Vatican's point of view they might even be accommodating protestant beliefs. "Therefore there is a kind of search for unidentified submarines below the surface of apparently tranquil waters."[19]

Christopher Hill, while defending the methodology of ARCIC I, also portrays its treatment of doctrine and practice in a light which suggests it should not be too difficult to present it as conforming to the criteria of the *Response*. In particular his discussion of the rubric in the 1662 rite concerning the consumption of the remaining consecrated bread and wine at the end of a eucharistic celebration adumbrates the ARCIC II reply which was to come in *Clarifications*.[20]

Edward Yarnold, as a Roman Catholic signatory of *The Final Report*, appears marginally embarrassed at the judgment of the *Response*, and discusses at length what might be the limits of the meaning of "consonant with the faith of the Catholic Church." Interestingly, he reckons the quest for strictly univocal agreement is a false trail, and, quoting from himself elsewhere, he states "the search for perfectly unambiguous formulas as a prelude to reunion is a wild-goose-chase."[21]

Francis Sullivan provides a critical comment in "The Vatican Response to ARCIC I." As a general point he asks "whether the authors of the Response fully understood the exact nature and limits of the claims made by ARCIC I" and then quotes a series of statements from the *Response*, and summarizes them by saying that their "negative character . . . is due to the fact that it criticizes ARCIC I for not achieving results which the Commission itself did not claim to have achieved."[22]

A fascinating further contribution was made by the learned John McHugh as "Marginal Notes on the Response to ARCIC I." He engaged in some literary dissection of the *Response*, not least in apparent contradictions within it, particularly exemplified in the section on "Authority," but

19. Hill and Yarnold, *Anglicans and Roman Catholics*, 214.

20. Hill and Yarnold, *Anglicans and Roman Catholics*, 231. See below on pp. 124–25.

21. Hill and Yarnold, *Anglicans and Roman Catholics*, 247.

22. Hill and Yarnold, *Anglicans and Roman Catholics*, 300–301. His schoolmasterly verdict of "could do better" is backed by a footnote on p. 300 stating he has found *no less than 17 points* at which the *Response* misquotes from the ARCIC I documents.

found elsewhere as well; and the treatment of the eucharist did not escape his scythe.

> But the most disturbing sentence is found under the heading *Eucharist* (para.22), where we read that "these earthly realities are changed into the reality of his body and blood, soul and divinity." However, what at first reading appears to be an egregious heresy is in fact quite obviously the result of mere human error in the word-processing of the final text![23]

This is spelled out—the Roman Catholic doctrine does not include the changing of the bread and wine into Jesus' "soul and divinity"—McHugh concluded that some other sentence about Jesus' presence in the sacrament had been allowed to run on when two thoughts were conflated.

His next paragraph, about the *Response's* insistence on "adoration of the reserved sacrament," also accused the text of inconsistency and a tendency to mislead. And finally, when he had dealt similarly with all three themes in the *Final Report* which the *Response* addressed, he summed up his "Marginal Notes" as follows:

> The general impression is that a final revision may have been entrusted to a sub-committee or a secretary charged with putting together a comprehensive response, but without authority to make more than minor modifications to proposed drafts of various sections of the document . . . the reader, especially any reader accustomed to the traditional practices, usage and style of the Roman Curia, is left genuinely perplexed concerning the precise degree of authority ascribed by the Holy See to the Response, and therefore to some of the statements which it contains.[24]

The literary criticism could go further, tracing out echoes of *Observations* from nearly ten years before, and speculating further on McHugh's "final impression" of a document cobbled together slightly inexpertly from different submissions. Such ecumenical impolitenesses were hardly open to Anglicans, or indeed to Roman Catholics on ARCIC II, to emulate. Christopher Hill had in 1991, when the *Response* was issued, articulated a discernment which others later echoed that the PCPCU understood the task differently from the CDF:

---

23. Hill and Yarnold, *Anglicans and Roman Catholics*, 329.
24. Hill and Yarnold, *Anglicans and Roman Catholics*, 331.

The CDF, it will be remembered, had already produced its "Observations" as a "contribution to the current dialogue" in March 1982,
only weeks after the publication of the *Final Report* itself. It comes
as no surprise therefore that the cautious reservations the CDF
expressed then are now reiterated with more authority. In essence,
what seems to have happened is that the Council for Unity [ie the
PCPCU] has persuaded the CDF to accept a genuinely positive
and ecumenical tone, while failing to persuade it to modify its
substantive judgments.[25]

However, muttering about the style or methodology of the *Response* would
hardly suffice. Instead the question for ARCIC II had to relate to its content,
whether to confront the *Response's* insistence on Statements being verbally
"identical" to official Roman doctrine, or whether to bow to the pressure
further to "clarify" the existing *Eucharistic Doctrine* and *Elucidation*, and
thus go as far as possible to meet the various, apparently non-negotiable,
requirements of Rome. While the personal verdict of Archbishop George
Carey and the actual resolution of ACC-9 might possibly have given scope
to ARCIC II to draft a confrontation, it is perhaps inherently unlikely that
Roman Catholic members would have been willing to take that course, and
in any case there is no evidence to suggest the Commission ever treated it
as a live option. Whether chosen by them or not, their path was to follow
out the Vatican's behest. As they were already addressing a full program of
new themes, the need to reply to the *Response* can have seemed little other
than a distraction from their existing task, one to be handled with as little
disturbance of their agenda as possible.

25. Christopher Hill, "Response to the Response" in *The Tablet*, December 7, 1991.

8

Clarifications (1994):
Text and Context

A RCIC II THUS RECOGNIZED that the ball was in their court, and, after earlier work in 1992 in which a possible procedure was drawn up, in December 1992 the co-chairs were together in Rome and met Cardinal Cassidy, the president of the PCPCU, to discover whether a reply from them would be a constructive next step. In the words of Stephen Platten, then Anglican co-secretary of ARCIC II, Cassidy "agreed to consult with the Congregation for the Defence of the Faith who confirmed that a formal response from ARCIC II could be a positive step forward."[1] So ARCIC II was already addressing this when in early 1993 ACC-9 remitted the question to them as "a matter of priority." While still engaged on their own identified projects, they had already asked a sub-committee to draft "clarifications" on both the eucharist and ministry. The sub-committee consisted of Jean Tillard, Pierre Duprey, Julian Charley and Christopher Hill, all of whom had been members of ARCIC I, the Commission which had agreed the documents which the Vatican *Response* was saying were inadequate.[2] Unlike the two Roman Catholics, the two Anglicans were no longer in 1993 members of ARCIC II, and they were summoned specifically for this task. The four met in February 1993, and obviously viewed themselves as seeking to satisfy the criteria Rome had set in the *Response*. We can but presume they had been convened on those terms. Their draft went before ARCIC II in September 1993; it was there marginally

---

1. Platten, "Unity and the Churches," 97–98.

2. Christopher Hill had not become a member until 1974, when he was appointed Anglican co-secretary, and thus had not been directly a signatory of the Windsor Statement, *Eucharistic Doctrine*.

amended[3]; and it was then sent as a relatively private communication to the PCPCU. Cardinal Cassidy took their text to the two "dicasteries" (i.e., the CDF and PCPCU), and then replied favorably in February 1994; the two co-chairmen thereupon provided an Introductory "statement" to both *Clarifications* and Cassidy's Letter, and passed the composite document to the ACC and the PCPCU, to be published for them by the Catholic Truth Society and Church House Publishing in London.

Before considering the text, it is worth emphasizing its provenance. The four who initially drafted the text are separately listed as sub-committee members on page v of *Clarifications*, but are not otherwise mentioned, not even to be thanked, by the two co-chairmen in their Introduction. They do get a later mention in the Cassidy Letter. The point is that, as a drafting sub-committee, they were demonstrably neither more nor less than what that name implies; they did the drafting and then submitted their draft to the Commission meeting in plenary; and the Commission as a whole first amended it, and then adopted it. ARCIC II must be held formally responsible for the resultant document. The emphasizing is needed as, after a period of complete official silence by Anglicans about *Clarifications*, when later its existence was noted, at least two official reports attributed it simply to the sub-committee (an attribution which I have also found in conversation even with members of ARCIC II).[4] This erroneous attribution in two official reports can surely only have arisen through casual disclaimers of responsibility by Anglican members of ARCIC II, thus, it would seem, exempting themselves from any need of an *apologia* for the document. However, it is actually not difficult within

---

3. See the report by Charles Sherlock in Denaux, Sagovsky, and Sherlock, *Looking Towards*, 309.

4. Thus IARCCUM reported in 2007:

> [The Vatican's Response] requested further work in these two areas. *Clarifications* prepared by an ARCIC sub-commission were subsequently judged by the Roman Catholic Church to have greatly strengthened agreement in these areas. (IARCCUM, *Growing Together*, 7)

Similarly, the "Kyoto" report in 2009, in its summary concerning the history of Anglican–Roman Catholic relationships, includes this sole reference to *Clarifications*:

> Official responses were made by the two Communions (through Resolution 8 of the 1988 Lambeth Conference on the Anglican side) to the work of ARCIC I, pointing to areas of convergence or agreement in understanding, and to outstanding areas of difference (giving rise to various "Clarifications" from an ARCIC sub-commission). (Jones, *Vision Before Us*, 172)

the original text of the documents to find ARCIC II itself taking full responsibility for it, and there the responsibility must lie.

TEXT K

A STATEMENT BY THE
CO-CHAIRMEN OF ARCIC-II

A STATEMENT

by the Co-Chairmen of the Anglican–Roman
Catholic International Commission

We present here ARCIC's *Clarifications of Certain Aspects of
the Agreed Statements on Eucharist and Ministry* and a letter
we have received in reply from Cardinal Cassidy, President of
the Pontifical Council for Promoting Christian Unity. These
mark a very significant moment in the work of ARCIC and
in its reception. Consequently, a few words recalling their
background may be helpful.

In September 1981, at the final meeting of the first ARCIC in
Windsor, England, the first phase of the Commission's work
was brought to a conclusion. This was marked by the publication in 1982 of the *Final Report*, containing all of the first
Commission's Agreed Statements and Elucidations. From the
beginning, the Commission's method had been determined
by the *Common Declaration* between Archbishop Michael
Ramsey of Canterbury and Pope Paul VI in 1966. This spoke
of "a serious dialogue which, founded upon the Gospels and
on the ancient common traditions, may lead to that unity in
truth, for which Christ prayed." The method was understood
by ARCIC as an endeavour "to get behind the opposed and
entrenched positions of past controversies" and the deliberate avoidance of the "vocabulary of past polemics, not with
any intention of evading the real difficulties that provoked
them, but because the emotive associations of such language
had often obscured the truth" (Authority in the Church 1.25).
When Pope John Paul II received the members of ARCIC

in audience at Castel Gandolfo in 1980 he observed that the method of ARCIC had been "to go behind the habit of thought and expression born and nourished in enmity, to clothe it in a language at once traditional and expressive of the insights of an age which no longer glories in strife."

By faithfulness to this method, through long, patient and charitable dialogue, in a context of common prayer, ARCIC claimed that it had "reached substantial agreement on the doctrine of the eucharist" (Eucharistic Doctrine, 12); and similarly, on the ordained ministry, a consensus where "doctrine admits no divergence" (Ministry and Ordination, 17). For ARCIC, substantial agreement meant that "differences of theology and practice may well co-exist with a real consensus on the essentials of . . . faith" (Eucharistic Doctrine: Elucidation).

ARCIC never claimed that its agreement on authority had quite the same quality. What was claimed here was highly significant but more limited: "a high degree of agreement 'on authority in the Church and in particular on the basic principles of primacy,'" (Preface to the Final Report). After careful study of the particular issues of papal primacy and infallibility ARCIC spoke of a "convergence" which, taken with its earlier agreements, appeared "to call for the establishing of a new relationship between our Churches" (Final Report, Conclusion). Both Churches have asked the Commission to continue to work on vital issues connected with authority.

From the beginning the Commission recognized that its agreements could not be ratified by the official authorities "until such time as our respective Churches can evaluate its conclusion" (Eucharistic Doctrine, Co-Chairmen's Preface). The ARCIC agreements do not therefore represent the end of a process. Rather, dialogue involves not only a readiness to put questions but also to be questioned. The formal presentation of the Agreements for evaluation, in fact, initiated a further vital stage in the process of seeking reconciliation, during which the appropriate authorities in both communions are called upon to test the adequacy of the Commission's Agreements in the light of their respective faith and practice.

For the Anglican Communion, the Lambeth Conference of 1988 marked a decisive stage in this process. Prior to this all the Provinces of the Anglican Communion had been asked by the Anglican Consultative Council whether the Agreements on the Eucharist and on Ministry and Ordination were "consonant in substance with the faith of Anglicans." In asking this question of the Provinces, the Council thus set in motion an official procedure to enable the bishops of the Lambeth Conference "to discern and pronounce a consensus" (ACC, Newcastle, 1981). The responses of the Provinces were officially collated, summarised and published in preparation for the Conference. After noting that the Provinces had given "a clear 'yes'" to these agreements, the Lambeth Conference went on to recognise "the Agreed Statements of ARCIC I on Eucharistic Doctrine, Ministry and Ordination, and their Elucidations as consonant in substance with the faith of Anglicans" (Resolution 8 and Explanatory Note).

After wide consultation and serious reflection, the Catholic Church produced its Response to the *Final Report* in 1991. It spoke very positively of ARCIC's work as "a significant milestone not only in relations between the Catholic Church and the Anglican Communion but in the ecumenical movement as a whole," acknowledging "points of convergence and even of agreement which many would not have thought possible before the Commission began its work." At the same time, concerning the work on Eucharist and Ministry and Ordination for which "substantial agreement" had been claimed, it raised specific issues which "would need greater clarification from the Catholic point of view."

The response of ARCIC to this request is contained in *Clarifications of Certain Aspects of the Agreed Statements on Eucharist and Ministry*. These Clarifications must, of course, be read in the context of the earlier Agreements or the issues they deal with will appear to be out of proportion. The *Clarifications* were submitted to the same (Roman Catholic) authorities from whom the request had come. The text is reproduced here, along with the assessment communicated in a letter from Cardinal Cassidy to us as Co-Chairmen of ARCIC. It will be seen that ARCIC's clarifications are judged to have "indeed thrown new light on the questions" so that, as the Cardinal says, "the agreement reached on Eucharist and Ministry by ARCIC-I is thus greatly strengthened and no further study would seem to be required at this stage." These clarifications and the Cardinal's letter constitute a very important element in the reception of ARCIC's agreements on Eucharist and the understanding of Ministry. It is well known, however, that there remains a serious disagreement between the Roman Catholic Church and the Anglican Communion about the ordination of women to the priesthood.

It is our hope that this positive step on the road of reception will assist both communions to recognize that what ARCIC has stated and now clarified does indeed represent agreement about our respective faith and practice. Though much still remains to be discussed, the agreements reached on the important subjects of Eucharistic Doctrine, Ministry and Ordination constitute an important stage in our growth towards fuller communion. We hope and pray that this now more definitive agreement will spur us on to overcoming other difficulties in the way of full visible unity which our two communions have committed themselves to seek.

+ MARK SANTER
+ CORMAC MURPHY-O'CONNOR
(Co-Chairmen ARCIC-II)

Text L

CLARIFICATIONS OF CERTAIN ASPECTS OF THE AGREED STATEMENTS ON EUCHARIST AND MINISTRY OF ARCIC I

In this paper we seek to answer the queries raised in the 1991 Response of the Holy See to the *Final Report* of ARCIC (1982) concerning the Eucharist and the Ordained Ministry (CTS D 0609). We are encouraged by what is said in the Response— that this may "serve as an impetus to further study."

The Commission was inspired by two official statements of the Roman Catholic Church. The first came from the address by Pope John XXIII at the opening of the Second Vatican Council, when he said: "The substance of the deposit of faith is one thing, and the way it is presented is another."* The second statement is para. 17 of *Unitatis Redintegratio* which, in speaking of East and West, includes the words, "sometimes one tradition has come nearer than the other to an apt appreciation of certain aspects of a revealed mystery, or has experienced them in a clearer manner. As a result, these various theological formulations are often to be considered as complementary rather than conflicting." This concept has been endorsed by the *Catechism of the Catholic Church* (1972), which affirms that when the Church "puts down her roots in a variety of cultural, social and human terrains, she takes on different external expressions and appearances in each part of the world. The rich variety of ecclesiastical disciplines, liturgical rites and theological and spiritual heritage proper to the local churches, in harmony among themselves, shows with greater clarity the catholicity of the undivided Church." In our study of Eucharist and Ministry we discovered beneath a diversity of expressions and practice a profound underlying harmony. This harmony is not broken when an element of the truth is more strongly affirmed in one tradition than in another, in which nevertheless it is not denied. Such is usually the case with Eucharistic adoration, as we shall later show.

EUCHARIST

The Response to the *Final Report*, whilst approving the main thrust of the statement on Eucharistic Doctrine, asks for clarification concerning the following points:

* The quotation is from Pope John XXIII's Italian text. However, the official Latin text in translation reads: "For the deposit of faith, or the truths which are contained in our venerable doctrine, are one thing, and the way they are expressed is another, with, however, the same sense and meaning."

a. the essential link of the one Eucharistic Memorial with the *once-for-all* sacrifice of Calvary which it makes sacramentally present;

b. "the propitiatory nature of the Eucharistic sacrifice, which can be applied also to the deceased." The Response stressed the fact that "for Catholics the whole Church must include the dead." It appears to want reassurance that the Anglican communion shares the same view;

c. certitude that Christ is present sacramentally and substantially when "under the species of bread and wine these earthly realities are changed into the reality of his Body and Blood, Soul and Divinity";

d. the adoration of Christ in the reserved sacrament.

The Response of the Holy See states that the Catholic Church rejoices because the members of the Commission were able to affirm together "that the eucharist is a sacrifice in the sacramental sense, provided that it is clear that this is not a repetition of the historical sacrifice." In the mind of the Commission the making present, effective and accessible of the unique historic sacrifice of Christ does not entail a repetition of it. In the light of this the Commission affirms that the belief that the eucharist is truly a sacrifice, but in a sacramental way, is part of the eucharistic faith of both our communions. As has been stated in the Elucidation on Eucharistic Doctrine 5: "The Commission believes that the traditional understanding of sacramental reality, in which the once-for-all event of salvation becomes effective in the present through the action of the Holy Spirit, is well expressed by the word *anamnesis*. We accept this use of the word which seems to do full justice to the semitic background. Furthermore it enables us to affirm a strong conviction of sacramental realism and reject mere symbolism."

When we speak of the death of Christ on Calvary as a sacrifice, we are using a term to help explain the nature of Christ's self-offering, a term which is not exhaustive of the significance of that self-offering. However, it has become normative for the Christian tradition because of its intimate relation with the unique propitiatory character of the death of Christ. This theme of propitiatory sacrifice is clearly emphasized in the classical eucharistic liturgies of the churches of the Anglican Communion (e.g., the English *Book of Common Prayer*, 1662), where the words immediately preceding the *Sursum Corda* have always included 1 John 2:1,2, "If anyone sin, we have an advocate with the Father, Jesus Christ the righteous, and he is the propitiation for our sins." So the Prayer of Consecration begins:

> Almighty God, our heavenly Father, who of thy tender mercy didst give thine only Son Jesus Christ to suffer death upon the Cross for our redemption; who made there (by his one oblation of himself once offered) a full, perfect and sufficient sacrifice, oblation, and satisfaction, for the sins of the whole world; and did institute, and in his holy Gospel command us to continue, a perpetual memory of that his precious death, until his coming again.

Similarly, the propitiatory dimension of the eucharist is explicit in the *Final Report* when it says that through the eucharist "the atoning work of Christ on the cross is proclaimed and made effective" and the whole Church continues to "entreat the benefits of his passion on behalf of the whole Church." This is precisely what is affirmed at the heart of the eucharistic action in both classical and contemporary Anglican liturgies (e.g., *The Book of Common Prayer*, 1662):

> O Lord and heavenly Father, we thy humble servants entirely desire thy fatherly goodness mercifully to accept this our sacrifice of praise and thanksgiving, most humbly beseeching thee to grant, that by the merits and death of thy Son Jesus, and through faith in his blood, we and *all thy whole Church* may obtain remission of our sins and all other benefits of his passion.**

** A nuanced example of propitiatory language in association with the eucharist is found in the writings of the seventeenth century Anglican divine, Jeremy Taylor: "It

"All thy whole Church" must be understood in the light of the article in the Nicene Creed which precedes it, "I believe in the one holy catholic and apostolic church . . . in the resurrection of the dead and the life of the world to come." For this reason commemoration of the faithful departed has continued to be part of the intercessions in Anglican eucharistic liturgies past and present (compare also the liturgical provision for a eucharist at a Funeral and in the Commemoration of the Faithful Departed in the *Alternative Service Book*, 1980, of the Church of England, pp.328ff, 834ff and 936ff).

The Holy See's Response gladly recognizes our agreement with regard to the real presence of Christ: "Before the eucharistic prayer, to the question 'What is that?,' the believer answers 'It is bread.' After the eucharistic prayer to the same question he answers: 'It is truly the body of Christ, the Bread of Life.'" It also acknowledges that, "The affirmations that the eucharist is the 'Lord's real gift of himself to his Church' (*Eucharistic Doctrine*, 8), and that the bread and wine 'become' the body and blood of Christ (*Eucharistic Doctrine, Elucidation*, 6) can certainly be interpreted in conformity with the catholic faith." It only asks for some clarification to remove any ambiguity regarding the mode of the real presence. The Response speaks of the earthly realities of bread and wine being changed into "the reality of his Body and Blood, Soul and Divinity." In its preparatory work the Commission examined with care the definition of the Council of Trent (DS 1642, 1652) repeated in the *Catechism of the Catholic Church* (1992) (No 1376). Though the Council of Trent states that the Soul and Divinity of Christ are present with his body and blood in the eucharist, it does not speak of the conversion of the earthly realities of bread and wine into the Soul

---

follows then that the celebration of this sacrifice be, in its proportion, an instrument of applying the proper sacrifice to all the purposes for which it was first designed. It is ministerially, and by application, an instrument propitiatory; it is eucharistical; it is an homage and an act of adoration, and it is impetratory, and obtains for us and for the whole church, all the benefits of the sacrifice, which is now celebrated and applied; that is, as this rite is the remembrance and ministerial celebration of Christ's sacrifice, so it is destined to do honour to God . . . to beg pardon, blessings, and supply all of our needs" (Discourse XIX, 4).

and Divinity of Christ (DS 1651). The presence of the Soul is by natural *concomitantia* and the Divinity by virtue of the hypostatic union. The Response speaks of the "substantial" presence of Christ, maintaining that this is the result of a substantial change in the elements. By its footnote on transubstantiation the Commission made clear that it was in no way dismissing the belief that "God, acting in the eucharist, effects a change in the inner reality of the elements" . . . and that a mysterious and radical change takes place. Paul VI in *Mysterium Fidei* (AAS 57, 1965) did not deny the legitimacy of fresh ways of expressing this change even by using new words, provided that they kept and reflected what transubstantiation was intended to express. This has been our method of approach. In several places the *Final Report* indicates its belief in the presence of the living Christ truly and really in the elements. Even if the word "transubstantiation" only occurs in a footnote, the *Final Report* wished to express what the Council of Trent, as evident from its discussions, clearly intended by the use of the term.

Reservation of the Blessed Sacrament is practised in both our churches for communion of the sick, the dying and the absent. The fear expressed in the Response that a real consensus between Anglicans and Roman Catholic is lacking concerning the adoration of Christ's sacramental presence requires careful analysis. Differences in practice do not necessarily imply differences in doctrine, as can be seen in the case of East and West. The difficulty is not with reservation of the sacrament but with devotions associated with it which have grown up in the Western Church since the twelfth century outside the liturgical celebration of the eucharist. To this day these devotions are not practised in the Eastern Churches, just as they had not been during the Church's first thousand years. Nevertheless, the belief concerning Christ's presence has been and remains the same in East and West. Obviously the distinction between faith and practice is especially pertinent here. We recognized the fact that some Anglicans find difficulty with these devotional practices because it is feared that they obscure the true goal of the sacrament. However, the strong affirmation that "the Christ whom we adore in the Eucharist is Christ glorifying the Father" (*Elucidation*, 8) clearly shows that in the opinion of the authors of the document there need be no denial of Christ's presence even for those who are reluctant to endorse the devotional practices associated with the adoration of Christ's sacramental presence. Provision for the reservation of the Sacrament is found within the Anglican Church, according to pastoral circumstances. In the Church of England, for example, this is regulated by the faculty jurisdiction of the diocesan bishop.

The 1662 *Book of Common Prayer* authoritatively expresses the historical Anglican teaching that the consecrated elements are to be treated with reverence. After communion the rubric instructs the minister to "return to the Lord's table, and reverently place upon it what remaineth of the consecrated Elements, covering the same with a fair linen cloth." A further rubric states that "the Priest . . . shall, immediately after the Blessing, reverently eat and drink the same." Such reverence remains the Anglican attitude, as can be seen from the collect provided for the Thanksgiving for the Institution of Holy Communion:

> Almighty and heavenly Father, we thank you that in this wonderful sacrament you have given us the memorial of the passion of your Son Jesus Christ. Grant us so to reverence the sacred mysteries of his body and blood, that we may know within ourselves and show forth in our lives the fruits of his redemption; who is alive and reigns with you and the Holy Spirit, one God, now and for ever.[5]

---

5. cf. *Alternative Service Book*, 1980, 920. This reference is provided as a footnote in the officially published text, and in a bracket in the main text in Hill and Yarnold, *Anglicans and Roman Catholics*. The collect is no part of historic Anglican liturgy, as, in the 1662 book and in many provinces worldwide, neither the collect nor the festival it marks has had any place. In the ASB the festival was optional, particularly meeting the desires of Anglicans who wished to adopt an approximation to the Roman Catholic festival of Corpus Christi.

MINISTRY AND ORDINATION

[The document then responds to the Vatican's concerns on this separate topic]

[September 1993]

Text M

THE LETTER OF CARDINAL CASSIDY IN REPLY

PONTIFICUM CONSILIUM AD CHRISTIANORUM UNI-TATEM FOVENDAM *E Civitate Vaticana, die* March 11th, 1994

PROT.N . . .

1278/94/e

To the Co-Chairmen of ARCIC-II

Bishop Mark SANTER	Bishop Cormac MURPHY-O'CONNOR
Bishop of Birmingham	Bishop of Arundel and Brighton

On September 4th last, you sent me a document containing "Clarifications of certain aspects of the Agreed Statements on Eucharist and Ministry" which had been submitted to and approved by the ARCIC-II meeting taking place in Venice at that time.

This document has been examined by the appropriate dicasteries of the Holy See and I am now in position to assure you that the said clarifications have indeed thrown new light on the questions concerning Eucharist and Ministry in the Final Report of ARCIC-I for which further study had been requested.

The Pontifical Council for Promoting Christian Unity is therefore most grateful to the members of ARCIC-II, and to those from ARCIC-I who prepared these clarifications. The agreement reached on Eucharist and Ministry by ARCIC-I is thus greatly strengthened and no further study would seem to be required at this stage.

There is one observation that I should like to bring to your notice in this connection. It concerns the question of *Reservation of the Blessed Sacrament*, and in particular the comparison which is made on page 4 of the Clarifications between the practice of the Orthodox Churches (and the Catholic Churches of the Eastern Rite) and that of the Anglican Communion. Orthodox and Eastern-rite Catholics have a very clear and uniform practice concerning the reservation of the Blessed Sacrament. While there are differences in respect of devotions connected with the Reserved Sacrament, adoration of the Reserved Sacrament is normal for both Orthodox and Greek-Catholics. The Clarifications do not seem to make clear that this can be said unreservedly and uniformly for Anglicans. In fact the Clarifications state that "provision for the reservation of the Sacrament is found within the Anglican Church according to pastoral circumstances" and that "in the Church of England, for example, this is regulated by the faculty jurisdiction of the diocesan bishop." It seems important to stress that the Response of the Holy See to the Final Report was concerned not with the question of devotions associated with Christ's presence in the Reserved Sacrament, but with the implications of diverse Anglican practice regarding Reservation itself and attitudes towards the Reserved Sacrament.

The remarkable consensus reached up to now on the themes dealt with by ARCIC-I will only be able to be seen in its full light and importance as the work of ARCIC-II proceeds. This would appear to be particularly the case in respect of the study of the questions still open in relation to the third part of the Final Report of ARCIC-I, dealing with Authority in the Church. It would seem urgent, then, that this question be taken up as soon as possible by ARCIC-II.

With the expression of my deep esteem and kind personal greetings,

Yours sincerely in the Lord
Edward Idris Cardinal Cassidy
President

Before we address any questions of the actual content of *Clarifications*, various issues of process and of the status of the document obtrude themselves. Three such issues are as follows:

1. was this, with Cardinal Cassidy's Letter, an ecumenical breakthrough?

2. should the Commission have been addressing the Vatican alone?

3. how (and why) was the publication ignored by Anglicans?

These issues bear strongly upon each other, and also relate closely to the content of the document. Clarity about them should assist an evaluation of the content of the report.

"Process Issue 1": Was This an Ecumenical Breakthrough?

We need to recapture the situation. The Anglicans had broadly agreed the two ARCIC I documents; the Vatican had accepted that much progress had been made, but had raised some outstanding problems which needed clarifying by ARCIC II; the ACC in turn had urged ARCIC II to address the problems "as a matter of priority"; and ARCIC II had now done that, and Cardinal Cassidy had confirmed that the problems were indeed solved. So what should happen next? All experience in the Church of England of ecumenical agreements has been that the two parties to any agreement have celebrated together, with the intensity and character of the celebration matching or even exceeding the importance and significance of the agreement. So what was to happen here, where two worldwide Communions, struggling to find agreement on one of the great issues dividing them, had now achieved through their representatives that common understanding, and, presumably, had moved measurably nearer to each other? If the 1991 *Response* had been a full acceptance of the *Final Report*, would there not have been some public celebration of the agreements thus certified and sealed? Cassidy had at least written of agreement "greatly strengthened." So was it not a breakthrough? Would there not be celebrations—publicity, thanksgiving to God, mutual felicitations, arguably another joint Statement by the Archbishop of Canterbury and the Pope?

But not only did nothing of this sort happen; quite the reverse, at least by the Anglicans a veil was gently but firmly drawn over the whole proceedings, with ARCIC II itself conniving (see "Process issue 3" below). Cardinal Cassidy's advice that "no further study is needed at this stage" became not the confirmation of an agreement, but, it seems, a cue for abandoning and even burying the project. The two Communions were not alerted in any way, and, as shown below, the ACC and the 1998 Lambeth Conference took no notice whatsoever: yet, from an objective standpoint, surely either the breaches were mended and there should have been celebrations, or, despite the Cassidy suspending phrase, further study *was* needed. What might have been an ecumenical breakthrough was treated, at least by the Anglicans, as the nearest approach imaginable to a slightly embarrassing non-event. But why?

"Process Issue 2": Should the Commission Have Addressed the Vatican Alone?

The formal character of *Clarifications* is that it is an explanation to the Vatican to answer the Vatican's problems with the ARCIC I treatment of the eucharist and ministry; and this formal character is confirmed by the published answer of Cardinal Cassidy, formally the sole recipient of the explanation, the sole judge of its adequacy.

But this is actually extraordinary. If we understand Cassidy as saying that the Vatican authorities are satisfied that the two bands of theologians on ARCIC II have now reached an agreement which Rome itself can agree and endorse, then at first sight the breakthrough has indeed happened. But the truth is otherwise. For consider: the 1988 Lambeth Conference had given broad acceptance to the Statements in *The Final Report*; but the Vatican had only agreed those Statements when they had been glossed by *Clarifications*—and in formal terms *the Anglicans had never seen the glossing*. The document had never been sent to us. We had not been asked to consider it. We had at most merely looked over the shoulder of the Commission writing to Rome. So the authorities of the two Communions had, at a five-year interval, been separately endorsing different documents from each other. This is formally absurd, and if, as has been widely concluded and will be further examined in the next chapter, *Clarifications* had actually gone far beyond merely tweaking the previous Statements, then the procedure was substantially perilous. Perhaps the lack of celebrations has been providential and appropriate; but equally the silence has allowed the assertion of full agreement, almost taken for granted by senior Roman Catholics, to lurk also in the back of the Anglican corporate mind.[6] So was *Clarifications* simply repeating, in language more readily understood and accepted in Rome, exactly the doctrine of the eucharist set out in the two ARCIC I documents and agreed by Lambeth 1988 as "consonant" with Anglican belief? Or, to meet the objections of the *Response*, had it strayed across a previously intact border into territory which was alien to major strands of Anglicanism? Much would depend upon that question of content.

"Process Issue 3": How (and Why) was the Publication Kept Largely Out of Sight?

This asserted disappearance from view of *Clarifications* below the Anglican radar is easy to establish. As noted above, ACC-9 in Cape Town in January 1993 had resolved that ARCIC II should "proceed as a matter of priority with its mandate to give attention to the official responses of both Churches [i.e., responses to *The Final Report* of 1982]."[7] ARCIC II had now done so. The co-chairmen, with the Cassidy Letter before them, had written to Rome of "this now more definitive agreement."[8] They had passed it to the Anglican Communion Office, who took steps to get it published in England. The published text went to *Church Times*, which gave it a brief notice on July 8, 1994. The Roman Catholic *The Tablet* followed on July 16, 1994, with, "A heartening response to the Vatican's questions."

So what sort of report was the next ACC, ACC-10, meeting in Panama in 1996, to expect?

The answer appears to be: no report at all. The co-chairmen had written of "reception," but *Clarifications* disappeared from view. So here we stop

---

6. This is wonderfully illustrated later by Michael Nazir Ali, a member of ARCIC II, quoting the assent of the authorities of the two Communions as though they were referring to the same set of documents as each other, when manifestly they were not: "[T]his Synod, and indeed the Lambeth Conference, was able to declare the agreements on the Eucharist and Ordination to be consonant with the faith of Anglicans, and the Roman Catholic church has also said that no further study would seem to be required at this stage" (Church of England General Synod, *Report of Proceedings* of February 14, 2008, in the debate on the IARCCUM report, *Growing Together*). The *verbatim* quotation at the end of his sentence from the Cassidy Letter betrays the phenomenon of the two Communions "agreeing" different documents from each other.

7. ACC-9, 140. See p. 86 above.

8. *Clarifications*, 3.

to examine the contents of the document before returning to this process question—"reception."

9

Clarifications (1994): Content and Significance

T HE 1991 *RESPONSE* OF the Holy See, as summarized in *Clarifications* by ARCIC II in 1994, had welcomed the acknowledgment that "the eucharist is a sacrifice" and had sought "clarification" on two points relating to Christ's sacrifice:

(a) The essential link of the eucharistic Memorial with the *once-for-all* sacrifice of Christ which it makes sacramentally present;

(b) "the propitiatory nature of the eucharistic sacrifice, which can be applied also to the deceased."

Of these two papal *desiderata*, the first looks to a suspicious Anglican as at least slippery, and probably also calling for a belief in an "actualization" of Calvary in our celebrations—not only making the sacrifice of Christ effectual, but also making it present. The second raises further issues about masses for the dead.

Along with the two *desiderata* concerning eucharistic sacrifice, Pope John Paul II had two more concerning the presence of Christ in relation to the eucharist.

(c) Certitude that Christ is present sacramentally and substantially when "under the species of bread and wine these earthly realities are changed into the reality of his Body and Blood, Soul and Divinity";

(d) the adoration of Christ in the reserved sacrament.[1]

---

1. The four points quoted are direct quotations from *Clarifications* (see p.102 above). The sentences within the points which are in quotation marks here are quoted

Here then are the agenda: does *Clarifications*, in addressing these four points, not only satisfy Cardinal Cassidy and the PCPCU, but also stay within the limits set by *Eucharistic Doctrine* and the *Elucidation*, and present an overall doctrinal position "consonant" with Anglican faith? I examine each in turn.

(a) The essential link of the eucharistic Memorial with the *once-for-all* sacrifice of Christ which it makes sacramentally present

The ARCIC II text meets this point by saying "In the mind of the Commission the making present, effective and accessible of the unique sacrifice of Christ does not entail repetition of it." The phrase "the making present . . . of the sacrifice of Christ" goes well beyond the "making effective" of *Eucharistic Doctrine*, and also beyond the cliff-edge of *Elucidation* which reads "the eucharist is a sacrifice in the sacramental sense." This latter text in 1979 was, as we have seen, sufficiently ambiguous to allow still the meaning that the eucharist is a proclamation and making effective in the present of the historic sacrifice of Christ, but the "making present" terminology here takes us over the cliff-edge into a far more exclusive domain, where the assertion that the eucharist is "a sacrifice" has become unambiguously an actualization of *the* sacrifice of Christ. The "making present" is, in some metaphysical sense, an assimilation of the "once-for-all" event in history into the liturgical celebration occurring daily and everywhere. It is very clear that, to those who use the terminology of "eucharistic sacrifice," it is the sacrifice which the church on earth is in its celebration offering to which they refer—as indeed is testified in the Roman Catholic liturgical texts "may the Lord receive the sacrifice at your hands" and "we offer you the pure victim, the holy victim, the undefiled victim"; and the Vatican *Response* moves in a similar sphere of thought, though using the passive. But if the statements are put together, then it appears we are supposed to say that the church offers the sacrifice of Christ; and such an assertion not only has no basis in scripture generally, but very specifically contradicts all the statements in the Epistle to the Hebrews that Jesus offered up himself *on our behalf*. Furthermore, we cannot think of a sacrifice which

---

in *Clarifications* directly from the *Response* (see pp. 79–80 above), whereas the rest of the four points are summaries in *Clarifications* of the points made in the *Response* in §§21–24. It is, of course, the doctrine of *Clarifications* that is under review here.

is "offered" unless there is a sequential set of stages (again made very clear in the Epistle to the Hebrews). The concept of the sacrifice of Christ being "present" is difficult to expound—surely a sacrifice is a sequential *action* (as indeed "we offer" implies an action), and saying that that action is "present" is in no sense comparable to saying that Christ himself is present (to which we come further on)? If, of course, when the *Response* and *Clarifications* refer to the sacrifice being "sacramentally present" they actually mean simply that the benefits of Christ's once-for-all death are conveyed to the communicants in the sacrament (i.e., are sacramentally conveyed), then we can all hang up our swords. But such language, near to the quotation from *Elucidation* §5, refers to the Lord ministering grace to us, not to our having a sacrifice (his sacrifice?) to offer to God. If we the church are in the eucharist offering Jesus' sacrifice, and that is the meaning of his sacrifice being made "present" at our eucharist, then *Clarifications* goes beyond the language of *Elucidation*, and takes us into territory which is unknown in Anglican formularies and alien to many Anglicans. Not only is such a concept in apparent breach of the teaching of the New Testament, it is also without warrant in 1662 and indeed in most contemporary Anglican eucharistic liturgies. What is expressed in *Clarifications* is not what is said in our liturgies, or believed in our congregations.

(b) "the propitiatory nature of the eucharistic sacrifice, which can be applied also to the deceased."

The assurance sought by the Pontifical Council to make good the implied lack in the *Final Report*, is met in *Clarifications* first by reference to the "propitiatory dimension" of the eucharist. The word "dimension" looks like a considerable weakening of the word "nature" (and indeed was, it seems, the key to the acceptance of the wording by Charles Sherlock), but the sequence of thought goes on to state; (a) that this "dimension" is "explicit" when "through the eucharist" Christ's work on the cross "is proclaimed and made effective"; (b) that the church "entreats the benefits of his passion on behalf of the whole church"; and (c) that "the whole church" includes the departed, simply because that is what "whole" must mean. We are therefore at the eucharist in some propitiatory way seeking "the benefits of Christ's passion" on behalf of the faithful departed.

Almost every line in this sequence of thought needs scrutiny. The exposition is anticipated in *Clarifications* by a renewed emphasis upon

Christ's historic death on Calvary as propitiatory sacrifice, with a particular quoting of the 1 John 2:1–2 "Comfortable Word" from 1662. But the insistence of this Comfortable Word that his death was the propitiation for our sins is there to round up the assurance of forgiveness conveyed by the whole penitential section—the text is not of itself in any way connected to the sacramental action, even though followed soon by it, but *Clarifications* seems to invoke it as though to add weight to the case for the "propitiatory dimension" to the eucharist itself. The line of thought runs on to quote from the opening of the Prayer of Consecration, further emphasizing that Christ's death was propitiatory—but equally stating that redemption was effected "there" upon the cross. There is no hint in either the Comfortable Word or the Prayer of Consecration that the action "here" is itself propitiatory.[2] The inclusion of the 1 John 2 verses does nothing at all to suggest a "propitiatory dimension" to the eucharist.

The real weight of the argument appears to rely upon the prayer, quoted in full at this point in *Clarifications*, which is often called the "prayer of oblation"[3]; for the present purpose it is this opening of the prayer which concerns us:

> O Lord and heavenly Father, we thy humble servants entirely desire thy fatherly goodness mercifully to accept this our sacrifice of praise and thanksgiving.

The argument appears to be that "this our sacrifice of praise and thanksgiving" *is* the eucharistic sacrifice, the offering up Christ himself. Such an exposition of the phrase runs wholly counter to its natural meaning and is unsustainable in the light of scripture and of both its other uses in 1662 and its particular location within the 1662 eucharist.

The natural meaning is, of course, that praise and thanksgiving are being offered sacrificially, and in modern use it echoes, "It is right to give our thanks and praise" from the opening dialogue. Cranmer, of course, inherited "sacrificium laudis" from the Sarum canon, recognized its origins in Hebrews 13:15–16 (where the sacrifice is explicitly articulated with our lips, not with our sacramental elements), and therefore recast the phrase to bring

2. Christopher Hill, who was on the drafting sub-committee, acknowledges this in a private communication: "On propitiation for example, the citing of the Prayer Book shows how such traditional language is found in classical Anglicanism, though of course in relation to Calvary rather than of the sacramental memorial of Christ's sacrifice."

3. Note this title used at the Malines Conversations on p. 11 above. A fuller treatment of the whole prayer comes on pp. 117–18 following.

out its true meaning. He confirmed this understanding when in 1552 he moved this section of the eucharistic prayer to come after communion—the offering of praise and thanksgiving was now by its very location identified as a grateful response of the congregation after receiving communion. However this identification of its meaning was further reinforced by a new use for the phrase in the 1662 revision of the Prayer Book; for, largely unnoticed by twentieth-century readers of the book, "our sacrifice of praise and thanksgiving" appeared in a new provision of 1662, the "Form of Prayers to be used at Sea"! This was, of course, a wholly non-sacramental liturgical collection, conducted by a ship's captain, and this particular prayer was an offering of praise and thanksgiving for deliverance from a storm.[4] Very evidently, the 1662 revisers did not attribute any specifically eucharistic meaning to it, but thereby precluded misinterpreting Cranmer's careful use of it.

What then of Cranmer's actual location of it, as we receive it within the 1662 eucharist? *Clarifications* states of this prayer that it comes "at the heart of the eucharistic action" both in 1662 and in "contemporary Anglican liturgies." Taking these two asserted locations in turn, one has to say first that the prayer is *not* replicated in many contemporary Anglican liturgies; but the key point concerns its place of origin, i.e., in 1662. In the 1662 BCP this prayer is *not* "at the heart" of the eucharistic action; it is a post-communion prayer, which is used when the eucharistic action is already completed; and in that position it is simply one of two alternatives between which a choice is made by the officiant, and thus it can well be omitted altogether over any period of time. So nothing vital to the understanding of the eucharist by Anglicans can be inferred from its use in that position in the rite. It does appear within some modern Anglican eucharistic prayers, but the onus of proof would be upon anyone seeking to fasten the meaning of eucharistic sacrifice upon it there—and in the ASB in the Second and Fourth Eucharistic Prayers the text says "*through him* [Christ] we offer this sacrifice" (emphasis mine). The one offering which we *cannot* be asking that Christ should mediate to the Father on our behalf is surely the offering of himself?[5] However the "sacrifice of praise" is expounded in such contexts, it cannot mean an offering of Christ himself.

4. The whole provision is printed at the end of the Prayer Book, and interestingly the need of such a provision was signalled by a precedent contained within the *Directory for Public Worship* authorized during the Commonwealth period—but the phrase examined here was provided in 1662 itself.

5. A lecture of mine on "Priesthood and Sacrifice and the Ordained Ministry" deals with twentieth-century Anglican authors who have wanted to expound the phrase as

Next is the treatment of "all thy whole church." An extraordinary link is made between the recital of the Nicene Creed (with its reference to the church[6]) and this phrase in the post-communion prayer—the latter, says *Clarifications*, "must be understood in the light" of the former. The "must" is unwarranted—it would be equally possible to insist that "all thy whole church" *must* be understood in the light of the bidding "Let us pray for the whole state of Christ's church militant here in earth." In both cases no necessity of logic is built into either the form of words used or any structural relationship of the post-communion prayer to the earlier liturgical item.[7] The employment of "must" totally overstates the matter. Petitions on behalf of the faithful dead were completely eliminated from the liturgical program of the Church of England at the Reformation; and, while they were not specifically forbidden in the XXXIX Articles, they were strongly denounced in the Third Part of the Homily Concerning Prayer, in the second *Book of Homilies*. And when in the formation of the 1662 rite mention of the departed was added to the Prayer for the Church Militant, it was done in a careful form of thanksgiving for the departed without any petition for them, and the "Church Militant here on Earth" title was retained and guards against misunderstanding. The Burial service was also scrutinized in 1662, and minor alterations were made, but not such as to introduce petitions for the dead. *Clarifications* smoothly refers to the "commemoration" of the departed, which has "continued to be part of the intercessions in Anglican Eucharistic liturgies," but this choice of words conceals the fact, inimical to *Clarifications'* stated purpose, that such "commemoration" has not necessarily itself taken an intercessory form. Similarly the citing of the provision, new for the Church in England in the ASB, for a eucharist at a funeral or at the Commemoration of the Faithful Departed, does *not* make the point those drafting *Clarifications* wished it to make—for the collect in each case is a prayer for the living, modelled upon the 1662 commemoration of the departed at the end of the Prayer for the Church Militant. The broad pre-

---

eucharistic sacrifice, as illustrated by the title of Bryan Spinks's *Festschrift* for Arthur Couratin—*Sacrifice of Praise*; the lecture is in my Alcuin Collection, *An Evangelical Among*, 148–66. The phrase has always meant "sacrificial praise" in popular hymnody.

6. Oddly, the text cited ("I believe in the one holy catholic and apostolic church") is not exactly either 1662 or the modern form.

7. Similarly the reference to "the whole church" in the quotation from Jeremy Taylor in the footnote on pp. 103–4 above does not self-evidently entail that he was including the dead as beneficiaries in his account of how the eucharist "is . . . applied . . . to . . . supply all our needs."

sumption must be that the eucharist on such occasions is an expression of the unity in Christ of the living and departed, with prayer that we the living may follow in the known steps of the departed. Furthermore there is no collect or other proper provided so worded as to relate such prayer to the celebration of communion; and therefore, without resort to the most extraordinary special pleading, such liturgical texts cannot be called in evidence, even for those occasions specially related to the departed, that the eucharistic action itself is the offering of the propitiatory sacrifice of Christ for the benefit of the departed. Yet the choice of words in *Clarifications* was surely intended to convey exactly that understanding of the Anglican eucharist to the Pontifical Council?

(c) certitude that Christ is present sacramentally and substantially when "under the species of bread and wine these earthly realities are changed into the reality of his Body and Blood, Soul and Divinity"

This requirement provides a straight statement that, according to Rome, Christ's presence is localized "in" the eucharistic bread and wine, or, in the exact phrase, "under" the "species of bread and wine" ("species" is a long-settled term to allow the consecrated elements to be identified by their "sensible form" (as the dictionary defines "species") without their being called "bread and wine"). Thus the term "species" protects the doctrine of transubstantiation; and the *Response* was here echoing the argument from *Observations* ten years earlier that ARCIC I had erred in still calling the elements "bread" and "wine" after they had been consecrated, and the elements were therefore wrongly being characterized as still in "their ontological substance."

The Commission was in a cleft stick here. ARCIC I had worked fairly hard to retain, at least as a possible interpretation, a "receptionist" understanding of the feeding on the body and blood of Christ, of which a major implication was that the "wicked" or un-faithful received only the outward sign of bread and wine, and not the inward part of the benefits of the death of Christ. The Commission had in 1971 fudged the use of the term "transubstantiation" by stating in its well-known footnote that "In contemporary Roman Catholic theology it [i.e., the term 'transubstantiation'] is not understood as explaining *how* the change takes place." But the *Response* treated the footnote as inadequate; it was requiring the Commission directly to address "*how* the change takes place," and consequently virtually to affirm the whole Aristotelian doctrine of the Fourth Lateran Council with its dependence on distinguishing substance and accidents—for the "ontological reality" (i.e., the substance) had now to change, leaving merely the "species" (i.e., the accidents) without visible or tangible alteration. *Clarifications* rightly muttered that the Tridentine doctrine did not involve the conversion of the elements into the "Soul and Divinity" of Christ, thus suggesting they were handling the objection critically.[8] But on the major point they went along unprotestingly with the major demand: "Even if the word 'transubstantiation' only occurs in a footnote, the *Final Report* wished to express what the Council of Trent, as evident from its discussions, clearly intended by the use of the term."[9] So ARCIC II is asserting the doctrine of Trent without qualification and claims that that is what ARCIC I in the *Final Report* had "clearly intended." My caution in the Introduction about inferring a "mind" (or here "intention") behind an agreed text is highly relevant. For a careful reading of the 1971 text is open to a very different understanding—the footnote in *Eucharistic Doctrine* had allowed, simply to the Roman Catholics, some flexibility in how Roman Catholics understood the doctrine of Christ's presence, without anything in the footnote infringing any liberty of interpretation for Anglicans: but *Clarifications* was now telling us that what ARCIC I meant overall was total inflexibility of understanding for both Anglicans and Roman Catholics. The doctrine of Trent held the field: *causa finita est.*

Jesus's words "Take, eat: this is my body" would seem to allow all kinds of shades of meaning to communicants, and Anglicans have traditionally exercised considerable liberty in understanding differently from each other the clear biblical terminology of the 1662 Book of Common Prayer. They can thus agree that they are indeed receiving the body of Christ, whether they believe his body to be strictly localized in some way "in" the bread, or they believe the bread to be a means of conveying the benefits of Christ's cross to them, or even whether they believe, in Hooker's famous phrase, that "the real presence of Christ's blessed body and blood is not therefore to be sought for in the sacrament, but in the worthy receiver of the sacrament."[10] But there are two fairly clear limits to this liberty: firstly, the insistence in

---

8. See the careful dissection of this careless phraseology in the *Response* by John McHugh on pp. 92–93 above.

9. *Clarifications*, 7.

10. Hooker, *Of the Laws*, ch. 67, §6

Article XXIX (conforming to the thrust of the 1662 BCP) that only the faithful receivers actually feed on the body and blood of Christ; and, secondly, that there is no basis for declaring consecrated bread as containing (or being) the body of Jesus Christ, in a context which is separate from the giving and consuming of it. This is where the element (actually only the bread, in the Roman form of the wafer) is reserved for the purpose of the adoration of Christ localized within the sacramental species, along with the provision for the "blessing" of the people from a monstrance containing a reserved wafer in the rite called "Benediction." While (as the documents say) there are Anglicans who practice these extra-liturgical devotions, there is nothing in the historic Anglican formularies to warrant such practices, and no liturgical provision in the main current Prayer Books of the Anglican Communion today to sanction them either.[11] Furthermore, ARCIC I had put down a very strong marker in its phrase "The Lord's words at the Last Supper . . . do not allow us to dissociate the gift of the presence and the act of sacramental eating."[12] Yet now in *Clarifications* ARCIC II had turned to asserting a presence of Christ through transubstantiation, a presence which can be, and frequently is, wholly "dissociated" from any context or overt purpose of "sacramental eating." The 1662 BCP, to which *Clarifications* tends to turn, asserts the exact opposite, as can well be illustrated from its main petition in "the prayer of consecration."[13] The Sarum petition terminated on the bread and wine (though the "unto us" could be viewed as qualifying its meaning); but in 1662 the petition concerns solely what the communicants are to receive; and they evidently receive the inward part of the sacrament through receiving bread and wine as the outward part— and, very clearly, at the point of reception these elements remain bread and wine ("these thy creatures").[14] The conveying of the benefits of communion through the outward sacramental elements is exactly comparable to

11. See Appendix C.

12. *Eucharistic Doctrine* §9 (*Final Report*, 15, see p. 41 above).

13. This may well be called the "epiclesis," or "the first epiclesis" or "the consecratory epiclesis"; but to some liturgists a petition for consecration should only be called an epiclesis if it asks that consecration should be effected by the agency of the Holy Spirit. The two texts lack that actual mention of the Spirit, but are nevertheless epicletic forms.

14. Cranmer's words of distribution reinforced the thrust of the prayer; and even in the combined form of 1559/1662 ("The body of our Lord Jesus Christ . . . preserve thy body and soul unto everlasting life; take and eat this in remembrance . . . and feed on him [Christ] in thy heart by faith with thanksgiving") the form is benedictional and injunctive, and not simply declaratory.

the conveying of the benefits of baptism through the outward sacramental element of water; 1552 and 1662 treated both sacraments alike, with no implication that the inward grace is contained within the physical element, or that the element has been in some way changed into the inward part. As with baptism, so also with the eucharist, the unbeliever receives the outward sign without receiving the inward grace. The unbreakable link in reformed doctrine is between receiving the elements by faith and being partakers of the body and blood of Christ; whereas with transubstantiation or similar doctrines the unbreakable link is between the outward elements and the body and blood of Christ, independently of the faith or unbelief of the recipients, and indeed independently of whether the elements are in fact consumed or are reserved for some other purpose.

Table 4

THE SARUM EPICLESIS	THE 1552/1662 EPICLESIS
Which oblation we beseech thee, O Almighty God, in all things to make blessed, appointed, ratified, reasonable and accepted; that unto us it may become the body and blood of thy most dearly beloved Son our Lord Jesu Christ;	Hear us, O merciful Father, we most humbly beseech thee; and grant that we, receiving these thy creatures of bread and wine, according to thy Son our Saviour Jesus Christ's holy institution, in remembrance of his death and passion, may be partakers of his most blessed body and blood.

The significance was reinforced when Article XXIX came into the XXXIX Articles and said

ARTICLE XXIX. OF THE WICKED WHICH EAT NOT THE BODY OF CHRIST IN THE USE OF THE LORD's SUPPER

The Wicked, and such as be void of a lively faith, although they do carnally and visibly press with their teeth (as Saint *Augustine* saith) the Sacrament of the Body and Blood of Christ, yet in no wise are they partakers of Christ: but rather, to their condemnation, do eat and drink the sign or Sacrament of so great a thing.

Now it would be absurd to proclaim that Anglicans are all persuaded of the fully reformed character of the eucharists in which they share; and clearly there has been in the last two centuries among Anglicans a considerable borrowing from Rome and even a teaching of its doctrines as our own. That cannot be denied; it is more explicit in some Anglican provinces than in others (or in some provinces it may, as in England, vary from parish to parish); Anglicanism has *de facto* been somewhat comprehensive about eucharistic doctrine; but it is improper and misleading (and constitutionally impossible) to accept Roman Catholic or quasi-Roman Catholic doctrine as *the* mainstream Anglicanism which can be asserted jointly as the basis of agreement between the two Communions.

(d) the adoration of Christ in the reserved sacrament

This fourth "clarification" desired by Rome's *Response* is the logical outcome of the third. If the person of Jesus Christ is present under the "species" of the wafer "in the reserved sacrament," then adoration of him thus locally present is the wholly appropriate response. But if the PCPCU's (c) is to be answered as above, what are we to make of the PCPCU's (d)? "The adoration of Christ in the reserved sacrament" begs all sorts of questions to a reformed theologian. The Anglican Communion at large has whole provinces which never reserve sacramental elements, and vast numbers of worshippers, even where reservation for the sick is practiced, who think the Roman practice of adoration is ill-based, unbiblical and frankly wrong. The question had not been addressed by ARCIC I in the initial *Eucharistic Doctrine* Statement in 1971. It had then figured in the *Elucidation* in 1979, where in §9 ARCIC I had said, in all honesty, "In spite of this clarification [i.e., a not very convincing attempt in §8 to link the purpose of adoration closely with the purpose of communion], others still find any kind of adoration of Christ in the reserved sacrament unacceptable." ARCIC I at that point had reckoned this division of views was not prejudicial to "substantial agreement." But the PCPCU was now insisting that a common adherence to such adoration *was* vital to substantial agreement, so how were ARCIC II to meet them?

The ARCIC II answer is a bold misrepresentation of Anglicanism backed by an astonishingly perverse use of the 1662 BCP. They say that Anglicans have no problem with reservation as such, but only with "devotions associated with it." That is to minimize the problem within Anglicanism. There are very large numbers of Anglicans who do *not* practice reservation even for communicating the sick, and it is somewhat superficial to assume they all have no problems with such reservation—the overall reasons for many Anglicans, indeed whole provinces, not following a relatively recent reintroduction of the practice into Anglicanism have simply not been examined. The 1662 Prayer Book (which is coming into discussion below) forbade any form of reservation, and, to take the mildest possible understanding of reservation, even distribution of consecrated elements to the sick and housebound at a distance from the actual celebration of communion is not accepted by a large swathe of Anglicans—and has never been part of pastoral ministry in whole provinces. But it is true that, once the issue of adoration towards or before reserved elements is then brought into the discussion, then Anglicans are much more fundamentally split. Yet it is on this point that the *Response* wanted assurance—"adoration of Christ in the reserved sacrament." If the Commission could not assure Rome that Anglicans all practice reservation, how could they possibly go the further step and tell him we are all ready to adore "Christ in the reserved sacrament"? Yet ARCIC II appears to have decided that they would find some way of reassuring the PCPCU on this point, at whatever cost to the facts of Anglican faith and practice. Such reassurance, we may reckon, would have best depended upon straight unequivocal evidence, such as rubrical instructions across the provinces of the Communion providing for both reservation and adoration of the consecrated elements.[15] There is, however, an almost total absence of such evidence in respect of adoration; so the Commission turned to a bizarre reliance upon a liturgical text (actually a rubric) to make a point to the PCPCU almost exactly the opposite of what the text in its plain sense had stated.

I refer of course to the final paragraph of *Clarifications'* treatment of the issue of adoration of Christ in the reserved sacrament. Christopher Hill had suggested that the rubrics following the end of the 1662 communion service provided the requisite evidence.[16] He duly acknowledges in correspondence that he did indeed bring this suggestion into play on the drafting sub-committee which proposed the text of *Clarifications* to ARCIC II. The Commission adopted it, and accordingly called the 1662 rubric in evidence for "the historical Anglican teaching that the consecrated elements are to be treated with reverence." They write:

> After communion the rubric instructs the minister to "*return to the Lord's Table, and reverently place upon it what remaineth of the consecrated Elements, covering the same with a fair linen cloth.*" A further rubric states that "*the Priest . . . shall, immediately after*

15. On this point, see Appendix C.

16. See p. 92 above for the reference in his chapter in Hill and Yarnold, *Anglicans and Roman Catholics.*

the Blessing, reverently eat and drink the same." Such reverence remains the Anglican attitude, as can be seen from the collect [there
follows a collect, not from the 1662 Book, for Thanksgiving for the
Institution of Holy Communion]."[17]

This argument needs line-by-line analysis, with particular scrutiny of:

1. The overall issue of the effects of consecration

2. The requirement to consume the remaining consecrated elements

3. The meaning of *"reverently"*

4. The relevance of the nature of the bread

5. The citing of the ASB collect

6. The text of the "Black Rubric"

7. The citation of "faculty jurisdiction" in England

I address these in order.

1. The Overall Issue of the Effects of Consecration

The "overall" issue provides the interpretative backdrop to the closing rubrics. While 1662 has, as noted, a very clear concept of effecting consecration by the repetition of the dominical words in the institution narrative,
it is also clear that what the communicants receive is "these thy creatures
of bread and wine." Consecration has therefore changed the significance
and use of the elements, but not affected their nature. Thus, before we
consider the treatment of consecrated remains, we note that there is no
hint whatsoever of "adoration of Christ" in the elements *during* the eucharistic action. Roman Catholics would generally expound adoration
directed to the reserved wafer after the rite as the logical follow-on from

17. *Clarifications*, 8, to be found here on p. 106 above. The collect of the Thanksgiving for the Institution of Holy Communion (a fudged Anglican way of not calling the
occasion "Corpus Christi"!) exists in some provinces of the Anglican Communion, but
this is not a major festival in most of those which have it in their calendars, and is quite
unknown in the calendars of several provinces. Its petition to Jesus Christ is that we may
"so reverence the sacred mysteries of your body and blood that we may know within ourselves . . . the fruits of your redemption." This appears to bid reverence toward the body
and blood of Christ *as received in communion*, and it is therefore in formal terms a collect
which could be used perfectly appropriately in a province where no reservation exists,
and it cannot be said to relate to the Pope's wish for Anglicans to affirm the "adoration of
Christ in the reserved sacrament." See also "Issue 5" on p. 128 below.

adoration directed to the consecrated elements within the rite. As 1662 completely lacks the latter practice of adoration, it is somewhat arbitrary to posit any follow-on from it.

2. The Requirement to Consume the Remaining Consecrated Elements

The sixth rubric at the end of the service reads:

> And if any of the Bread and Wine remain unconsecrated, the Curate shall have it to his own use; but if any remain of that which was consecrated, it shall not be carried out of the Church, but the Priest and such other of the Communicants as he shall then call unto him, shall immediately after the Blessing, reverently eat and drink the same.

It is at this point that the argument in *Clarifications* ceases to be arbitrary and becomes bizarre. The argument about adoration is entirely about the attitude people take towards the reserved elements. But this rubric in 1662 *prohibits reservation altogether*. Indeed, if a different ecumenical conversation had led to a request that Anglicans should show that reservation is *not* part of their historic practice, then the reply would have had to cite this same rubric for exactly the opposite purpose to that for which ARCIC II was adducing it. Without pressing that point, we still have the absurdity of the Commission making a case for "adoration of Christ in the reserved sacrament" from a rubric which precludes any reservation whatsoever of the consecrated elements. In the Church of England all reservation, whether for the sick or any other purpose, was wholly illegal until alternative services began in the 1960s. It was in fact the proposed legitimizing of a very limited use of reservation which led to the defeat of the 1927/1928 Prayer Book revision proposals.

3. The Meaning of *"Reverently"*

The adverb "reverently" is used in both the rubric following the distribution and in the sixth rubric, quoted above, which comes after the end of the service. But the adverb is being asked to bear a weight of meaning which it is not equipped to carry. "Reverently" indicates an attitude of mind in the presence of God whatever the action; and it does not imply that reverence is due to some object of the action. The adverb *"reverently"* is used in these rubrics to warn against casual or irreverent disposal of the consecrated elements. It implies an outward dignity in behaviour and a heart set on God, but it has nothing to do with adoration of Christ in the consecrated elements, and those Anglicans who do not conceive of Christ as being "in" the consecrated elements have no difficulty in conforming to this rubric. We may compare the 1662 use of "reverently" in matrimony (marriage is to be entered "reverently, discreetly, advisedly, soberly and in the fear of God"), and in the ordination rites (the candidates are asked "Will you reverently obey your Ordinary?"). Neither of these is about giving divine adoration to a marriage partner or a bishop as though to a divinity! The rubrical "*reverently*" re consuming the remaining elements has obviously no implications of adoration, and no particular connection with sacramental theology.

4. The Relevance of the Nature of the Bread

The fifth rubric after the communion service reads as follows:

> *And to take away all occasion of dissension and superstition, which any person hath or might have concerning the Bread and Wine, it shall suffice that the Bread be such as is usual to be eaten; but the best and purest Wheat Bread that conveniently may be gotten.*[18]

It appears that, in citing the sixth rubric of 1662 as favoring reservation, the Commission overlooked the fifth rubric's regulation of the kind of bread to be used. This is understandable, as in England and in many other parts of the world in the twentieth century the wafer, although illegal in England until the 1960s, almost displaced the *"purest Wheat Bread"* of the rubric. Nevertheless the provision of the 1662 book was for a form of bread which firstly produced crumbs when it was broken (and often when being distributed) and secondly went stale and soon moldy if kept. And many Anglican parishes in many provinces retain the use of such bread to this day, or even revive its use after decades of using wafers. The character of "purest wheat bread" makes it wholly unfit for medium-term reservation or for adoration purposes. Had ARCIC II quoted this rubric to the PCPCU, the Roman authorities might have had much more difficulty in imagining how Anglicans believe in the adoration of Christ in the reserved sacrament.

---

18. This rubric largely dates from 1552, and the implication of "*to take away all occasion . . . of superstition*" must on any reading be labeling the previous use of wafers as occasioning "superstition." This would hardly have read well in the message to the PCPCU.

5. The Citing of the ASB Collect

Clarifications concludes this section with what appears to be viewed as a crowning argument, the "collect provided for the Thanksgiving for the Institution of Holy Communion":

> Almighty and heavenly Father, we thank you that in this wonderful sacrament you have given us the memorial of the passion of your Son Jesus Christ. Grant us so to reverence the sacred mysteries of his body and blood, that we may know within ourselves and show forth in our lives the fruits of his redemption; who is alive and reigns with you and the Holy Spirit, one God, now and for ever.

As noted in the footnote on p.125 above, this collect does not belong to 1662, as its printed form within this argument from 1662 would suggest, but comes from the Church of England's *Alternative Service Book* of 1980, as indicated in a footnote. It is in fact adapted from the form proposed in 1927 and 1928 (with medieval roots), and the occasion became an optional lesser feast in the Church of England in the ASB calendar and lectionary, and has been retained in that way in the Common Worship provision since 2000. It has no claim, in the way that 1662 has, to belong to the Anglican Communion's history; nor is it in use in many parts of worldwide Anglicanism. But, even if it were to meet the larger claim of being typical or archetypical Anglican liturgy, it is still doubtful whether it would serve the purpose for which it is quoted; for it is surely emphasizing what we *receive* in communion, so that we recognize the fruits of communion *within ourselves*. This differs quite markedly from "recognizing" that objective divine presence within the sacramental elements, apart from reception and apart from the liturgical celebration, the presence which the *Response* required to be adored.

6. The Text of the "Black Rubric"

Semi-finally we come to the final rubric, the so-called "Black Rubric"

> *Whereas it is ordained in this Office for the Administration of the Lord's Supper, that the Communicants should receive the same kneeling; (which order is well meant, for a signification of our humble and grateful acknowledgement of the benefits of Christ therein given to all worthy Receivers, and for the avoiding of such profanation and disorder in the holy Communion, as might otherwise ensue;) yet,*

lest the same kneeling should by any persons, either out of ignorance and infirmity, or out of malice and obstinacy, be misconstrued and depraved; It is hereby declared, That thereby no adoration is intended, or ought to be done, either unto the Sacramental Bread and Wine there bodily received, or unto any Corporal Presence of Christ's natural Flesh and Blood. For the sacramental Bread and Wine remain still in their very natural substances, and therefore may not be adored; (for that were Idolatry, to be abhorred of all faithful Christians;) and the natural Body and Blood of our Saviour Christ are in Heaven and not here; it being against the truth of Christ's natural Body to be at one time in more places than one.

This rubric was actually restored in 1662 after a century of absence. It was marginally amended, but its thrust is clear: there is no place even within the celebration of the rite for adoration directed towards the elements. The reference to idolatry would not be helpful in the context of the Anglican–Roman Catholic dialogue; and it may seem over-disjunctive or even rationalistic to assert that Christ's natural body is "there" and "not here," but it is true to our credal confession that "He ascended into heaven." The main point being made is that, once the Commission had decided they must go to the 1662 communion service (and it was they who decided that), to the 1662 text and rubrics entire they ought to go. And as text and rubrics are quite forcefully hostile to the purpose of the Commission, one has to conclude either that their task had driven them to a counsel of despair, or that they were quite notably unacquainted with the contents of the service they were so ready to quote.[19]

7. The Citation of "Faculty Jurisdiction" in England

A final blunder about reservation comes in the citation in the penultimate paragraph of the example, from the Church of England, of regulation "by the faculty jurisdiction of the diocesan bishop." The current legal position in England about responsibility for reservation lies within the modern rubrics for the communion of the sick or (since 2000) for a corporate distribution of communion for a congregation distant in time or space from a full

---

19. A full round-up of their stretching the meaning of 1662 would include the prayer in relation to the dead (see pp. 103–4 above), the citing of 1 John 2:1–2 as though affirming that the eucharistic action is itself "propitiation for our sins" (see p. 103 above), the misapplication of "all thy whole church" (see p. 104 above), and the erroneous understanding of "sacrifice of praise and thanksgiving" (see p. 103 above).

celebration. The president at a celebration of the eucharist may reserve for these purposes without reference to the bishop; and faculty jurisdiction is only relevant if a parish wishes to install a specially designed new place of storage, as, e.g., a pyx or a tabernacle. Ordinary storage in a locked cupboard or safe fulfills the liturgical criteria, and is not subject to further "regulation." Faculty jurisdiction touches simply the fittings and furnishings of church buildings; and, as these do not have to be re-designed if reservation is practiced for pastoral needs, the faculty jurisdiction is wholly irrelevant. Nothing in this erroneous example touches upon the adoration question; it is simply unclear what use the "example" is to the argument.

After seven months Cardinal Cassidy said, in reply to *Clarifications*, that they had "thrown new light" on the questions. That appears to be a diplomatic way of saying that the *Clarifications* made it clear that the previous ARCIC I statements should not be taken at face value (as the *Response* had done), but now could be seen to be affirming what could not be seen in them before. This goes beyond Mary Tanner's phrase, that what had been "implicit" before, *Clarifications* was making "explicit," for in the process it had ruled out any other "implicit" meanings, and indeed went beyond what was even implicit. It crossed the line for many Anglicans from the acceptable to the indefensible—but somehow the Anglicans managed not to have to make a judgment about it at all.

Half of Cassidy's Letter concerns his "observation" that he is not persuaded that for Anglicans "adoration of the Reserved Sacrament" is "normal": "The Clarifications do not make clear that this can be said unreservedly and uniformly for Anglicans." His lack of persuasion on the point was 100 percent accurate: not only is such "adoration" only found in a somewhat specialized stream of Anglicans, but no Anglican Prayer Book in the world has any rubrical or other direction for reservation other than for ministering communion at a spatial or temporal distance from the original celebration, and none has any authorized rites for Benediction, exposition, or Corpus Christi processions.[20] Worldwide experience suggests that today not reserving at all is still "normal" for Anglicans; that reserving for the absent is a recognized regular variant on this; and that adoration of the reserved sacrament is a specialized minority devotion. There are clergy and congregations who have such practices, but they do so on a local basis only—and their practices cannot be cited as in any way official Anglican rites or devotions.

20. See Appendix C.

It is slightly odd to read Cassidy as saying that the *Response* had been "concerned not with the question of devotions associated with Christ's presence in the Reserved Sacrament," for the *Response* certainly reads as expressing that concern, and *Clarifications* certainly reads as addressing it.[21] He expounds the *Response* as more concerned with "diverse Anglican practice regarding Reservation itself and attitudes towards the Reserved Sacrament." True, diversity among Anglicans was reported in *Elucidation*, and, without much open admission, is clearly still part of the picture in *Clarifications*. However, at this stage, for whatever reason, Cassidy, having made his "one observation," does not press it, but says the Commission has done enough— "no further study would seem to be required at this stage."

How then are we to assess the drafting which so readily drew upon 1662? The drafters' inversion of the straightforward protestantism of 1662 to meet the very strongly Roman Catholic *desiderata* can only be attributed to a recognition that they had little else to offer in order to demonstrate an Anglican position to meet their terms of reference. But one also wonders whether there is not be detected some ignorance or misunderstanding of Anglican eucharistic history among both Anglicans and Roman Catholics on the Commission itself which adopted the draft. As Cardinal Cassidy noted, *Clarifications* had "thrown new light on the questions." Indeed it had, but what value-judgments does the adjective "new" carry?

---

21. It is ironic to find him quoting in illustration the "faculty jurisdiction" error of *Clarifications* (see p. 106 above), but here, as there, it makes no difference to the line of thought.

10

Reception?

A Prospect of "Reception"?

THE CO-CHAIRMEN OF ARCIC II introduce *Clarifications* and Cardinal Cassidy's Letter by saying "These mark a very significant moment in the work of ARCIC and in its reception." Later they speak of "this positive step on the road of reception" which will "assist both communions." Although the term "reception" is in regular Anglican use in this sense, it had not been so used in the earlier ARCIC I Statements on the eucharist. It would be easy to query this whole use of the term "reception"—for surely it can only be used confidently in retrospect, that is, when the particular idea, doctrine or policy has duly been adopted, i.e., actually received? In recent decades ecumenists and other reformers have become accustomed to using the term prospectively, as if the initiators of an idea were somehow building in a covert future necessity for their pet scheme to be widely adopted. That is how it appears here. So what force does the term "reception" bear in this co-chairmen's Introduction?

Anglican Reception—Initial Steps

We pick up the story where chapter 9 ended. The threefold document was sent in 1994 from the co-chairmen to the Anglican Communion Office who passed it to Church House Publishing in London, for them to publish it in conjunction with the Catholic Truth Society. It was duly published in July 1994 at the same time and in exactly the same format as the ARCIC II agreed Statement, *Life in Christ*. But sending for publication was apparently not quite the same as formal reporting. Admittedly, the co-chairmen wrote that "this positive step . . . will assist both communions to recognize that what ARCIC has stated and now clarified does indeed represent agreement."[1] But, despite the "both communions," the formal reporting was being made to the PCPCU alone; and, although the Cassidy Letter was presumably of relevance to both Communions, and the co-chairs' Introduction was addressing both, the threefold document was not apparently viewed thereafter as of significance to the Anglican Communion. ACC-10 was not meeting until 1996, in Panama. When it met, it was not that ARCIC II itself had escaped attention, for the Council did receive a round-up, an overview by its Ecumenical Advisory Group, of ecumenical relations. This was the Agros Report, which went to considerable length to describe ecumenical work across the worldwide Communion since ACC-9 had met in Cape Town in 1993, and it included a focused section on the work of ARCIC II, specifically mentioning *Church as Communion*. But this Agros Report had *no mention whatsoever* of *Clarifications*, and accordingly not a hint of "a matter of priority."

The onus must in theory have then fallen upon the members of ACC-10 themselves. Their predecessor, ACC-9, on which many of them had sat, had resolved that a consideration by ARCIC II of the Vatican's *Response* was "a matter of priority." Now they met, and the Agros report before them signally omitted any mention of *Clarifications*. So, whether they lacked minutes from 1993, or continuity of persons, or corporate memory, or enquiring minds, as far as researches can so far tell, *Clarifications* never appeared above the horizon during their meetings; and it certainly never got mentioned by name, or otherwise, in the Council's report, *Being Anglican in the Third Millennium* (1997).[2] ACC-10 made *no mention whatsoever* of *Clarifications*.

Such an omission is very hard to ascribe to a responsible well-managed semi-authoritative body, but unless some such odd contingency subtly disabled ACC-10 from doing its own acknowledged business, are we driven to thinking some positive concealment was being practiced somewhere?

1. *Clarifications*, 3.

2. In 2018 Stephanie Taylor, Executive Officer and Information Manager in the Anglican Communion Office, did an exhaustive search of the archives covering this period on my behalf. With a nil return from each line of enquiry she concluded with political caution: "On balance it would appear that the documentation suggests that *Clarifications* was not formally received by the ACC."

Roman Catholic Reception

Roman Catholics, on the other hand, have at intervals referred to *Clarifications* as an agreed document, without any qualifying reservations. Pope John Paul II seems to have welcomed it; for in the record of Archbishop George Carey's visit to Rome in December 1996, the Pope is recorded as saying "The Final Report of the first stage of our international dialogue has highlighted points of convergence and even agreement not thought possible before ARCIC began its work."[3] If his "convergence" identified the Authority Statements, did his "even agreement" have *Clarifications* in view, reckoning that it was simply explaining the previous statements? Rome had not agreed anything else from ARCIC, so it seems more than possible.

Roman Catholic readiness to quote from *Clarifications* is not surprising, as the contents of *Clarifications* contained no embarrassment for them. Thus, for instance, Donna Geernaert, describing the work of ARCIC I and II, reported:

> In 1993 ARCIC II published *Clarifications on Eucharist and Ministry*, which answered specific questions raised in the Roman Catholic Response to the Final Report.[4]

Cardinal Cassidy himself was unsurprisingly ready:

> A first Vatican response was not so positive, and it was possible only after much discussion within the Vatican for the Pontifical Council for Promoting Christian Unity to respond with a more encouraging reply. The discussions led to "clarifications," which in turn were accepted by ARCIC, and eventually, as president of the Pontifical Council, I was able to confirm officially that no further work needed to be done on the presentation of the Anglican and Catholic faith in the eucharist.[5]

"A more encouraging reply" is hardly how Anglicans would have generally characterized the *Response*, but it is perhaps a relative assessment, in comparison with the earlier CDF *Observations*. Thereafter to Cassidy it looked like plain sailing.

A good instance of Roman Catholic use of *Clarifications* in England is provided by *One Bread One Body: A teaching document on the Eucharist in*

---

3. Anglican Communion Office, *New Spirit*, 16.

4. Geernaert, "Achievements," 124.

5. Cassidy, *Ecumenism*, 56.

the Life of the Church which, in its chapter on the eucharist, quotes freely from both *Eucharistic Doctrine* and *Elucidation*, but just as freely includes:

(a) (Re the "making present" of the sacrifice of Christ) "cf ARCIC's *Clarifications on Eucharist and Ministry* (1994): 'In the celebration of the eucharistic memorial, the self-offering of Christ is made present. The community, gathered around the ordained minister who presides in Christ's name, enters into communion with this self-offering.'"[6]

(b) (Re offering the eucharistic sacrifice, and with reference to the Vatican *Response*) "The Anglican–Roman Catholic International Commission's *Clarifications* state that 'the one who presides is the minister of the sacramental self-offering of Christ.'"[7]

Thus the Roman Catholic bishops treated *Clarifications* as a useful teaching document, without any hint of controversy attached. Even more strikingly, Cardinal Walter Kasper, who had succeeded Edward Cassidy as president of the PCPCU in 2001, when writing of the eucharist very specifically in the context of the Anglican–Roman Catholic dialogue, cross-referred to *Clarifications* three times in four pages.[8] Later, in an expanded footnote, he then wrote as follows:

On the official Anglican and Roman Catholic responses, and the ensuing *Clarifications*, see footnote 25 [ie an earlier discussion]. This official response process allows us to see in ARCIC's *Final Report* a consensus on basic truths pertaining to the nature of the eucharist.[9]

So Kasper seems to have been treating *Clarifications* as all of a piece with the ARCIC I *Eucharistic Doctrine* and *Elucidation*, treating it in fact exactly as "clarifying" material, not in any way adding to the original two documents in the *Final Report*, but simply expounding them—and assuming they were agreed by the Anglicans as much as by the Roman Catholics. Arguably he

6. Catholic Bishops' Conferences, *One Bread One Body*, 25n71, quoting from the "Ministry and Ordination" section of *Clarifications* (not shown in Text L above).

7. Catholic Bishops' Conferences, *One Bread One Body*, 28, also quoting from the "Ministry and Ordination" section of *Clarifications* (also not shown in Text L above).

8. Kasper, *Harvesting the Fruits*, 172, 173, 176. There are also references to *Clarifications* in his section on "Ordained Ministry," 103, 106, 108, and 156n25, to which there is a cross-reference in the extract quoted above.

9. Kasper, *Harvesting the Fruits*, 194n42.

thus fulfilled exactly the suggested analysis above—that he was treating as an agreed ecumenical statement, one wholly within the public arena, that which the Anglicans had never officially seen, let alone endorsed. In his address to the 2008 Lambeth Conference he spoke in the same vein:

> The *Clarifications* (1993) produced by members of the Commission were seen to "have greatly strengthened agreement in these areas" according to Catholic authorities.[10]

Anglican Reception—The Story Continues

The Anglican handling of *Clarifications* was very different. If we return to ACC-10 in 1996, the Council had almost by definition no resolutions to debate on an issue which, it seems, had never risen above its horizons. It did the normal kind of routine ecumenical business: in Resolution 16 it accepted the Agros Report proposal that the Ecumenical Advisory Group be replaced by an Inter-Anglican Standing Commission on Ecumenical Relations (this became IASCER); and in Resolution 17 it thanked the Advisory Group for the Agros Report and requested that the Report be published as a companion booklet to the Report of ACC-10 itself. At this level, ecumenical life without *Clarifications* was clearly to be the norm.

And so the story continued. The Lambeth Conference in 1998 welcomed the agreed Statements of ARCIC II and duly listed them: *Salvation and the Church* (1987), *Church as Communion* (1991), *Life in Christ: Morals, Communion and the Church* (1994). Of *Clarifications* not one hint was heard. One wonders whether Bishops Mark Santer and John Baycroft, who were signatories of *Clarifications* and were members of the Lambeth Section IV on "Called to be One," attempted to get its findings endorsed, or at least noticed, by the Conference?[11] If they wanted their work *not* to be noticed, they took apparently effective steps towards that end, for their Section not only did not refer to it in the Section Report, but they brought to the plenary session this Resolution IV.23 (c):

10. Kasper, "Roman Catholic Reflections," 202. The quotation in this is inexact; the reference to "members of the Commission" perhaps betrays the mistaken impression that only a sub-committee was responsible for it; and "according to Catholic authorities" tells us, whether or not consciously on Kasper's part, exactly who had seen the agreement as "strengthened."

11. Michael Nazir Ali, then Bishop of Rochester, was also a signatory of *Clarifications*, but was in a different Lambeth Section.

> [This Conference] . . . recognizes the special status of those Agree-
> ments which have been affirmed by the Lambeth Conference 1988
> as "consonant in substance with the faith of Anglicans" (*Eucharis-
> tic Doctrine*, *Ministry and Ordination*, and their *Elucidations*) and
> urges the provinces to receive them into their life.

This was passed on the nod. But who present would ever have guessed, from either the Report or the Resolution, that Rome in the PCPCU *Response* had *not* agreed what the bishops were promoting, and that ARCIC II had given a controversial interpretation of the two ARCIC I agreements on the eucharist, and that Rome had then accepted that interpretation as meeting the problems raised in the 1991 *Response*? None of this was men- tioned—the resolution simply harked back to 1988, so both the *Response* and *Clarifications* were being silently written out of history: for Anglicans the story stopped in 1988. So we face the extraordinary scenario where the Anglicans responsible for *Clarifications* had reported to Rome with a joint Statement meeting the Vatican's requirements, while the Anglicans worldwide were to know nothing about it whatsoever, and were to go on happily with simply the 1988 Resolution on "substantial agreement" on the basis of texts which Rome had distinctly *not* agreed.

ARCIC Itself

I said earlier that ARCIC II itself had contributed to a procedure which it is becoming tempting to call "airbrushing out of existence." How so? Well, when the Commission's next agreed Statement, *The Gift of Authority*, was published in 1999, both the Introduction and the blurb on the cover acknowledged only three previous Statements, i.e., just as were listed at Lambeth 1998, *Salvation and the Church* (1987), *Church as Communion* (1991), *Life in Christ: Morals, Communion and the Church* (1994). And the same occurred again when *Mary: Grace and Hope in Christ* was published in 2005—the Commission listed its previous publications, but was again not acknowledging among them even the existence of *Clarifications*. The apologia for this I have most frequently encountered is that *Clarifications* was not a "statement" of ARCIC, and so its existence did not qualify for a mention.[12] But will that suffice?

---

12. The distinction of status between "statements" and *Clarifications* was made in the Church of England General Synod as the reason for not circulating *Clarifications*. But not being a Statement was near to not being anything. The suspicion also arises that ARCIC

IARCCUM

After the Mississauga Consultation in 2000 the International Anglican–Roman Catholic Commission for Unity and Mission (IARCCUM) was formed in 2001. It produced its first major report, *Growing Together in Unity and Mission* in 2007, which is considered in the next chapter. Although *Clarifications* is mentioned twice in its text, it does not appear in the professedly full list of all ARCIC documents in its Appendix 2.[13] Of its two mentions in the text one is in the four pages on the eucharist, which consist of excerptive quotations from *The Final Report*.[14] Worse than that was the "Briefing Paper for General Synod" of the Faith and Order Advisory Group to assist the General Synod debate on *Growing Together* (GS 1673) in February 2008, where the group of experts quoted the 1988 Lambeth approval of the ARCIC I documents, and then listed the "five reports" of ARCIC II without any reference at all to *Clarifications*.[15]

Finally we come to the official account of ARCIC II and its work in Adelbert Denaux, Nicholas Sagovsky, and Charles Sherlock (eds.), *Looking towards a Church Fully United* (SPCK, 2016). I asked Nicholas Sagovsky in advance of publication what space would be given to *Clarifications*, and he replied quite simply "You won"t find *Clarifications* mentioned in it." As a member of ARCIC II, and here as its chronicler, he was quite openly treating *Clarifications* as in some way not qualifying to count as part of ARCIC II's work. When the 350-page volume was published, it proved that Charles Sherlock had nevertheless slipped in just one half-page (in

---

II were simply not acknowledging the document as theirs, a possibility outlined on p.96 above—or that it had somehow dropped below their horizon of awareness.

13. The actual mentions are on p. 7 including n. 6 (see p. 96, n. 4 above) and p. 29, n. 103 (see p. 144 below here). The listing on p. 63 is under the heading of "The Documents of ARCIC"; such listings elsewhere are of "statements" and the omission of *Clarifications* can, it seems, in those cases be justified on the grounds that it was not a "statement," but one would expect here the inclusive term "documents" to include *Clarifications* (the existence of which, as noted, IARCCUM had registered, for it cited it in these mentions in its main text). Yet the listing of "documents" still omits it. What category beyond that of "documents" could it be said to occupy?

14. See IARCCUM, *Growing Together*, 25–29. The "almost" in my sentence reflects a single mention of *Clarifications* in the last footnote of the section, where it appears to be cited to confirm a position taken in *Elucidation*. The general summarizing of *Eucharistic Doctrine* and *Elucidation* in the report is considered on p. 145 below.

15. The sole possible reference to *Clarifications* in the debate on *Growing Together* was made by Bishop Michael Nazir Ali, as quoted on p. 96, n. 4 above; but he reached the bottom line of "no further study is needed" by eliding any identification of its source.

pp.308–9) which simply described the Commission's agreement to the text without mention of its contents.[16] This one-paragraph nod towards *Clarifications* appears as a tiny exception in a weighty book otherwise wholly devoted to the five "statements" of ARCIC II, each having fifty to sixty pages of commentary; and these five are presented as fulfilling the agenda of the Commission without remainder.[17]

It is arguable that, from the Roman Catholic point of view, the reception had already occurred with Cardinal Cassidy's Letter. Cassidy had taken seven months sounding out the "dicasteries" (i.e., the CDF and the PCPCU), and he wrote representatively on their behalf. His "No further study would seem to be required at this stage" must surely rank as "reception"—that is, from the point of view of the Roman dicasteries, after due scrutiny they reckoned the needs of "clarifying" identified by the *Response* had been met. In Rome reception is done by authority, and it had been done. But from an Anglican standpoint the document, at the point of publication, had not been seen by any official or representative body, and any "reception" of it was strictly prospective and hypothetical. So what steps towards Anglican reception were set in motion? If this was, as the chairmen said, "a significant moment" and "a positive step" in reception, what was to come next? The subsequent history suggests that rarely, if ever, has such a "significant" moment been addressed more silently to its intended recipients. In summary, as far as Anglicans were concerned, *Clarifications* gained practically no media notice; it was not reported to the ACC or the Lambeth Conference; at the Lambeth Conference its own signatories apparently did not raise it; it was not distributed in any measure through the Anglican Communion; it was not expounded or defended by its signatories; it was not the subject of any synodical debate or vote; it was ignored by the ARC-USA conversationalists; it had minimal exposure in journals; and even the Commission which produced it declined to acknowledge it thereafter

16. To be scrupulously exact, *Clarifications* is also mentioned by name in a footnote on p. 258 and in the text on p. 313, where it is, very unusually, bracketed with *The Final Report* as "agreements reached."

17. Curiously, when writing on his own, the Roman Catholic Denaux states, "ARCIC II has issued *six* documents [emphasis mine]" and his list duly includes *Clarifications* (Denaux, "Anglican–Roman Catholic Dialogue," 5n1), and he continues with nearly a full page (22) discussing this "document of a special nature." He quotes Cassidy's "greatly strengthened," adds the co-chairmen's "very important element in the reception of ARCIC I's agreements," and then goes on the ordination of women. He does not appear to have noticed that the Anglican Communion has not officially seen, let alone agreed on, *Clarifications*.

among their far-reaching agreements. It was very rarely reviewed. If this is how a "significant moment" opens the prospective way to "reception," we are finding ourselves in ARCIC's Adventures in Wonderland.

Rejection Attempt

There was, however, another possible doorway to publicity. The proactive alternative to silent reception proved to be vocal rejection. Soon after publication *Clarifications* had been picked up at a slightly less official level in the Church of England. The evangelical theologian Tim Bradshaw was a member of English ARC (i.e., the Anglican–Roman Catholic conversations in England), and had been highly critical years before of the ARCIC I Statements.[18] Now he wrote an equally critical, equally scholarly, "Appraisal" of *Clarifications* for English ARC in September 1994, and was encouraged there by the verdict of the Roman Catholic theologian, Sr. Cecily Boulding, who had herself been a member of ARCIC II until 1990:

> It would seem that the care and precision that characterized the language of *The Final Report* has not always been maintained in *Clarifications*. In view of the embarrassing carelessness and imprecision evident in the *Response to F.R* by the CDF, it would seem all the more important that ARCIC should maintain its standards in the careful expression of its statements.[19]

I was then myself prompted by Tim Bradshaw, who was with me on the CCU. I deliberately wrote my own assessment before I read his critique, in order to be sure I was writing strictly from my own initial judgment. My somewhat polemical review of *Clarifications'* treatment of the eucharist then formed an editorial in the journal I edited, *News of Liturgy* [*NOL*].[20] This led to considerable correspondence, and then a series of questions in General Synod which followed over the next three years. My correspondence included a private letter to Archbishop George Carey asking his verdict. He replied on April 21, 1995:

> I have read *NOL* with interest and agree with it substantially. I have to say that, when I saw *Clarifications*, I said to Bishop Mark Santer

18. See e.g., Bradshaw, *Olive Branch*, 89–100.

19. Cecily Boulding, Memorandum for English ARC "evoked by the critique of the Rev Tim Bradshaw," March 21, 1995.

20. See *News of Liturgy* (April 1995) 1–4.

and to Stephen Platten that this did not reflect my theology and felt it had gone too far towards Rome.

George Carey could, no doubt, have brought his criticism to bear at ACC-10 in Panama, but, as noted above, the ACC took no account of *Clarifications*.[21] I reckoned his letter had then to be treated as confidential (the quoting of it here is by permission). Meanwhile the Council for Christian Unity invited its theological sub-committee, the Faith and Order Advisory Group (FOAG), to prepare notes on *Clarifications*, and they produced a memorandum ("a confidential internal document") in August 1995. This was highly critical of the affirmations about both the asserted propitiatory nature of the eucharist and the presence of Christ in the consecrated elements. It described the attempt to make 1662 support these affirmations as "special pleading" (but the memorandum was "not for wider circulation"). FOAG agreed that further discussion of the document by the churches would be needed; but the Standing Committee of Synod declined to provide copies of *Clarifications* for members. Consequently in 1996 one member of Synod, Eric Bramhall, tabled a Private Member's Motion: "That this Synod reject the conclusions of the recent report of the Anglican–Roman Catholic International Commission entitled 'Clarifications.'" Despite members having to find their own copies of *Clarifications*, over 130 of them (around twenty-five percent of the total numbers of Synod) signed up for this debate to happen, but they were outbid by other back-benchers' proposals for the small space for private members' motions on the Synod agenda. The frustration built up not only at the content of *Clarifications*, but also at the apparent unwillingness of anyone in authority to discuss or defend the document. The reasons given varied: the document could not be circulated to Synod members (lest they undiscerningly think it to be on the same level as *Life in Christ*); there was no need to have a debate on it, as a comprehensive treatment of all the ARCIC Statements was coming up when they had all been published (it never did); and that fairly critical assessment of *Clarifications* which was made for the Council by the FOAG was also confidential and not to be released to Synod members. Some of this frustration was recognized very soon after in print by Mary Tanner, who was at the time secretary of the CCU, when she wrote,

21. George Carey, in his memoirs, *Know the Truth*, reports his dismay at the Vatican *Response* but does not take the story as far as *Clarifications*. He describes his visits to Pope John Paul II (including that mentioned on p.134 above), but provides no account as president of ACC-10.

However [despite the Cassidy favourable verdict], there are now indications that some Anglicans consider *Clarifications* has gone too far in the direction of using the language of one partner. The *Clarifications* add nothing which is not implicit in the *Final Report* itself. But it needs to be asked how helpful it was to make the implicit explicit in terms set up by one side only.[22]

After Mary Tanner had retired, when it was clear that the motion to reject *Clarifications* was going to run out of time, the CCU did arrange a "fringe" meeting at lunch-time in General Synod in July 1998. No *verbatim* record of this is available, but this is my contemporary account:

> The Bishop of Birmingham, who chairs ARCIC-II, and the Bishop of Stafford, Christopher Hill, who was a member of ARCIC-I, and, it appears, was brought back to help draft *Clarifications*, occupied the platform. In effect they acknowledged that they had been in untried circumstances when they decided to respond to the Pope's criticism of the ARCIC-I's agreements on eucharist and ordination and had got it wrong procedurally. On the question of content, Eric Bramhall, who put down the original Private Member's Motion, accused the Commission of moving in the sphere of transubstantiation. There were several other probing attacks upon both procedure and content, and little comfort for the Commission. The CCU now has to ask what steps to take—or whether simply to let Eric Bramhall's Private Member's Motion come up.[23]

Alongside this, there was a sustained attack upon *Clarifications* in Ireland by the scholarly Michael Kennedy in *Search—A Church of Ireland Journal*. The force of his criticisms was intensified by his own position, for here was no hardline evangelical automatically protesting against leanings towards Rome, but a learned constitutionalist who in his own person might well have preferred a more catholic ambience than the Church of Ireland provided. He was simply demonstrating that the position taken by *Clarifications* was incompatible with the constitution and formularies of the Church of Ireland. Even so the authorities of the Church of Ireland never took up the issue; *Clarifications* was not subjected to any official debate or verdict.

One only of the signatories of *Clarifications* went public to explain and defend his acceptance of it—Charles Sherlock from Australia. He was carrying the label of "evangelical" (having succeeded Julian Charley in

22. Tanner, "In Defence of Dialogue," 181.
23. *News of Liturgy* (July 1998) 5.

1991), but was from Melbourne and not to be thought a typecast "Sydney evangelical." Nevertheless, as a signatory, he recognized that the evangelical opposition to the document in England and elsewhere needed an answer. He wrote a chapter on "Eucharist, Sacrifice, and Atonement: The *Clarifications* of ARCIC" in the symposium which brought together papers on the eucharist from the 1995 International Anglican Liturgical Consultation in Dublin.[24] His defence rested on scholarly fine distinctions (such as a difference between "propitiatory value" and "propitiatory dimension"[25]) and only related to the issue of eucharistic sacrifice—he did not discuss the issue of Christ's presence in the elements or attempt to defend *Clarifications* on this point.

So where else in the Anglican Communion did *Clarifications* penetrate? It is hard to discover any awareness. Even provinces which had discussed the *Response* of the Vatican in 1992–93, such as The Episcopal Church in the USA and the Anglican Church in Canada, showed no sign of interest in *Clarifications*. In Aotearoa New Zealand a welcome for the report was expressed at the General Synod in 1998 and then ARCCNZ considered it—and apparently liked it. But, despite enquiries around the world, no further sightings have been reported from elsewhere. To this day it remains uncertain how far and to what places the yellow-ochre booklet had travelled or been studied. The document had the Cassidy cachet that the earlier agreements had by it been "greatly strengthened"; it had its co-chairmen's commendation for "reception"; but in Anglican circles no-one had promoted it, very few had even welcomed it, and not many more had even noticed it. But for a process of "reception" supposed to begin from publication, was ever reception so passive and so hidden, perhaps because it was also embarrassing?

There is a view of the 1990s that there was a general *ennui* in relation to ecumenism, and, if so, the Anglican lack of "reception" of *Clarifications* can well be seen as symptomatic of it. But in any case, in 1999 the arrival of the next agreement from ARCIC II, that on authority entitled *The Gift of Authority*, swept away any residual interest Anglican–Roman Catholic conversations at any level might have had in the eucharist. There is little reason to think the interest has since returned.

24. Holeton, *Our Thanks and Praise*, 117–28.
25. See his own account in Denaux, Sagovsky, and Sherlock, *Looking Towards*, 308–9.

I I

The Twenty-First Century

T HERE CAN BE DISCERNED in the new millennium some modest echoes
in Anglican–Roman Catholic dialogue of the eucharistic issues charted above. However, a range of other controversial items has dominated the
agenda, and so those echoes have been been regularly drowned out by the
official ARCIC II agreements on Authority (1999) and on Mary (2005), and
by the unofficial rumblings in the atmosphere from Anglican disputes over
same-sex unions, and other lesser issues.

IARCCUM and *Growing Together*

A major new initiative came in 2000 from the convening by the Archbishop of Canterbury and Cardinal Cassidy at Mississauga in Ontario of
a consultation of bishops to consider relationships between the two Communions in the sphere of action as well as belief. From this consultation
came in 2001 the International Anglican–Roman Catholic Commission
for Unity and Mission (IARCCUM). This was formed as an "episcopal
commission" to monitor and encourage the practical outworking of the
ecumenical partnership between the two Communions, not least in mission. The Commission's actual working was delayed by those troubles
mentioned above which affected the Anglican Communion in 2003–2005,
but later meetings led to a serious publication in *Growing Together in Unity
and Mission: Building on 40 Years of Anglican–Roman Catholic Dialogue*
(London: SPCK, 2007). As noted in chapter 8 above, the Introduction in
§2 acknowledges *Clarifications* and attributes it to a "sub-commission."
It quotes Cardinal Cassidy as saying that agreement had been "greatly
strengthened" by the document, but adds in an informative footnote that
"No formal Anglican response to Clarifications has been initiated"; and

144

this confirms the whole story from 1994 onwards, and must call in question whether any agreement has even been attempted, let alone has been strengthened. The report goes on to summarize a common set of beliefs, and within these it addresses "Eucharist." This summary is largely composed of quotations lifted from *Eucharistic Doctrine* and *Elucidation,* identified by quotation marks, and of footnoted attributions. No quotation is here attributed to *Clarifications* and only one reference to it appears among twenty-three footnotes. As that one reference relates to "some Anglicans who would find difficulty in these devotional practices [ie adoration of Christ in the reserved sacrament]" there is no problem in recognizing its truth. Nevertheless, the section includes in §40 "The eucharistic memorial, however, makes present this once-for-all-sacrifice of Christ." This is clearly drawn from *Clarifications*, but, almost uniquely in the whole summarizing process, it is not presented in quotation marks and has no footnoted reference. It goes beyond the text of *Eucharistic Doctrine* and *Elucidation* and tells Anglicans and Roman Catholics that they have agreed what from the Anglican side they have not agreed. Where the summary addresses the "real presence of Christ" in §§41 and 42, there is no quoting of the key qualifying sentence in *Eucharistic Doctrine*, "The Lord's words at the Last Supper . . . do not allow us to dissociate the gift of the presence and the act of sacramental eating." The summary as a whole has no standing save as a witness to how the twenty or so participants read the actual agreements; but its composition as an arbitrarily chosen catena of sentences lifted from their original context does require a critical reading, and the summary should not be viewed as an accurate précis of the three Statements. The report, as noted earlier, lists on page 63 "The documents of ARCIC," and divides them into the work of the two successive Commissions. But *Clarifications* appears in neither half: it has disappeared once more.

Growing Together was accompanied on publication in February 2007 by two weighty "Commentaries," one by the Anglican Bishop Paul Richardson, and the other by Bishop Bernard Longley, a Roman Catholic deeply immersed in ecumenical relationships in Britain, who later became the Roman Catholic co-chair of ARCIC III.[1] Neither was a member of IARCCUM, and it is not clear from the website by what authority they were asked to provide these resources. Both further summarize the

---

1. These are available by links from the website "Anglican–Roman Catholic Dialogue—IARCCUM."

account of eucharistic agreement in §§39–49. Richardson does not refer to *Clarifications*, but Longley does:

> The 1993 "Clarifications," produced by an ARCIC sub-commission to respond to these concerns in so far as they addressed the Agreed Statements on Eucharist (1971) and Ministry (1973), was seen to have greatly strengthened the agreements reached. Yet *GTUM* does not explicitly appeal to these "Clarifications": it makes reference to them but does not extensively draw upon them.

There is no surprise in Richardson's omission: whether deliberate or not, it is almost routine among Anglicans. Longley's paragraph is interesting, as it appears cautious about giving *Clarifications* too lofty a status, yet quotes Cassidy's "greatly strengthened" without qualification, as though both Communions had equally evaluated it.[2]

General Synod and *Growing Together*

The Church of England General Synod was to debate *Growing Together* in February 2008, and in preparation for it FOAG circulated the Briefing Paper GS 1673. The section on "Anglican–Roman Catholic Dialogue" duly lists the work of ARCIC I and ARCIC II, and, in almost predictable terms, completely omits any mention of *Clarifications*—the "second phase" (i.e., ARCIC II) was "producing five reports."[3] Yet, when it goes on to note "what has been agreed thus far," under the heading of "Eucharist" comes a nine-line summary, and this contains the characteristic wording of *Clarifications* "They [Anglicans and Roman Catholics] see the Eucharist as a memorial (*anamnesis*), which makes present the once-for-all-sacrifice of Christ." So was *Clarifications* forming minds on FOAG, while eluding actual mention by name in the Briefing Paper?

In the actual debate Bishop Michael Nazir Ali delivered his summary of ARCIC treatment of the eucharist noted earlier, conflating Anglican agreement to the two ARCIC I statements with Cassidy's favourable verdict on ARCIC II's *Clarifications*.[4] The wide-ranging debate, while evincing

2. Longley simply repeats here from *Growing Together* that the authorship of *Clarifications* was by a "sub-commission" (see p. 96, n. 4 and p. 144 above).

3. FOAG obviously lacked corporate memory—it was but fourteen years since they had delivered a very critical memorandum on *Clarifications* (see p. 141 above).

4. See p. 111, n. 8 above, where his actual wording is recorded.

concerns about eucharistic sharing, did not otherwise touch on doctrinal questions about the eucharist.

A Critic from the Touchlines

At this point mention must be made of Brian Douglas, an Anglican sacramental theologian, a teacher of theology from Canberra, Australia—and by no means evangelical. In the early years of the century he established a website providing a careful summary of the eucharistic theology of around a hundred and sixty Anglican sources, mostly summarizing individual theologians, but also including the ARCIC Statements. He presents four basic categories for understanding the ways in which the presence of Christ relates to the bread and wine of communion: immoderate realism; moderate realism; moderate nominalism; immoderate nominalism.[5] He is less than charmed by *Clarifications*, and part of his analysis provides an appendix to this chapter.

IARCCUM has since 2012 conducted an enquiry about progress in Anglican–Roman Catholic local dialogues around the world. No evidence has appeared touching on the eucharistic documents.

Two American Authors

While issues other than the eucharist were dominating concerns through the Anglican Communion in the first decade of the century, two American authors, both published in 2007, reflected at length on Anglican–Roman Catholic relationships, and included examination of the eucharistic agreements. The Episcopalian Mary Reath gives her whole book to a reporting of ARCIC matters, and in her Epilogue on "Agreed ARCIC Documents" she lists "Eucharist" in her heading and mentions *Elucidation* in her exposition; but there is mention of neither the PCPCU's *Response* nor *Clarifications*.[6] The Roman Catholic Owen Cummings, writing to appraise "the

---

5. These categories do not really allow for the "conveyancing" role of the sacrament outlined in principle in the historic formularies, as it surely has to be located between the "realism" and the "nominalism" adopted by Douglas? There is a case for further dialogue on that point. But Douglas has his place in this chapter as a theologian who has coolly evaluated *Clarifications*, even while so many have either ignored it or have smoothly assumed it decided an ecumenical issue which on inspection it did not decide.

6. Reath, *Rome and Canterbury,* 106–8.

eucharist in contemporary Anglican Theology" gives separate chapters to English Anglican theologians, including a generous survey of "Evangelical Anglican Eucharistic Theology" (a rare chapter heading indeed), and has a chapter of twenty pages on "Formal Statements and the Eucharist." This latter examines *Eucharistic Doctrine* very carefully, saying that he wants the text "to speak for itself."[7] But, having said he will "look briefly at the official responses," he then merely mentions *Elucidation* in passing. The Anglican response which he charts is the Church of England 1986 one, not the Lambeth 1988 one. He thinks that the Vatican *Response* had been rather too heavy. He writes later on IARCCUM. But he too never mentions *Clarifications*. And glancing at these two books leaves us wondering whether *Clarifications*, unnoticed in North America in the 1990s, had ever actually crossed the Atlantic in the new millennium.

Lambeth 2008

A next possible reference to the eucharistic agreements might have been expected at the Lambeth Conference in July 2008. However, the "indaba" mode of meeting and discussing without reporting or resolving precluded any close study of documents, and the capturing of conversations and reflections ended in listed "resources" where *Growing Together* had a simple mention by its title and ARCIC had a six-line paragraph referring to the Authority and Mary reports from the preceding decade. There was, however, the major address by Cardinal Walter Kasper in which he began with an "Overview of relations in recent years," and included *Clarifications* more or less within the work of ARCIC I, adverting then to the "greatly strengthened" phrase which Roman Catholics have regularly repeated.[8]

The Kyoto Report—*The Vision Before Us*

The Kyoto Report of the Inter-Anglican Standing Commission on Ecumenical Relations 2000–2008 (IASCER) was published as Sarah Rowland Jones (ed), *The Vision Before Us* (London: ACO, 2009). The twelve pages on relations with the Roman Catholic Church include a brief account of "two phases" of ARCIC with a listing of the respective documents of ARCIC I

---

7. Cummings, *Canterbury Cousins*, 84–94.
8. His actual wording is on p. 135 above.

and ARCIC II. Typically, *Clarifications* is not in the lists. However there comes lower down on the same page a paragraph about "difficulties around providing a formal Communion-wide response" in relation to ARCIC I documents. Here *Clarifications* is mentioned as though from ARCIC I. The relevant part reads:

> Official responses were made by the two Communions (through Resolution 8 of the 1988 Lambeth Conference on the Anglican side) to the work of ARCIC I, pointing to areas of convergence or agreement in understanding, and to outstanding areas of difference (giving rise to various "Clarifications" from an ARCIC sub-commission).

This, while giving *Clarifications* some bare existence, is a most minimal account of the events covered. It is impossible to learn from it that on the Anglican side Lambeth 1988 had raised no difficulties, that the Vatican *Response* had raised serious "areas of difference," that *Clarifications* was answering Rome only, that Cassidy had stated that on that basis no further study was required, and that *Clarifications* had not been agreed by Anglicans.

The Final Report of ARCIC II

The Final Report of ARCIC II, which was published in 2016, has been mentioned earlier, as the conclusive part of the evidence of ARCIC II sidelining *Clarifications*.[9] In the Preface Bishops David Moxon and Bernard Longley, the co-chairmen of ARCIC III, who commissioned the volume, write that, in respect of the "five Agreed Statements of ARCIC II," the report "offers critical analyses of their contexts and of responses made, and resources to 'promote the reception of its previous work by presenting the previous work of ARCIC as a corpus' (from the mandate of ARCIC III)."[10] The key words here are "five" (i.e., *Clarifications* is excluded) and "promote the reception" (the process from which it is excluded).[11] The editors tell us in the Introduction that the "mandate" to ARCIC III at its inauguration in 2009 came from Archbishop Rowan Williams and Pope Benedict XVI in just those terms "to promote the reception of its previous work."

9. See pp. 138–39 above.

10. Denaux, Sagovsky, and Sherlock, *Looking Towards*, v.

11. In the earlier mention of *Looking Towards* (see pp. 138–39 above) we noted a single paragraph that gave the barest mention to *Clarifications*, as over against fifty to sixty pages for each of the five Statements.

We have then a mandate to ARCIC III and to its chosen three authors re the five Statements to promote their reception; we have alongside that the exclusion of *Clarifications* from that process. The authors were kicking into the long grass the task of reception which, as shown in chapter 10 above, the co-chairmen of ARCIC II had originally said they were putting in motion for *Clarifications*. While this was fully in accord with the actual Anglican tendency towards inertia or amnesia, one wonders why the Roman Catholics on the Commission settled for it. They had been regularly assured that agreement was "greatly strengthened" by *Clarifications*; but, if they now agreed that it was not worth more than Charles Sherlock's single paragraph, were they setting aside what purported to be such a key element in "reconciling" the two Communions?

Appendix to Chapter 11: Assessment of *Clarifications* by Brian Douglas[12]

The Anglican–Roman Catholic International Commission published a document in 1994 called *Clarifications on Eucharist and Ministry*, which as its name implies, sought to clarify certain aspects of the Agreed Statements on Eucharist and Ministry as published in *The Final Report* of 1982. In these *Clarifications* the Commission attempted to reaffirm moderate realism by arguing that "the making present, effective and accessible of the unique historic sacrifice of Christ does not entail a repetition of it" (*Clarifications*, 1994: 5). While the object of this statement seems clear, that is, to affirm no repetition of the historic sacrifice in the Eucharist, the wording seems problematical. What *Clarifications* argues is that the historic sacrifice of Christ is made present, effective and accessible in the Eucharist. This has the danger of associating the historic sacrifice too closely with the Eucharist, identifying one particular (the historic sacrifice) with another (the eucharistic sacrifice) and of failing to distinguish in an adequate way between the sign and the signified and thereby leading to an understanding of the sacrifice which could be seen to be based on immoderate realism. The historic sacrifice and the eucharistic sacrifice are really both particulars of a

12. This appendix is taken, with permission, from Brian Douglas's website, www. anglicaneucharistictheology.com, a resource that reports 160 "case-studies," mostly of single authors, covering the years from the Reformation to the end of the twentieth century, and compiled in the years 2001–2006. Douglas has also written at length on "Anglican–Roman Catholic International Commission."

more universal event, that is, Christ's sacrificial activity, however *Clarifications* seems to treat the "historic sacrifice of Christ" as a universal, arguing that this event can be made "present, effective and accessible" in the present, that is identified with the Eucharist. It may have been better to have argued that the historic sacrifice is an instantiation of Christ's saving work which is also instantiated in the Eucharist.

12

The Future

T HIS BOOK IS ENTITLED "Did the Anglicans and Roman Catholics Agree on the Eucharist?" The answer should by now be clear—no, they did not; and not only did they not agree, but it is doubtful whether they knew they had not agreed. The Anglicans at least have never looked the situation in the face. It is simple in logic—if the PCPCU were to agree that Roman Catholic criteria for agreement had been satisfied by *Clarifications*, then some Anglican process for evaluating the document also was needed; and any assertions of agreement being "greatly strengthened" should have been delayed until both sides had agreed the same document. From the point of view of history, the handling of this issue has been bizarre.

On the other hand, it is seems to have become entirely reasonable not to look for Communion-wide agreement to the ARCIC documents. That is in fact how the five ARCIC II Statements have increasingly been handled—they have been on record, perhaps as points of theological and ecumenical reference, but not as being deployed to demonstrate any particular convergence of the two Communions. In England the first Statement, *Salvation and the Church* (1987), was referred to the dioceses and answers were received; but nothing like "consonant with our faith" was brought from round the Communion to the 1998 Lambeth Conference. The next two Statements did not for many years receive in England even that diminishing attention. However, Lambeth 1998 gave a broad welcome to both of them. The two most controversial Statements of ARCIC II, on Authority and on Mary, had not been published in 1998, so no evaluation of them occurred—and it is surely likely that, had they been available, they would have stirred great controversy. Lambeth 2008 was not engaged in formal evaluation, and the Kyoto Report draws a contrast between the two ARCICs in respect to the treatment of their Statements:

> Official responses were made by the two Communions . . . to the
> work of ARCIC I. . . . While no comparable official response to
> the agreed statements of ARCIC II has been sought, IASCER has
> encouraged Anglican leaders and churches . . . to indicate their
> support for the continuing work of ARCIC.[1]

So the overall picture is that ARCIC II Statements have, thus far, only the authority attaching to their own signatories. No Anglican synod or other representative body or persons has committed us to, say, papal authority.

However, at this point *Clarifications* was a particular instance of ARCIC II overtly seeking to finish ARCIC I business, where the two Communions had indeed sought to sign up corporately for the agreements. It has run into the sand procedurally, quite apart from the demerits of its content; but, instead of a frank admission that this is the case, official reports and individual commentators either disregard it, or, with minimal side-reference to it, claim it has brought agreement. The ground-clearing of this present volume is intended to bring a clear-eyed grasp of the impossibility of spelling out any such agreement which is so claimed. For, in the shortest terms possible, Anglicans and Roman Catholics, called upon to sign up to ARCIC I on the eucharist, have in fact signed up to different documents from each other.

Nicholas Sagovsky, writing from inside ARCIC II near the end of its time, envisaged a "Joint Declaration" comparable to the "remarkable" joint declaration made by the Lutherans and Roman Catholics on Justification in 1999. He wrote,

> An Anglican–Roman Catholic joint declaration would need . . .
> to cover the grounds of explicit community-breaking division,
> would have to take in the Eucharist, ministry, authority, justification, and the communion of saints (including Mary). . . . It is to be
> hoped that by the end of the current round of dialogue, the second
> Anglican–Roman Catholic International Commission (ARCIC II)
> will have ensured there are texts to draw on in all these areas.[2]

This was written before the Statement on Mary was issued by the Commission (though after the one on Authority, which gets no mention here). But what could be sought in 2003 in the way of "texts to draw on" in the matter of the eucharist? Clearly re-touching existing texts was not on the residual agenda of ARCIC II, so it is the three texts considered thus far in this volume

1. Jones, *Vision*, 172.
2. Sagovsky, "Anglicans and Roman Catholics," 29.

which must have been in view. Sagovsky goes on on the next page to take note of *Clarifications*, though quoting the standard "greatly strengthened" attribute as commending it, and thus failing to disclose the problem it would cause to many Anglicans. He then sketches instructively and imaginatively what drawing upon the texts to compile a "Declaration" on the eucharist might accomplish. However, he concentrates on *Eucharistic Doctrine*, and (apart from one brief mention) ignores *Clarifications*. Thus he has, for instance, no assertion that Christ's sacrificial death is "made present" in the eucharist. He only builds in from *Clarifications* an acceptance of "permissible diversity" concerning adoration of the reserved sacramental elements, diversity which is certainly stated to be *de facto* Anglican practice in both *Elucidation* and *Clarifications*.[3] Whether, however, Cassidy's muttering that this had slipped past the Vatican's guard without condemnation would be sufficient commendation of it as a principle must be an open question.

There must be a strong temptation to hail the Sagovsky proposal as both closing off great difficulties in the existing position between the two Communions about the eucharist, and, presumably, assisting the formation of a sound base for building towards intercommunion and full *koinonia* in the future. If a Commission (ARCIC IV?) came up with such a comprehensive proposed "Declaration," we would all be under great pressure to assent to it. But Sagovsky's draft text would bring us back much nearer to the original *Eucharistic Doctrine*; and if we ignore the mistakes of history which this account has tried to disclose, we might well be led into having to repeat them. Sagovsky himself, in quoting "greatly strengthened" in one place, has surely made it all the harder to omit the thrust of *Clarifications* from the final Declaration in another? The role in history of a document which functions on a "Now you see it—now you don't" basis is destabilizing, and the two Communions need to come to terms with that.

So is there an alternative to the Sagovsky proposal? Could a joint declaration (which has much in principle to commend it) come about on some other basis? Are there Anglicans who can share peaceably in the life of an Anglican–Roman Catholic Commission, can "hear" what moves those of a different persuasion, but can also broadly hold to a reformed position and put down *ne plus ultras* when necessary? Anglicans at least, if given the chance, can live in communion with those with whom they disagree and work at finding the appropriate common wording of their eucharistic faith from within a position of communion. It would be wonderful to get

3. Sagovsky, "Anglicans and Roman Catholics," 40.

the chance: but it cannot be done by fudge or by creeping undermining of one's own or one's Communion's convictions. Here is a task for godly scholarship, divine discernment, patience in the Spirit, and love for those from whom we differ. Charley and Tillard, *Clarifications* notwithstanding, provide from the last century a lasting model. But the warning has to be that sometimes we have to differ and we have simply to state it honestly that way—and be ready nevertheless to resume the dialogue, and, if possible, to go on to true eucharistic sharing.

Eucharistic sharing, or intercommunion, has not figured sharply in this volume, not least because, however strongly it may be sought on a local basis, the ARCIC documents under examination have not been addressing it as such a major presenting issue. There is no doubt that there is desire to be found in both Communions to cut all the corners and to get to shared communion quickly; but it is clear that issues of the validity of orders and the nature of ecclesial structures and authority cannot be sidelined in order to promote that desired end. It is indeed possible that answers, even provisional answers, relating to those larger issues, may precede any return to the eucharistic question. Charles Sherlock reports that Cardinal Cassidy himself was asked, at an ARCIC II meeting which he was visiting after *Clarifications* had been published, what next "stage" he was envisaging which would re-open "study" of the eucharistic questions. His reply was that this might well come in association with the intercommunion question. And this is quietly confirmed by the present president of PCPCU, Cardinal Kurt Koch, who writes:

> Firstly agreement on the Eucharist is closely related to recognition of orders. The judgment of Leo XIII on Anglican orders given in his encyclical *Apostolicae Curae* is in effect while Catholic scholarship is seeking to move from a canonical mode of expression to a more theological vision of what is involved in Anglican ordained ministry. Secondly, Cardinal Cassidy's letter points to the question of authority, which is not unrelated to that of the Eucharist. The dispersed structure of authority within the Anglican Communion means that a breadth of understandings of the Eucharist are accepted which is a cause of serious misgivings to the Catholic Church. Thirdly, as was pointed out in the International Anglican–Roman Catholic Commission for Unity and Mission's document, *Growing Together in Unity and Mission*, "Anglicans and Catholics acknowledge that there is an intrinsic relationship between sharing the Eucharist and full ecclesial communion, but diverge on the way that is expressed on the way to full communion. Churches

of the Anglican Communion and the Roman Catholic Church therefore have different disciplines for Eucharistic sharing" (§46).[4]

So perhaps a glimpse of the future agenda is being given us.

Meanwhile the constructive work of ARCIC III has been under way for nearly a decade, and that Commission's only publication at the time of going to press had been the "final report" of ARCIC II.[5] What is to be expected from them? However, through the astonishing timing noted here in the Introduction and spelled out in the Postscript in chapter 13 below, the publication of *Walking Together on the Way* has gone a long way to answer this question. This particular history, covering the eras of ARCIC I and ARCIC II, has been at intervals marked by considerable unease. It may well be that ARCIC III will show us clearly that no amount of unease arising in and from the past history ought to daunt us from looking for better ways of working, for better upshot from our meetings, for better reception in our ranks, for better eucharistic worship in our lives, to be worked out under the good hand of our God in the years to come.

---

4. Quoted by permission from a personal letter of Cardinal Koch of February 9, 2018.
5. I.e., Denaux, Sagovsky, and Sherlock, *Looking Towards.*

13

Postscript: ARCIC III and *Walking Together on the Way*

THE WHOLE VOLUME OF the previous chapters was written and in the hands of the publishers in early 2018. However, in the brief period before the production process was begun, on July 3, 2018, ARCIC III, seven years from its formation, produced its first report, *Walking Together on the Way: Learning to Be the Church—Local, Regional, Universal*. This is a far more comprehensive Statement than any of the agreements of ARCIC I and ARCIC II, and its central concern is ecclesiology. Had it been to hand when I began this book, I might have conceived the plan differently. As it is, I have thought it best to let the story run as it appeared prior to the publishing of *Walking Together*, and then let this new Statement shed its own light upon the path hitherto taken.

Walking Together not only draws in, integrates, and reviews all the work of the previous two Commissions, but, pursuing its own work on the nature of the church, it adds elements of its own, as, for instance, a useful focus on baptism in §§52–55. The baptismal theme, coming as it does in a section on building the Christian community, then quite naturally runs on into a similar discussion of the eucharist in §§58–60. Here, however, ARCIC III is consciously reverting to the earlier findings on the eucharist, and that, for the purpose of this present investigation, means that these three paragraphs have to be evaluated in respect to their relationship to the three previous documents on the eucharist by ARCIC I and ARCIC II, and measured by the degree to which they reflect or nuance the earlier teachings. The evaluation will prove enlightening; but we begin with the actual three paragraphs from the ARCIC III text itself.

Text N

Paragraphs 58–60 of *Walking Together on the Way*, 2018

Note that *"ED"* stands for *Eucharistic Doctrine*, i.e., the 1971 Statement (Text E above); *"LG"* stands for *Lumen Gentium*, The Vatican II Dogmatic Constitution on the Church (1964); and *"Gift"* for the ARCIC II Statement, *The Gift of Authority* (1999).

The eucharist constitutes and builds up the communion of the Church

The whole Christ is present throughout the action of the eucharist

58. Anglicans and Catholics hold that the communion entered into in baptism reaches its sacramental fullness in the celebration of the eucharist. We believe that "in the whole action of the eucharist . . . the crucified and risen Lord, according to his promise offers himself to his people" (*ED* §3). The entire celebration of the eucharist makes "sacramentally present the whole mystery of salvation" (*ED* §7). Here, through the power of the Spirit, Christ instructs us with his Word and feeds us with his very self. For both traditions, to participate in the eucharist is to be nourished by and taken more deeply into Christ's own life: "Its purpose is to transmit the life of the crucified and risen Christ to his body, the Church, so that its members may be more fully united with Christ and with one another" (*ED* §6).* Reconciled in the eucharist, the

---

* See also "Our sharing in the body and blood of Christ leads to no other end than that of transforming us into that which we receive." St Leo the Great, *Sermon 63*, 7, PL 54, 357; and "The life-giving Word of God by uniting himself with his own flesh made it also life-giving. And so it was right that he should be united with our bodies through his sacred flesh and precious blood, which we receive as a life-giving blessing in the bread and wine." St Cyril of Alexandria, Commentary on Luke 22:19, PG 72, 92.

faithful are called to be servants of reconciliation, justice, and peace, and witnesses to the joy of the resurrection.**

In the eucharist the Church both meets Christ and is there disclosed to itself

59. As in baptism, eucharistic participation in Christ is not merely individualistic but is necessarily collective and ecclesial: "The cup of blessing that we bless, is it not a sharing [*koinonia*] in the blood of Christ? The bread that we break, is it not a sharing [*koinonia*] in the body of Christ? Because there is one bread, we who are many are one body, for we all partake of the one bread" (1 Cor 10:16–17). The eucharist celebrates and affirms the traditional understanding of the identity of the entire Church as born from the blood (signifying the eucharist) and water (signifying baptism) that flowed from the side of the crucified Christ (John 19:34). Furthermore, the risen and ascended Christ, present in the eucharist, always resides within the Church which is his Spirit-filled, charism-endowed body (1 Cor 12–14). In the eucharist, the Church both meets Christ and is there disclosed to itself. St Augustine famously gave eloquent expression to this in the context of exploring with the newly baptized what it means to receive communion:

> If you are the body and members of Christ, it is your mystery which is placed on the Lord's table; it is your mystery you receive. It is to that which you are that you answer "Amen", and by that response you make your assent. You hear the words "the body of Christ"; you answer "Amen". *Be* a member of Christ, so that the "Amen" may be true. . . . Be what you see; receive what you are. (*Sermon 272*)

** See 1 Cor 11:17–34, particularly 22 and 29; also Matt 25:31–46; Gal 2:10; 1 Cor 16:1–4; 2 Cor 8:1–15; 9:6–15. For St. John Chrysostom's development of this theme, see "The Gospel of St Matthew: Homily L.4", PG 58, 508–9.

The eucharist both celebrates communion and deepens the desire for communion

60. Authentic eucharistic participation in Christ is, then, always an ecclesial participation. Eucharistic communion with Christ is communion with all who similarly share in Christ through the Spirit (*Gift* §13; see also *LG* §7). The eucharist nourishes and feeds this ecclesial body of Christ and impels those who share in it towards the overcoming of all that obstructs or weakens this communion.*** For this reason, as is often noted in ecumenical contexts, the eucharist both celebrates the communion that already exists and intensifies in us the desire to move to deeper communion, for "has Christ been divided?" (1 Cor 1.13). In celebrating and living the eucharist the Church becomes more fully what it is. St Augustine describes the eucharist as the sacrament "through which in the present age the Church is made" (*Contra Faustum*, 12, 20). The eucharist is the living memorial of Christ's sacrificial death in which the Church entreats the benefits of his passion and enters into the movement of his self-offering (see *ED* §5).

[§61 re "*The eucharist celebrated in communion with the bishop actualizes the fullness of ecclesial reality*" completes the treatment of the eucharist in *Walking Together*.]

There appears to be no expectation of asking the two Communions for authoritative judgments on this ARCIC III Statement; and, even if there were, as the three paragraphs about the eucharist are included to contribute to a much larger ecclesial picture, their significance would lie not so much within their own argument as in that larger relationship. There seems to be little else in *Walking Together* which bears upon the eucharist, so it is these three paragraphs which particularly stand in sequence to the documents of 1971, 1979, and 1994.[6]

*** See *LG* §11; also *LG* §3. Contemporary Anglican eucharistic piety and liturgy celebrate the same conviction in the adaptation of St Paul's plea for the unity of the Corinthian Church: "Though we are many, we are one body, because we all share in one bread."

6. *Walking Together* was released with two semi-official Commentaries accompanying it, by Orme Rush, an Australian Roman Catholic, and James Harvey, an English Anglican, neither of them a member of the Commission. The two Commentaries barely touch upon

Nevertheless, for the purpose of the present enquiry, these three paragraphs, amounting to less than 5 percent of the whole Statement, do claim
to be summarizing the previous ARCIC work on the eucharist; and they
obviously depend most heavily upon *Eucharistic Doctrine* for their shaping
and formulation. There is no mention of *Elucidation* or discernible quotation from it; and, when all the previous documents are listed in a "resumé"
in §2, *Clarifications* does not figure in that list. However, a footnote on that
same page, citing the sources of the collected documents of ARCIC I and
ARCIC II, adds: "ARCIC II also issued *Clarifications of Certain Aspects of
the Agreed Statements on Eucharist and Ministry of the First Anglican–Roman Catholic International Commission* (London: CTS/Church House,
1994)." As with some earlier references noted here, this gives no indication
of the reason for *Clarifications*' compilation, nor of its content, nor of its
"reception." It is minimally noted merely to exist. However, in contrast with
the more arbitrary summary about the eucharist in *Growing Together*, the
actual text of these three paragraphs 58–60 do not appear to be drawing
upon anything at all from *Clarifications*; furthermore, they also show no
sign of dependence upon *Elucidation*; they appear to be rooted almost entirely in the original *Eucharistic Doctrine* of 1971. The only cited quotations
are from *Eucharistic Doctrine*. Are we perhaps back in 1971, spared the
later ARCIC glosses and explanations, approaching an agreed text if not
with a mental *tabula rasa*, at least with an open mind ready to put brackets
around some of the subsequent history recorded above? Indeed, we might
ask, did ARCIC III deliberately side-line the controversies of the past, either despatching them as irrelevant or declining even to consider them?

If we then compare §§58–60 with *Eucharistic Doctrine*, we find ourselves back in a discussion of how the eucharist builds up and bonds the
people of God. In §58 the church is "nourished" by the eucharist; in §59 the
church meets with Christ in the eucharist and finds itself in Christ through
participation; and in §60 the church thereby moves into an ever-closer mutual unity of its members. The whole passage has a dynamism about how
God works profoundly within his people through the sacrament.

If we are to press the comparison further, we need to address the categories of historic controversy signalled by the section headings in *Eucharistic Doctrine*—eucharistic sacrifice and "the presence of Christ." And here

---

the eucharist: Rush affirms "The eucharist makes Christ sacramentally present throughout the world, at all levels"; while Harvey sees in the eucharistic treatment "Much of the
language employed in these paragraphs is reminiscent of the theological tone of classical
Anglican eucharistic theology evidenced in the Book of Common Prayer."

the astonishing feature of *Walking Together* is what it does not say, what it does not ask its readers to endorse.

Eucharistic sacrifice comes first in 1971. There and here the eucharist is not described as being itself a sacrifice; in neither Statement is it identified with the unique sacrifice of Christ on Calvary; and in neither does it come nearer to these difficult formulations than in the 1971 wording, repeated here as sufficient, that the church "enters into the movement of his [Christ's] self-offering"—wording discussed at length on pp. 44–45 above. The only point where the new text may be straying beyond 1971 is in §58 where it quotes as from 1971 that the eucharist makes "sacramentally present the whole mystery of salvation." This might conceivably be expounded as expressing the doctrine that the eucharist is in itself the historic sacrifice of Christ or makes it present (which is what the PCPCU *Response* of 1991 required and *Clarifications* expressed); but the use of "mystery" actually precludes univocal clarity; and thus other more immediate understandings of the eucharist as simply conveying the grace of salvation to the recipients are equally possible. The quotation does, however, present a different underlying problem—astonishingly, this quoted phrase, while attributed to "*ED* §7," is not in fact a quotation from *Eucharistic Doctrine* at all![7] I note above that *Eucharistic Doctrine*, having cited the term "mystery" as a cross-heading, does not then utilize it or expound it in its text. ARCIC III seems to have invented a referenced quote—the Commission must have blinked.

What then of the presence of Christ in the eucharist? §58 is entitled, "The Whole Christ is present throughout the action of the eucharist," which might itself be viewed as a semi-polemical gambit, certainly as putting down a marker. Then the text itself begins by citing 1971 that "in the whole action" is where Christ offers himself to his people; §59 states that Christ is "present in the eucharist"; and §60 emphasizes communion with Christ through the eucharist. Nothing here is controversial—almost all of it might be confidently affirmed by any Christian church that celebrates the sacrament at all. But have the Fourth Lateran Council and the Council of Trent and the findings of the PCPCU all escaped notice?

So is there here an agreement? Does not the PCPCU, whether stiffened by the CDF or not, have to invoke the four criteria in the 1991 *Response*, which demonstrated how the Roman Catholics had in ARCIC I understated their own sacramental faith?[8] If the four criteria have disappeared

7. See the text on p. 40 above.
8. See p. 79 and p. 102 above.

from view, how fundamental were they when they were first delivered? In the light of this new text, could not the PCPCU have agreed on *Eucharistic Doctrine* in the first place? The point is strongly reinforced by our examining what is not said in *Walking Together*, which the *Response* said should have been in *Eucharistic Doctrine* and *Elucidation*. Here now in these §§58–60, the sole treatment of the eucharist in the Report, we find no mention of the presence of Christ within the consecrated elements, no mention of ontological change in them, no adoration of Christ in them, and no reservation of them. We find no identification of the celebration with the sacrifice of Christ, no "propitiatory value" ascribed to the eucharist, and no such value applied for the benefit of the dead. Virtually every feature of the *differentia*, which have traditionally helped demarcate Roman Catholic eucharistic belief as distinct from Anglican, has disappeared.

So the initial reaction of an Anglican reader has to be to ask whether this is a true presentation of "substantial agreement" (the key wording from 1971, which is admittedly not present here). If it is, was so much of the post-1971 history recounted above actually an unsteady march up a *cul de sac*? Do we go back and give the authors of 1971 a deserved pat on the back? But if this is *not* "substantial agreement," who is going to admit it or expose it, and how? What then are its status and usefulness? And what are the implications for ecclesiology?

Surely, then, we have to take it seriously as substantial agreement? If, of course, we are in a generation when ARCIC Statements exist primarily for study and pondering, but are not being referred to the Churches for endorsement or correction or registration of true agreement, what status will this passage have in future relationships? Indeed, is there here the seedbed for the idea explored in chapter 12 above of a "Declaration"? It is an early point at which to put out the flags and blow the trumpets, but is it possible that, looking forward, we now discard the title-question of this book, "Did the Anglicans and Roman Catholics agree on the Eucharist?" and ask instead with hope, "Could the Anglicans and Roman Catholics now agree on the Eucharist?"

Appendix A

*Anglican Liturgical
Use of "Memorial"*

T HE RENDERING OF ἀναμνησις (*anamnesis*) as "memorial" is a regular
feature of the ARCIC documents, and in *Elucidation* §5 it is stated to
be "found at the very heart of the eucharistic prayers of both East and West,
not only in the institution narrative, but also in the prayer which follows
and elsewhere." This reference to liturgies prompts a fuller survey of the
use of "memorial" in Anglican eucharistic prayers. Is it indeed "at the very
heart" of them?

Within the institution narrative itself the regular Anglican usage has
been "in remembrance of me" (and the Roman Catholic translations, of
both 1969 and 2011, have "Do this in memory of me"). We may then set the
narrative aside, and look for the use of "memorial" in what *Elucidation* calls
"the prayer which follows." The first paragraph after the institution narrative usually responds to Jesus" command, and sets out how we respond
to it to keep the "remembrance," and the paragraph is usually known to
liturgists by the name "anamnesis."

Cranmer wrote his successive Prayer Books against a background of
the Roman text "Wherefore, O Lord, we . . . being mindful [of Jesus's death,
resurrection, and ascension] . . . do offer unto thy excellent majesty . . . a pure
victim, a holy victim, an undefiled victim, the holy bread of eternal life, and
the cup of eternal salvation." So in 1549 (in complicated language) he wrote,
"We . . . do celebrate and make here before thy divine majesty . . . the memorial which thy Son hath willed us to make." Here he left virtually no hint
of offering, but remained reticent about *how* the church should obey Jesus'
command. At root he was simply saying, "Whatever Jesus willed is what we

are doing here," without unpacking its significance. But in 1552 he was so clear that the command was to eat and drink, that he removed the spoken anamnesis and put the physical distribution of communion in its place—doing in fact what he understood that Jesus had told his followers to do.[1] The word "memorial" disappeared with the anamnesis—there was no "prayer which follows"; and the text remained unchanged through 1559, 1604, and 1662; and 1662 endures until today and is a main point of reference within *Elucidation* and *Clarifications*. Thus, *Elucidation*, as noted on pp.58 and 64 above, reports a use of "memorial" in 1662 in a wholly non-existent prayer.

The Scottish Liturgy of 1637 was at this point in the rite drawn not from 1552 but broadly from 1549, and so it kept the use of "memorial." This was retained through the successive Scottish rites in the eighteenth century, and thus was also fed into the USA liturgical tradition. It remained in the American Book of 1979 (but not in the additional eucharistic prayers of 1998), but was elided from the Scottish Liturgy of 1982 (and from all the Scottish 1996 additional prayers).

When liturgical revision began in England, the drawing upon Frere's proposal of an "interim rite" did not entail the use of "memorial" in the Series 1 communion in 1966. It came into Series 2 in 1967 because, when I had dissented from the (Hippolytan-based) proposal to "offer unto thee this bread and this cup," one of the counter-proposals I made was for a return to 1549 and "make the memorial." This was adopted as a (politically) unitive wording at a late stage, and took the form "we make the memorial of his saving passion *etc.*" The Liturgical Commission viewed this as an unsatisfactory stopgap, not only because of its unclarity, but also because in popular use "memorial" strongly suggests the poignant memory of those who are lost and gone. In 1971, when we first used contemporary language we introduced into Series 3 "we celebrate his perfect sacrifice, etc." This was revised in Synod then and later subjected to major scrutiny in 1978–79, and at one point the House of Bishops bid briefly for a return to "make the memorial." The Commission resisted this, and brought it through the Synod marginally refined as The First Eucharistic Prayer in the Alternative Service Book 1980. This then read:

> Therefore, heavenly Father,
>
> we remember his offering of himself . . .
>
> As we look for his coming in glory,

1. For further on this see Buchanan, *What Did Cranmer.*

we celebrate with this bread and this cup

his one perfect sacrifice.

However, people who had taken to Series 2 in the 1960s, and been able to continue the use when the ASB came in, pleaded that the eucharistic prayer from Series 2 should be put into contemporary language and included in the ASB rite. Thus it became there the Second Eucharistic Prayer; it retained the stopgap "memorial"; and it was called in evidence in the extract from *Elucidation* quoted above. But its place was simply to reassure the lovers of the tradition (twelve years were sufficient to establish tradition); and in the event, the introduction of a Third Eucharistic Prayer, self-evidently an adaptation of the Roman Catholic Prayer II, which had been drawn from so-called Hippolytus, drew most of them away from the Second Prayer. This Third Prayer also used "memorial," though "memorial" did not itself come from the Roman Catholic Prayer, which has no echo of "*in meam commemorationem*" beyond "*Memores igitur*," but had been slipped in by the proposers of the prayer to the General Synod Revision Committee, almost certainly as giving a "traditional" Anglican atmosphere to it.[2] However its meaning remains as undecided as in its origins in 1549, traceable certainly to ἀναμνησις in the narrative, but thereby engaging it in the uncertainty of meaning of ἀναμνησις.

More happily, Series 3 had provided a precedent for the Anglican world. The verb "to celebrate" had been rare in 1662, and when used in the warning exhortation it had simply meant to perform or execute a BCP service. This had allowed the word "celebrant" to be employed in its Roman Catholic usage. But now the congregation would "celebrate," and they would celebrate the "feast"; they would celebrate the "gifts and graces of God"; they would celebrate the mighty acts of God; and this latter use of "celebrate," with the works of redemption as its object, proved irenic, a delight on the ears, and acceptable to all strands in the church.[3]

The result of this trend can be seen in the Anglican eucharistic rites of the last forty years. My own most recent collection of these, spanning 1985

2. It has to be acknowledged that there is a slightly sad follow-on from these texts. When Common Worship was prepared in 1998–99, the Liturgical Commission, with, I venture to say, little understanding of the history, decided to assimilate the little-used Second Eucharistic Prayer into the First, and in doing so elided "we celebrate" and brought back in from the Second Prayer "we make the memorial." Thus, it is anachronistically in Eucharistic Prayer A in Rite One today.

3. It had precedent elsewhere, and its scholarly roots were well written up by Paul Bradshaw, "Celebration," in Jasper, *Eucharist Today*.

to 2010, has just over one hundred eucharistic prayers in it, authorized in thirty-one of the thirty-eight Anglican provinces of 2010 in it.[4] Only seven provincial rites retain "memorial," mostly in rites still largely in seventeenth- or eighteenth-century forms, and some of them (as in the Church of England) do so only for one or two of a variety of eucharistic prayers. Only sixteen of those one hundred prayers contain it. "Celebrate" occurs as a major verb in the anamnesis in the eucharistic prayers of around sixteen different provinces and has clearly come to stay.

In the light of this evidence, the phrase about "memorial" that it was "at the very heart of the eucharistic prayers," which was a highly dubious assertion about Anglican rites in 1979, has now in 2018 become impossible to assert. At the most "memorial" is a residual and marginal use, retained because of some particular meaning or even nostalgia associated with it, but actually open to interpretations varying from Zwinglianism to Trent. It is thus equally impossible to cite "memorial" as across-the-board evidence that Anglicans believe that in the eucharist the historic sacrifice of Christ is made "present." Nor can "celebrate" possibly carry that meaning.

4. Buchanan, *Anglican Eucharistic.*

Appendix B

Eucharistic Sacrifice

I T IS RASH TO attempt to say something succinct on eucharistic sacrifice to undergird the even shorter passing mentions in the main text, but putting down a few further markers may assist an appreciation of a mainstream Anglican position, rooted in the historic formularies.

The starting-point is the scriptures. None of the four institution narratives (including 1 Cor 11) nor any of the flanking references (such as in John 6 or 1 Cor 10) gives any hint that the church, when it obeys the Lord's command to "do this," is to offer a sacrifice, or to offer his sacrifice. Where the scriptures hold supreme authority, as with the various churches of the Reformation, the eucharist is not celebrated as an offering of the sacrifice of Christ to the Father. It is only found where historic developments have overlaid the simple accounts of scripture.

How then did it happen in the "traditional" Churches of West and East? While the evidence of the first two centuries is scanty, one key to the early Christians' understanding of the eucharist is regularly encountered, namely a citing of Mal 1:11 as a prophecy which has been fulfilled in the eucharist. The text reads:

> "From the rising of the sun to its setting my name is great among the Gentiles, and in every place incense is offered to my name, and a pure offering; for my name is great among the Gentiles" says the Lord.

This is found in the Didache, Justin, Irenaeus, Tertullian, *et in multis*. The first uses we can trace clearly invoke the text as demonstrating how a Gentile people of God with a "pure" sacrifice has superseded a Jewish dispensation with "polluted" sacrifices (Mal 1:7) which God will not accept

(Mal 1:10). The prophecy was just what was needed to establish a largely Gentile church, and, once employed, "the sacrifice" became a regular title for the eucharist. But, it must be recalled, there was no New Testament precedent or warrant for this, and the happy lighting upon it in the Septuagint by Gentile apologists not only should not canonize the title, but should also invite critical evaluation of it. The Council of Trent cited the same Malachi text as fulfilled in the eucharist, and exemplified in the offering of the "puram hostiam."[1] In fact it looks as though the heart of the Roman doctrine lay in that "*offerimus,*" rather than in *anamnesis* (on which see Appendix A above).

It does not appear that those early uses entailed any notion that the church was offering Christ's own sacrifice. It was most probably understood as a "thankoffering," and the early use does not suggest it was intended to gain some specific benefit from God. I have noted elsewhere that Edward Kilmartin, the great historian of eucharistic sacrifice in the West, gives no place to Justin or other first- and second-century writers, but begins his account with Tertullian.[2] It is not difficult to see how by the third and fourth centuries the offering to God of the bread and wine which were accounted as the body and blood of Christ naturally phased into a doctrine that the church offers the sacrifice of Christ to the Father. Tradition works that way; but for Anglicans not all tradition has to be viewed as the inevitable flowering of truth under the guidance of the Spirit; there is always the possibility of unbiblical teachings becoming self-authenticating and not open to critical revision. Thus it was that, from a biblical point of view, the whole use and understanding of the Roman mass deteriorated over the centuries until in the sixteenth century it called for radical reform.

The Anglican Reformers worked by exactly that process, radical reform. Cranmer's liturgy distinguished wholly between Jesus's sacrifice "there" upon the cross and our sacrifice of self-offering "here" in response to his gift to us in the eucharist. Thus no Anglican liturgy today, as far as my knowledge goes, could ever say "May the Lord accept the sacrifice at your hands." And, although there are a very few modern rites which in the anamnesis offer the bread and cup to God, there are none that offer the "pure victim." The kind of texts required to give expression to the line in *Clarifications* that in the eucharist the sacrifice of Christ himself—the

1. A clear citation of it comes in modern times in the post-Sanctus of the Roman Catholic Eucharistic Prayer III.

2. Kilmartin, *Eucharist*, 8.

once-for-all sacrifice of Calvary—is made present (and therefore offered by the church to the Father) do not exist in Anglican liturgy.

There has been a strand of Anglicanism which has wanted to call the eucharist a "sacrifice" without defining what that means; and clearly the use of the term by the two archbishops in *Saepius officio* (see p. . . . above) meant "representing" the sacrifice of Christ to the Father, quite a step distant from "presenting" the sacrifice, though still unwarranted. The desire to call the eucharist a "sacrifice" is not confined to anglo-catholics, but it nevertheless appears to spring at several removes from the far more substantial wording associated with the Roman mass. Without biblical warrant, liturgical expression or actual definition such a verbal usage has little claim to enduring currency, and we would be well rid of it.

Appendix C

What Provision Do Anglicans Make for Extended Communion and Adoration of the Reserved Sacrament?

THIS TABLE PROVIDES A summary of provision made in thirteen modern Prayer Books of the Anglican Communion; many other provinces are in the process of experimental rites, or are not English-speaking; so this listing is not comprehensive but is strongly illustrative.

Liturgy Book	Rubrical Regulations for Consumption of Remains	Provision for Use of Reserved Elements
American 1979 BCP	*If any . . . remain, apart from any which may be required for . . . the sick* [or absent or for an administration as a separate service] *the celebrant or deacon, and other communicants, reverently eat and drink it . . .* (pp. 408–9)	Administration to the sick from the reserved Sacrament (p. 457)
Aotearoa New Zealand *A New Zealand Prayer Book* 1989	No rubrical direction given	*To meet special pastoral needs . . . by use of the sacrament which has been consecrated elsewhere.* (p. 729)

Liturgy Book	Rubrical Regulations for Consumption of Remains	Provision for Use of Reserved Elements
Australia *A Prayer Book for Australia* 1995	No rubrical direction given	*[The priest takes the bread and wine for the communion and says this or another authorized Prayer of Thanksgiving and Consecration.]* (p. 685)
Canada 1985 *Book of Alternative Services*	Remains to be consumed (unless reserved for the communion of persons not present) (p. 184)	Distribution by a deacon (p. 406) Communion under Special Circumstances: For those not present at the celebration (pp. 256–60)
Congo Swahili BCP 1997	No rubrical direction given	(No provision is made)
England *Common Worship* 2000	Remains "*not required for purposes of communion*" are consumed. (p. 182)	Distribution of communion to sick and housebound is provided (*Pastoral Services* pp. 74–78)
Ireland 2004 BCP	Remains to be "*reverently consumed*." No exceptions mentioned. (p. 77)	(No provision made)
Kenya 2002 *Our Modern Services*	*Whatever has been consecrated should all be consumed* (p. 66)	(No provision made)
Nigeria 1996 BCP	*If any of the consecrated Bread and Wine remains, it is to be consumed reverently . . .* (p. 372)	(No provision is made)
Southern Africa 1989 *An Anglican Prayer Book*	What remains "*which is not required for the purposes of communion*" is consumed.(p. 128)	Communion of the Sick "*from the reserved sacrament . . . is provided*" (p. 508)
Tanzania 1996 Swahili BCP	No rubrical direction given	(No provision is made)

Liturgy Book	Rubrical Regulations for Consumption of Remains	Provision for Use of Reserved Elements
Wales 2004 BCP	*Any consecrated bread and wine which is not to be reserved for purposes of communion is consumed.* (Vol I, p. 81)	*. . . he may set aside the elements for the Communion of the Sick at a Celebration of the Holy Eucharist in church . . .* (Vol II, p. 756)
West Indies 1995 BCP	No rubrical direction given	If communion to the sick is *"to be administered from the reserved sacrament,"* a rite follows (p. 348)

For the purposes of this present volume, we may safely conclude the following from this table:

i. The use of "extended communion" is widespread in the Anglican Communion, but is by no means universally provided in the official forms, and is therefore technically illegal or irregular in a number of the provinces shown.

ii. Where the provision for consuming the remaining consecrated elements at the end of a eucharistic celebration admits of exceptions, those exceptions are always and only for the purposes of communion.

iii. None of the thirteen Prayer Books has any provision for other extra-liturgical use of the consecrated elements.

iv. While it is difficult to prove a negative, it is probably safe to say there is no evidence in the Anglican Communion of any officially authorized extra-liturgical devotions to or before reserved sacramental elements.

Bibliography

Anglican Communion Office (ACO). *A New Spirit: The Documents of the Visit of His Grace the Archbishop of Canterbury, the Most Revd George L. Carey, to His Holiness Pope John Paul, Advent 1996, in Rome.* London: ACO, 1997.

Anglican Consultative Council (ACC). *ACC-4: Report of the Fourth Meeting 1979.* London: ACC, 1979.

———. *ACC-5: Anglican Consultative Council, Fifth Meeting, Newcastle upon Tyne, 8–18 September 1981.* London: ACC, 1981.

———. *ACC-6: Bonds of Affection: Proceedings of ACC-6, Badagry, Nigeria, 1984.* London: ACC, 1984.

———. *ACC-9: A Transforming Vision: Suffering and Glory in God's World, Cape Town 1993: The Official Report of the Joint Meeting of the Primates of the Anglican Communion and the Anglican Consultative Council.* London: for ACO by CHP, 1993.

———. *ACC-10: Being Anglican in the Third Millennium, The Official Report of the 10th Meeting of the Anglican Consultative Council,* Harrisburg: Morehouse, 1997.

ARCIC I. *The Final Report.* London: CTS/SPCK, 1982.

ARCIC II. *Clarifications of certain aspects of the Agreed Statements on Eucharist and Ministry of the First Anglican–Roman Catholic International Commission together with a letter from Cardinal Edward Idris Cassidy.* London: CHP/CTS for ACC and PCPCU, 1994.

Arrnentrout, Don S., and Robert Boak Slocum, eds. *An Episcopal Dictionary of the Church: A User Friendly Reference for Episcopalians.* New York: Church Publishing Inc., 1999.

Aveling, J. C. H., D. M. Loades, and H. R. McAdoo. *Rome and the Anglicans.* Edited by Haase, Wolfgang. New York: de Gruyter, 1982.

Barrett, Clive, ed. *Unity in Process: Reflections on Ecumenism.* London: DLT, 2012.

Beckwith, Roger T. "The Agreed Statement on Eucharistic Doctrine." *The Churchman* 87 (Spring 1973) 14–28.

Beckwith, R. T., G. E. Duffield, and J. I. Packer. *Across the Divide.* Basingstoke: Lyttelton Press, 1978.

Bird, David, et al. *Receiving the Vision: The Anglican Roman Catholic Reality Today.* Collegeville, MN: Liturgical, 1995.

Bishops' Conference of England and Wales. *Response to the Final Report of ARCIC I.* London: Catholic Media Office, 1985.

Böntert, Stefan (hg). *Gemeinschaft im Danken: Grundfragen der Eucharistiefeier in ökumenischen Gespräch.* Regensburg: Verlag Friedrich Pustet, 2015.

Bradshaw, Tim. *The Olive Branch: An Evangelical Anglican Doctrine of the Church*. Carlisle: Paternoster, 1992.

Buchanan, Colin. *An Evangelical Among the Anglican Liturgists*. London: Alcuin/SPCK, 2009.

———. *ARCIC and Lima on Baptism and Eucharist*. Grove Worship Booklet 86. Bramcote: Grove Books, 1983.

———. "Can the Anglicans and Roman Catholics Agree on the Eucharist?" In *Gemeinschaft im Danken: Grundfragen der Eucharistiefeier in ökumenischen Gespräch*, by Stefan Böntert, 263–79. Regensburg: Verlag Friedrich Pustet, 2015.

———. *The End of the Offertory*. Grove Liturgical Study 14. Bramcote: Grove Books, 1978.

———. *Is Papal Authority a Gift to Us?* Cambridge: Grove Books, 2003.

———. "The New Communion Service—Reasons for Dissent." In *An Evangelical Among the Anglican Liturgists*, by Colin Buchanan. London: Alcuin/SPCK, 2009.

———. *News of Liturgy* (monthly journal of liturgy) 1975–2003.

———. *Taking the Long View: Three and a Half Decades of General Synod*. London: CHP, 2006.

———. *What Did Cranmer Think He Was Doing?* Grove Liturgical Study 7. Bramcote: Grove Books, 1976, 1982.

———. ed. *Anglican Eucharistic Liturgies 1985–2010*. London: Canterbury, 2011.

Buchanan, Colin, et al. *Growing Into Union: Proposals for Forming a United Church in England*. London: SPCK, 1970.

Buchanan, Colin, Trevor Lloyd, and Harold Miller, eds. *Anglican Worship Today*. London: Collins Liturgical, 1980.

Carey, George L. *Know the Truth: A Memoir*. London: HarperCollins, 2004.

Cassidy, Edward Idris. *Ecumenism and Interreligious Dialogue*. Mahwah, NJ: Paulist, 2005.

Catholic Bishops' Conference of England & Wales. *General Instruction of the Roman Missal*. London: CTS and Colloquium, 2005.

Catholic Bishops' Conferences of England & Wales, Ireland, Scotland. *One Bread One Body: A Teaching Document on the Eucharist in the Life of the Church*. London: CTS, 1998.

CCU. *Anglican and Roman Catholic Response to the Work of ARCIC I*. GS Misc 384. London: General Synod of the Church of England, 1992.

Charley, Julian. *The Anglican–Roman Catholic Agreement on the Eucharist: The 1971 Anglican–Roman Catholic Statement on the Eucharist with An Historical Introduction and Theological Commentary*. Grove Booklet on Ministry and Worship 1. Bramcote Grove Books, 1971.

———. *Rome, Canterbury, and the Future*. Bramcote: Grove Books, 1982.

Clark, Alan, and Colin Davey. *Anglican/Roman Catholic Dialogue: The Work of the Preparatory Commission*. Oxford: Oxford University Press, 1974.

Cocksworth, Christopher J. *Evangelical Eucharistic Thought in the Church of England*. Cambridge: Cambridge University Press, 1993.

Craig, David, ed. *Equipping Bishops as Leaders in God's Mission*. London: ACO, 2015.

A Critique of Eucharistic Agreement. London: SPCK, 1975.

Cummings, Owen F. *Canterbury Cousins: The Eucharist in Contemporary Anglican Theology*. Mahwah, NJ: Paulist Press, 2007.

Denaux, Adelbert. "The Anglican–Roman Catholic Dialogue and Its Reception." *Rocznike Teologiczne* 61 (2014) 5–34.

————. *From Malines to ARCIC: The Malines Conversations Commemorated*. Leuven: Leuven University Press, 1997.

Denaux, Adelbert, Nicholas Sagovsky, and Charles Sherlock. *Looking Towards a Church Fully Reconciled: The Final Report of the Anglican–Roman Catholic International Commission 1983-2005*. ARCIC II. London: SPCK, 2016.

Dix, Gregory. *The Shape of the Liturgy*. London: Dacre Press, 1945.

Douglas, Brian. "Anglican–Roman Catholic International Commission (ARCIC) and the Eucharist: Review and Prospects." *The Journal of Religious History* 36 (2012) 351–67.

Dowden, J. *Further Studies in the Prayer Book*. London: Methuen, 1908.

The Emmaus Report: A Report of the Anglican Ecumenical Consultation 1987. London: ACC, 1987 .

Evans, Gillian, and M. Gourgues, eds. *Communion et Réunion: Mélanges Jean-Marie Roger Tillard*. Leuven, Belgium: Leuven University Press, 1995.

Franklin, William, ed. *Anglican Orders: Essays on the Centenary of* Apostolicae Curae. London: Mowbray, 1996.

————. "ARC-USA: Five Affirmations on the Eucharist as Sacrifice." *Worship* 69 (1995) 380–90.

Gasquet, F. A., and E. Bishop. *Edward VI and the Book of Common Prayer*. London: John Hodges, 1890.

Geernaert, Donna. "Achievements of ARCIC and IARCCUM." In *Celebrating a Century of Ecumenism*, edited by John A. Radano, 122–40. Geneva: WCC, 2012.

Green, Michael. "Christ's Sacrifice and Ours." In *Guidelines: Anglican Evangelicals Face the Future*, edited by J. I. Packer, 89–117. London: Church Pastoral Aid Society, 1967.

————. "Eucharistic Sacrifice in the New Testament and the Early Fathers." In *Eucharistic Sacrifice*, edited by J. I. Packer, 53–83. London: Church Book Room Press, 1962.

Halifax, Lord, ed. *The Conversations at Malines 1921–1925, Original Documents*. London: Philip Allan, 1930.

Hierarchy of England and Wales. *Instruction on Putting into Effect the Constitution on the Sacred Liturgy*. London: CTS, 1964.

Hill, Christopher J., and Edward Yarnold, eds. *Anglicans and Roman Catholics: The Search for Unity*. London: SPCK, 1994.

————, eds. *Anglican Orders: The Documents in the Debate*. London: Canterbury, 1997.

Holeton, David R., ed. *Our Thanks and Praise: The Eucharist in Anglicanism Today*. Toronto: Anglican Book Centre, 1998.

Hooker, Richard. *Of the Laws of Ecclesiastical Polity*. Vol 5. London, 1597.

IARCCUM. *Growing Together in Unity and Mission*. London: SPCK, 2007.

Church of Ireland. *The Response of the General Synod of the Church of Ireland to the Final Report of ARCIC-I*. Oxford: APCK/Oxford, 1987.

Jasper, Ronald C. D. *The Development of the Anglican Liturgy 1662–1980*. London: SPCK, 1989.

————, ed. *The Eucharist Today: Studies on Series 3*. London: SPCK, 1974.

Jones, Sarah Roland, ed. *The Vision Before Us: The Kyoto Report of the Anglican Standing Commission on Ecumenical Relations 2000-2008*. London: ACO, 2009.

Kasper, Walter. *Harvesting the Fruits: Basic Aspects of Christian Faith in Ecumenical Dialogue*. London: Continuum. 2009.

————. "Roman Catholic Reflections on the Anglican Communion." In *Equipping Bishops as Leaders in God's Mission,* edited by David Craig, 202. London: ACO, 2015.

Kilmartin, Edward J. *The Eucharist in the West: History and Theology*. Edited by Robert J. Daly. Collegeville: Pueblo, Liturgical, 1998.

The Lambeth Conference of 1897 with the Official Reports and Resolutions. Edited by R. T. Davidson. London: SPCK, 1907.

The Lambeth Conference 1968: Resolutions and Reports. London: SPCK, 1968.

The Lambeth Conference 1978 Preparatory Articles: Today's Church and Today's World. London: CIO, 1977.

The Lambeth Conference 1988, The Truth Shall Make You Free: The Report, Resolutions and Pastoral Letters from the Bishops. London: ACC, 1988.

The Official Report of the Lambeth Conference 1998, Transformation and Renewal. London: ACC, 1998.

The Report of the Lambeth Conference 1978. London: CIO, 1978.

The Lambeth Conference of 2008, Equipping Bishops as Leaders in God's Mission [listed under "Craig, David"].

McAdoo, Henry R. "Anglican/Roman Catholic Relations, 1717–1980: A Detection of Themes." In *Rome and the Anglicans*, by J. C. H. Aveling, D. M. Loades, and H. R. McAdoo, 224–34. New York: de Gruyter, 1982.

Modern Eucharistic Agreement. London: SPCK, 1973.

Morris, Jeremy, and Nicholas Sagovsky, eds. *The Unity We Have and the Unity We Seek*. London: T & T Clark, 2003.

Murray, Paul, ed. *Receptive Ecumenism and the Call to Catholic Learning*. Oxford: Oxford University Press, 2010.

National Evangelical Anglican Congress 2. *The Nottingham Statement*. London: Falcon Books, 1977.

Nilson, Jon. *Nothing Beyond the Necessary: Roman Catholicism and the Ecumenical Future*. Mahwah, NJ. Paulist Press, 1995.

O'Callaghan, Dermot. *Rome, Canterbury and Armagh*. Church of Ireland Evangelical Fellowship, 1984.

Pierce, Joanne M. "The Eucharist as Sacrifice: Some Contemporary Roman Catholic Reflections." *Worship* 69 (1995) 394–405.

Platten, Stephen. "Unity and the Churches: Focusing the Vision." In *Unity in Process: Reflections on Ecumenism*, edited by Clive Barrett, 97–98. London: DLT, 2012.

Price, Charles P. "Anamnesis in Episcopal Ecumenical Dialogues." *Worship* 69 (1995) 391–93.

Purdy, William. *The Search for Unity: Relations between the Anglican and Roman Catholic Churches from the 1950s to the 1970s*. London: Geoffrey Chapman, 1996.

Radano, John A., ed. *Celebrating a Century of Ecumenism*. Geneva: WCC, 2012.

Ratcliff, Edward. "The Communion Service of the Prayer Book." In *E. C. Ratcliff: Reflections on Liturgical Revision*, edited by David H. Tripp. Grove Liturgical Study 22. Bramcote, Grove Books, 1980

Ratzinger, Joseph. *Church, Ecumenism and Politics*. Slough: St. Paul, 1988.

Reath, Mary. *Rome and Canterbury: The Elusive Search for Unity*. Lanham: Rowman & Littlefield, 2007.

Root, Howard. "Some Remarks on the Response to ARCIC I." In *Communion et Réunion: Mélanges Jean-Marie Roger Tillard*, edited by Gillian Evans and M. Gourgues, 165–76. Leuven, Belgium: Leuven University Press, 1995.

Sachs, William L. *The Transformation of Anglicanism: From State Church to Global Communion*. Cambridge: Cambridge University Press, 1993.

Sagovsky, Nicholas. "Anglicans and Roman Catholics: A Joint Declaration of Agreement." In *The Unity We Have and the Unity We Seek*, edited by Jeremy Morris and Nicholas Sagovsky, 27–52. London: T & T Clark, 2003.

———. "Gregory Dix and the Shape of the Liturgy: Critical Assessment." In *Liturgies et Liturgistes: Fructification de leurs Apports dans l'aujourd'hui des Églises*, edited by A. Lossky and H. Brakmann. Semaines d'Études Liturgiques Saint-Serge 59, Studia Oecumenica Friburgensia 69. Münster, Aschendorff, 2015.

Sandford, E. G. *Memoirs of Archbishop Temple*. Vol. 2. London: MacMillan, 1906.

Santer, Mark, ed. *Their Lord and Ours*. London: SPCK, 1982.

Sherlock, Charles. "Eucharist, Sacrifice, and Atonement: The *Clarifications* of ARCIC." In *Our Thanks and Praise: The Eucharist in Anglicanism Today*, edited by David R. Holeton, 117–28. Toronto: Anglican Book Centre, 1998.

Tanner, Mary. "In Defence of Dialogue." In *Communion et Réunion: Mélanges Jean-Marie Roger Tillard*, edited by Gillian Evans and M. Gourgues, 181. Leuven, Belgium: Leuven University Press, 1995.

Tavard, George. "The *Final Report*, Witness to Tradition." *One in Christ* 32 (1996) 118–29.

Tillard, Jean M. R. *Église d'Églises: l'ecclésiologie de communion*. Paris: Editions du Cerf, 1987; English Translation: *Church of Churches: The Ecclesiology of Communion*. Translated by R. C. De Peaux. Collegeville, MN: Order of St. Benedict, 1992.

———. *What Priesthood has the Ministry?* Grove Booklet on Ministry and Worship 13. Bramcote: Grove Books, 1973.

World Council of Churches. *Baptism, Eucharist and Ministry*. Geneva: WCC, 1982.

Wright, Robert J. "The Reception of ARCIC I in the USA." In *Communion et Réunion: Mélanges Jean-Marie Roger Tillard*, edited by Gillian Evans and M. Gourgues, 217–30.

Names Index

Subject Index

185

Scripture Index

Lightning Source UK Ltd.
Milton Keynes UK
UKHW02f1201241018
331114UK00003B/280/P

9 781532 633836